USENIX Association

Proceedings of the

Workshop on Intrusion Detection

and Network Monitoring

(ID '99)

April 9–12, 1999
Santa Clara, California, USA

Contents

Workshop on Intrusion Detection and Network Monitoring

April 9–12, 1999
Santa Clara, California, USA

Network Data Processing and Storage
Session Chair: Dan Geer, CERTCO

Statistics and Anomalies
Session Chair: Marcus Ranum, Network Flight Recorder, Inc.

Message from the Program Chair

Welcome!

A few years ago, a wise old programmer complained that in "Internet Time" technologies go from "Interesting research" to "overhyped" before the researchers get a chance to actually make any progress. Hopefully this workshop will help prove that his complaint is wrong—a lot of smart people are doing research in intrusion detection (ID) today, and are willing to share their ideas with their peers. We have a line-up of papers that we think represent some of the most interesting work being done in the field; we're happy to be able to share them with you.

As program chair, it's an honor to help organize such a workshop: the real work is done by the authors and the USENIX staff. I'd like to thank our authors for submitting their work, and taking on the additional effort of sharing their thoughts with the community. Thanks also to the program committee for reviewing papers, choosing among them, and helping the authors edit their final drafts. Lastly, deep thanks to the USENIX staff, who kept an eye on the schedules, locations, publications, formats, and made sure the "i"s were dotted and "t"s were crossed. Without USENIX's ongoing commitment to spreading knowledge, the computing world would be a little darker. Thank you all.

I welcome you, and hope you enjoy and learn from the workshop.

Marcus J. Ranum
Program Chair

Analysis Techniques for Detecting Coordinated Attacks and Probes

John Green
Naval Surface Warfare Center
David Marchette
Naval Surface Warfare Center
Stephen Northcutt
Ballistic Missile Defense Organization
Bill Ralph
ATR Corporation

Abstract

Coordinated attacks and probes have been observed against several networks that we protect. We describe some of these attacks and provide insight into how and why they are carried out. We also suggest hypotheses for some of the more puzzling probes. Methods for detecting these coordinated attacks are provided.

1. Introduction

For approximately the last year, SHADOW analysts have been detecting a new class of network traffic. Although the probes and attacks embedded within this traffic consist mostly of known exploits, subsequent analysis reveals that multiple IP addresses are working together toward a common goal. Therefore, we have coined the phrase "coordinated attacks" to describe the activity that has been observed.

Indications of these concerted efforts appear in network traffic logs as multiple external IP addresses targeting a single address of the protected network. Similarly, a coordinated attack can also look as though multiple attackers are working together to execute a distributed scan on many internal addresses or services. It is believed that probes of this nature have been developed in an attempt to elude the scan detection code present in many intrusion detection systems.

In most of the cases observed, the number of cooperating IP addresses is rather small; four or five is common. However, as many as fifteen different coactive, scanning hosts have been uncovered by SHADOW analysts. Due to their distributed nature, these attacks were well below the threshold for a structured attack in terms of targeting, lethality and scope.

"We distinguish two fundamental types of threat. The unstructured threat is random and relatively limited. It consists of adversaries with limited funds and organization and short-term goals. While it poses a threat to system operations, national security is not targeted. This is the most obvious threat today. The structured threat is considerably more methodical and well-supported. While the unstructured threat is the most obvious threat today, for national security purposes we are concerned primarily with the structured threat, since that poses the most significant risk."

Air Force Lt. Gen. Kenneth A Minihan, director of the National Security Agency - brief to the Senate Government Affairs Committee, June 24 1998.

What is a structured attack? Interviews with premier intrusion detection researchers revealed that they consider structured attacks to be on the order of thousands of related exploits, probes, viruses, scans, denials of service, and ruses over a short period of time. Even though this definition doesn't accurately describe the patterns discussed earlier, we cannot call this activity unstructured. It definitely has structure!

This paper will examine various coordinated attacks and probes, including coordinated traceroutes, NetBIOS scans, Reset scans, SFRP scans and coordinated DNS server exploit attempts. Some of these probes are certainly the work of multiple computers working together; others appear to be fraudulent or decoy mechanisms.

2. Coordinated traceroutes

Coordinated traceroutes serve as a reminder that sites are always vulnerable, even if their firewalls are impenetrable. Information gleaned from this technique can be used to direct a denial of service attack against a site's external connectivity, effectively isolating the facility. Detection of coordinated traceroutes is simple; look for about five traceroutes within two seconds of one another, often with similar names.

Figure 1 shows an example of this activity. Here, five different sources, each from a different backbone network, are shown probing the same target. Most often, the target is a DNS server, or DNS serving firewall, and packet arrival is usually within tenths or hundredths of seconds of each other.

```
12:29:30.01  proberA.39964  >  target.33500:  udp
12 [ttl 1]
12:29:30.13  proberA.39964  >  target.33501:  udp
12 [ttl 1]
12:29:30.25  proberA.39964  >  target.33502:  udp
12 [ttl 1]
12:29:30.35  proberA.39964  >  target.33503:  udp
12 [ttl 1]

12:27:55.10  proberB.46164  >  target.33485:  udp
12 [ttl 1]
12:27:55.12  proberB.46164  >  target.33487:  udp
12 [ttl 1]
12:27:55.16  proberB.46164  >  target.33488:  udp
12 [ttl 1]
12:27:55.18  proberB.46164  >  target.33489:  udp
12 [ttl 1]

12:27:26.13  proberC.43327  >  target.33491:  udp
12 [ttl 1]
12:27:26.24  proberC.43327  >  target.33492:  udp
12 [ttl 1]
12:27:26.37  proberC.43327  >  target.33493:  udp
12 [ttl 1]
12:27:26.48  proberC.43327  >  target.33494:  udp
12 [ttl 1]

12:27:32.96  proberD.55528  >  target.33485:  udp
12 [ttl 1]
12:27:33.07  proberD.55528  >  target.33486:  udp
12 [ttl 1]
12:27:33.17  proberD.55528  >  target.33487:  udp
12 [ttl 1]
12:27:33.29  proberD.55528  >  target.33488:  udp
12 [ttl 1]

12:27:30.55  proberE.21337  >  target.33475:  udp
12 [ttl 1]
12:27:30.56  proberE.21337  >  target.33476:  udp
12 [ttl 1]
12:27:30.58  proberE.21337  >  target.33477:  udp
12 [ttl 1]
12:27:30.59  proberE.21337  >  target.33478:  udp
12 [ttl 1]
```

Figure 1. Coordinated traceroute example.

Coordinated traceroutes do have a commercial use. Some Internet Service Providers (ISP) use them to cal-

culate the best routes back to clients in an attempt to provide optimum web response. The stimulus for this type activity is a host from the protected network visiting a web server supported by an ISP that uses coordinated traceroutes.

As mentioned above, coordinated traceroutes can be a benign effort to improve the performance of a server. As such they can be viewed as providing a useful service. However, they can also be used to determine all the routes into your protected network. Thus it should be of interest to determine who is performing these traceroutes and why.

3. NetBIOS deception

One of the first things that a network analyst learns is that network traffic is not always what it appears to be. Source address spoofing is a classic example of this. Many commonly available exploit tools include this capability. In fact, the latest version of nmap takes spoofing a step further; it includes a decoy option. This option allows the hacker to make an attack appear as though it is coming from multiple sources. Even if an analyst at the targeted site detects the attack, it is very difficult to determine which of the IP addresses were spoofed, and which one was real.

The trace in figure 2 is from a site that receives very few NetBIOS session connection attempts. The traffic shown was detected over a single twenty-four hour period. These source addresses correlate with NetBIOS session connection attempts seen at other sites over several days. The signature of this massive scan is: four connect attempts for each address, the do not fragment option is set, a window size of 8192, and the TTL fields cluster. Perhaps the most interesting signature of this coordinated activity is that the traffic is destined only for IP addresses that are not populated by hosts. The first two traces show all four attempts, the rest have been edited for space.

The source addresses spanned several countries, but certainly could have been spoofed. The scan rate is slow enough that the entire probe could have been generated from a single computer. The fact that the Time To Live (TTL) field is within three hops for all packets is also interesting and points to a single computer. Different operating systems have different TTL defaults. The probes were sent to hosts that do not exist, therefore the TCP three-way handshake was never completed. That would be evidence this was actually a probe. Could this be a hoax?

If this is a hoax, what is the purpose? One possibility is that fake attacks may create fear, uncertainty, and doubt in the same vein as virus hoaxes. Another possibility is an "attacker honey pot". [Even a mediocre fake attack will tie up analyst and CIRT resources, and possibly serve as a distraction so that a much lower signal precision attack can get through undetected] *decoy*

Another hypothesis is that the attacker is only interested in "brand new" systems that are brought online. Since most security patches are available from vendor websites, many administrators bring up vulnerable systems with the intent of downloading and installing the patches at a later date. This process may take several days, leaving new systems and the networks that they reside on vulnerable to attack.

The fact that only non-existent systems are targeted makes these probes particularly puzzling. It also makes them worthy of concern, since it implies that the attackers have a precise map of the protected network.

Trace 1:

```
00:56:22.78 proberD.3506 > 172.20.124.23.139:
S 14300153:14300153(0) win 8192   (DF)
00:56:25.69 proberD.3506 > 172.20.124.23.139:
S 14300153:14300153(0) win 8192   (DF)
00:56:31.70 proberD.3506 > 172.20.124.23.139:
S 14300153:14300153(0) win 8192   (DF)
00:56:43.69 proberD.3506 > 172.20.124.23.139:
S 14300153:14300153(0) win 8192   (DF)
```

Trace 2:

```
06:49:55.47 proberA.4197 > 172.20.139.137.139:
S 596843772:596843772(0) win 8192   (DF)
06:49:58.44 proberA.4197 > 172.20.139.137.139:
S 596843772:596843772(0) win 8192   (DF)
06:50:04.44 proberA.4197 > 172.20.139.137.139:
S 596843772:596843772(0) win 8192   (DF)
06:50:16.43 proberA.4197 > 172.20.139.137.139:
S 596843772:596843772(0) win 8192   (DF)
```

Additional traces, only the first packet is shown:

```
12:57:56.94 proberE.2038 > 172.20.216.29.139:
S 294167370:294167370(0) win 8192   (DF)
13:37:51.75 proberI.4186 > 172.20.215.205.139:
S 22881687:22881687(0) win 8192   (DF)
13:50:23.64 proberB.3293 > 172.20.53.123.139:
S 355997160:355997160(0) win 8192   (DF)
14:11:01.95 proberC.3491 > 172.20.245.182.139:
S 57370977:57370977(0) win 8192   (DF)
15:41:59.50 proberG.3278 > 172.20.252.141.139:
S 266305199:266305199(0) win 8192   (DF)
22:49:15.39 proberH.3658 > 172.20.124.23.139:
S 14035939:14035939(0) win 8192   (DF)
```

Figure 2. Netbios deception example.

4. Reset scans

If you examine the Internet traffic to your site, there is a very good chance you will find a large number of inbound Resets and SYN/ACKs for which there is no corresponding SYN packet. Generally, these scans originate from a multitude of source addresses and often appear to be coordinated due to their concurrency. Several questions come to mind: "What is going on?" and furthermore, "What are some of the events that cause Reset generation?" Section 4 will explore some of the events that can generate Reset scans, the motivations for Reset scanning, and will also discuss the methods that SHADOW uses to detect them.

4.1. Natural function of TCP/IP

Resets are a normal part of TCP/IP communications. If something goes wrong with a TCP connection, a reset may be generated. Typically, in this case only one would be observed between the server and client. If a connection is attempted to a service that does not exist, a reset may be generated. A single SYN attempt/Reset response from a mscan probe is shown in figure 3. Note that the acknowledgement number is the sequence number incremented by one.

```
13:13:10.670000 www.1880 > mailrelay.6000: S
1393635005:1393635005(0) win 512
13:13:10.680000 mailrelay.6000 > www.1880: R
0:0(0) ack 1393635006 win 0
```

Figure 3. SYN attempt/Reset response example.

Client systems generally attempt to establish connections multiple times. Four SYN "active open" attempts to the same destination address and source port is commonly seen for most services. Electronic mail and web (TCP port 25 and TCP port 80) active opens often try larger numbers of attempts ranging from twelve to twenty five.

From an intrusion detection standpoint, we generally expect to see outbound Resets as a result of activity caused by inbound traffic. Examining the trace in figure 3, we see that the inbound traffic from www to Mailrelay attempts to initiate an X Windows connection. Mailrelay wants no part of this; so an outbound and Reset to www is generated.

If we detect inbound Resets we expect that these were caused by outbound connections from our systems. In the next two possible causes for the generation of Resets, we will look at situations where we observe a medium to large number of Resets, (or SYN/ACKS) inbound. In these cases, there is no corresponding SYN packet.

4.2. Second order effect

The inbound Resets (or Syn/Acks) could also be explained as a "second order effect" of a denial of service attack, or scan on another site. [For this to be a second order effect, we must not have initiated the connections with SYN packets and our IP addresses are used (spoofed) to attack someone else.] This last case is a dominant factor in the generation of large numbers of inexplicable Resets. IRC servers seem to be the primary targets in a large number of these cases.

A wide variety of Internet addresses have been used for this sport; we have received traces of excessive Resets from all over the globe. Figure 4 illustrates example traffic at two sensor locations: SITE_A and SITE_B. It shows the activity that each site detected on the same day. The time stamps indicate concurrent activity from Irc_victim to multiple destination hosts. This denial of service attack generates Resets from Irc_victim, since the attack was to Irc_victim's inactive ports.

Excerpts from SITE_A tcpdump at ~02:00:

```
02:13:23.55 Irc_victim.37762 >
192.168.129.191.18602: R 0:0(0) ack 1940197743
win 0
02:14:00.07 Irc_victim.25013 >
192.168.251.67.26831: R 0:0(0) ack 397924438
win 0
02:14:20.68 Irc_victim.32824 >
192.168.123.30.17807: R 0:0(0) ack 1747849368
win 0
```

Excerpts from SITE_B tcpdump at ~02:00:

```
02:13:21.54 Irc_victim.4723 >
172.20.96.61.7790: R 0:0(0) ack 172384509 win
0
02:14:09.39 Irc_victim.45991 >
172.20.72.145.18363: R 0:0(0) ack 578682865
win 0
02:14:12.35 Irc_victim.58839 >
172.20.46.51.51347: R 0:0(0) ack 1901339874
win 0
```

Figure 4. Expected behavior for inactive ports.

In contrast, figure 5 depicts the network traffic pattern for active ports. Note the change in the 12:00 hour activity to the active port 6667 with the expected

SYN/ACK response from Irc_victim, followed by the RST/ACK segment indicating an aborted connection.

For the truly paranoid, we offer an alternate interpretation of the traces shown in figure 5. A "man in the middle" scan could create this signature. In this case, the attackers must compromise our site, or a node on the route to our site. They must place a sniffer that is tuned to collect Resets and Syn/Acks on a compromised site. They then port scan the target from another location spoofing our address space. The sensor located on the compromised host collects the results and sends them to the attacker. This is unlikely to be the case in attacks against multiple sites.

It is important to point out that this kind of secondary effect will appear as a coordinated attack against the protected network if the attacker targets multiple hosts or networks, and always spoofs our IP addresses in the attack.

Sample trace from SITE_A at ~12:00:

```
12:47:03.65 Irc_victim.6667 >
192.168.140.187.10496: S 157348803:157348803(0)
ack 687865857 win 16384 <mss 1460> (DF)

12:47:03.87 Irc_victim.6667 >
192.168.140.187.10496: R 1:1(0) ack 1 win 16384
(DF)

12:48:38.57 Irc_victim.6667 >
192.168.246.165.33026: S 2670541452:2670541452(0)
ack 2164391937 win 16384 <mss 1460> (DF)

12:48:39.07 Irc_victim.6667 >
192.168.246.165.33026: R 1:1(0) ack 1 win 16384
(DF)
```

Sample trace from SITE_B at ~12:00:

```
12:47:07.43 Irc_victim.irc >
172.20.246.181.36126: S
1105399373:1105399373(0) ack 2367553537 win
16384  (DF)

12:47:07.56 Irc_victim.irc >
172.20.246.181.36126: R 1:1(0) ack 1 win 16384
(DF)
12:47:20.35 Irc_victim.irc >
172.20.64.221.18178: S
1443077754:1443077754(0) ack 1191313409 win
16384  (DF)

12:47:20.35 Irc_victim.irc >
172.20.64.221.18178: R 1:1(0) ack 1 win 16384
(DF)
```

Figure 5. Expected behavior for active ports.

4.3. Resets for intelligence gathering

Reset scanning works like any other inverse mapping method. This is because the routers are thinking IP, not TCP and the IP address is in the IP layer. When destination IPs or ports are inactive, the routers simply want to be helpful and return an address unreachable message. There are a variety of techniques (including Reset scanning) to locate the hosts, nets, and active service ports that do not exist. The attacker simply has to take the converse of the map to get a first order understanding of what does exist.

Figure 6 is an example from the point of view of the Reset scanner. They know the address of the system(s) they have scanned, so they wait for icmp error messages from the destination network's router. The results of interest could look like net (or host) unreachable or time exceeded.

```
20:38:11.783596 router > 192.168.32.192: icmp:
time exceeded in-transit [tos 0xc0]
20:38:55.597130 router > 192.168.31.15: icmp:
time exceeded in-transit [tos 0xc0]
20:41:41.824191 router > 192.168.52.99: icmp:
time exceeded in-transit [tos 0xc0]
20:43:50.750498 router > 192.168.52.99: icmp:
time exceeded in-transit [tos 0xc0]
20:44:01.280339 router > 192.168.61.209: icmp:
time exceeded in-transit [tos 0xc0]
20:44:27.790505 router > 192.168.59.164: icmp:
time exceeded in-transit [tos 0xc0]
```

Figure 6. Results from a reset scan.

In the early days of this technique, Reset scans were easy to detect due to common "signature acknowledgement numbers"; the TCP header ACK field was always a fixed number, usually 674719802 or 674711610. Figure 7 shows a Reset probe from two attackers that can trivially be detected due to the signature Ack number.

```
17:40:45.87 hook.24408 > target1.1457: R
0:0(0) ack 674719802 win 0
17:40:53.03 hook.33174 > target2.1457: R
0:0(0) ack 674719802 win 0
17:41:12.16 hook.36250 > target3.1979: R
0:0(0) ack 674719802 win 0
17:43:37.61 router > hook: icmp: time exceeded
in-transit
17:43:43.14 hook.44922 > target4.1496: R
0:0(0) ack 674719802 win 0
17:42:30.40 grin.3532 > target1a.1167: R
0:0(0) ack 674719802 win 0
17:42:40.58 grin.33233 > target2a.1797: R
0:0(0) ack 674719802 win 0
17:44:28.84 grin.52504 > target3a.1634: R
0:0(0) ack 674719802 win 0
```

```
17:47:52.58 grin.46657 > target4a.2121: R
0:0(0) ack 674719802 win 0
17:47:52.70 router > grin: icmp: time exceeded
in-transit
```

Figure 7. Example of "signature acknowledgement numbers".

Unfortunately, some of the more recent probes have random acknowledgement numbers. Probes of this type have been observed from at least fourteen different cooperating Internet addresses, primarily ISPs, all within a twenty-four hour period. And of course, how do you sort between the scans and second order effects?

Many people want to label all Resets as a second order effect and just not deal with it. This is foolish; when there is this much smoke, find the fire. These probing systems are working together to map multiple target sites. Reset traces from all over the world provide strong evidence that this activity is a long-term, Internet wide effort. The scan rate from some attacks is as low as 2 packets per day per target site, well below commonly set thresholds for scan detectors.

This begs the question: "Without a signature Ack how can we detect Reset scans?" In this case, the primary signature is the Reset code bit set with no other activity from that source, (such as an active open [SYN] from the source or target). An obvious solution is to keep track of the state of each TCP connection and alarm: if a Reset, Syn/Ack, or Fin is detected without the active open. However, this solution can be compute intensive for large networks. The answer lies in less expensive mechanisms; namely scan detectors.

Inverse mapping is best detected over a longer time window, such as an hour, or even a day. In this case, we can test for an external host making connections to n internal hosts where n is a small value, (Shadow systems default to 7, but this is configurable). This technique will detect any scan that meets or exceeds the tally trigger over the time window. Figure 8 shows how SHADOW displays detected scans.

```
Hourly Tally Counter

8          192.168.2.1      hook
7          172.20.20.20     grin
7          10.32.21.12      false_positive.net
```

Figure 8. SHADOW scan detection output.

The advantage of such a technique is that it will detect any scan, so it will detect scans for which there is no signature. The disadvantages of this approach are threefold: scans below the tally trigger point will be missed, the scan detector has no provision for a focusing filter, collecting low and slow probes on an hourly basis is a manual technique and therefore prone to error.

Some attackers are patient enough to scan at rates as low as two packets per day; in these cases an hour clearly is not a reasonable time window. Figure 9 illustrates example output from a 24 hour scan detection tool called look4scans.pl. This tool was part of the version 1.5 Shadow software release.

```
10.9.8.7 :    Reset.host.net
10.9.8.7 > 192.168.103.90 : R
10.9.8.7 > 192.168.114.15 : R
10.9.8.7 > 192.168.122.80 : R
10.9.8.7 > 192.168.137.149 : R
10.9.8.7 > 192.168.157.224 : R
10.9.8.7 > 192.168.164.44 : R
10.9.8.7 > 192.168.174.161 : R
10.9.8.7 > 192.168.201.148 : R
10.9.8.7 > 192.168.202.85 : R
10.9.8.7 > 192.168.204.79 : R
10.9.8.7 > 192.168.213.156 : R
10.9.8.7 > 192.168.29.38 : R
10.9.8.7 > 192.168.41.157 : R
10.9.8.7 > 192.168.43.145 : R
10.9.8.7 > 192.168.45.174 : R
10.9.8.7 > 192.168.85.28 : R
10.9.8.7 > 172.20.107.109 : R
10.9.8.7 > 172.20.113.214 : R
10.9.8.7 > 172.20.115.6 : R
10.9.8.7 > 172.20.13.168 : R
10.9.8.7 > 172.20.140.69 : R
10.9.8.7 > 172.20.145.25 : R
10.9.8.7 > 172.20.191.30 : R
10.9.8.7 > 172.20.205.137 : R
10.9.8.7 > 172.20.207.56 : R
10.9.8.7 > 172.20.224.98 : R
10.9.8.7 > 172.20.23.185 : R
10.9.8.7 > 172.20.31.98 : R
10.9.8.7 > 172.20.41.248 : R
10.9.8.7 > 172.20.42.114 : R
10.9.8.7 > 172.20.62.140 : R
10.9.8.7 > 172.20.71.217 : R
10.9.8.7 > 172.20.84.178 : R
```

Figure 9. Example 'look4scans.pl' output.

Slow coordinated attacks are particularly difficult to detect using these methods. If the attackers can guess your detection threshold they can ensure that no single IP address sends enough packets to trip that threshold. Unless the attackers are foolish enough to include some

other signature in the scan, these will be particularly difficult to detect.

4.4. Resets as an indicator of TCP session hijacking

The nmap scanning tool released December 1998 has a sequence number evaluator as part of its most basic functionality, so hijack will be with us for a while yet! The idea is to find an active connection, and predict the sequence numbers on both sides of the connection. Hit the side you *don't* want to penetrate with a Reset to break off the connection from their point of view. Assume the connection and attack the other side. The signature for this attack is the correct sequence number and wrong IP address.

4.5. ISS RealSecure kill

We have seen this only twice. If an ISS RealSecure thinks the site it is protecting is under attack, it may generate a connection Reset. In this case, the packet contains the ID Number of the RealSecure engine.

4.6. Deception

As stated earlier, several freely available scanners can generate Resets with spoofed addresses simply as a smokescreen. They accomplish no purpose except possibly to consume analyst and CIRT resources.

How big of a problem is this? There are a few areas of concern:

A.   If some portion of the inexplicable Resets is related to mapping attempts, then external actors are gaining intelligence about the networks that we are supposed to defend. In this case, the solution is to implement a firewall that can drop these packets.

B.   Though we aren't particularly bothered by the second order effect problem, it is bad from a public perception standpoint if it is widely thought that our sites are attacking other sites, since our address space is being used.

5. SFRP scans

In the previous scan examples, the attackers came to us. This is not always the case. Scanning can happen when we visit the attacker. In this case, malformed packets with SYN, Reset, FIN and Urgent are detected coming from web servers to the browsing client. The most common pattern is one SFRP (SYN/FIN/Reset/PUSH) packet sent to each browsing client per session. Sometimes SRP's are also sent, Figure 10 illustrates the pattern.

```
10:47:36.61 media.com.2048 > target.48579: SFR
2842082:2842590(508) ack 2642669109 win 768
urg 2571 (DF)
11:23:42.97 media.com.2048 > target.47720: SFP
4820865:4821409(544) win 3840 urg 2571 (DF)
13:49:44.33 gm.com.49608 > target.49606: SFP
7051:7607(556) ack 2147789506 win 7768 (DF)
13:49:44.72 gm.com.22450 > target.1591: SFRP
2038:2074(36) ack 116065792 win 0 urg 0 (DF)
```

Figure 10. TCP stack analysis.

Figure 11 shows related activity that is not from the original site but is within the same general timeframe. The stimulus here is the client visiting the web server. These are examples of what comes back. Each client gets at least one packet and as many as four, (with different combinations), during a visit to a web server.

```
12:18:46.25 im.com.5500 > target.1137: SFP
3241821:3242365(544) win 13234 urg 55134 (DF)
13:37:30.33 im.com.22555 > target.22555: SF
8440982:8441538(556) win 10240 (DF)
14:52:57.45 scannernet.30975 > target.16940:
SFRP 2029994540:2029995068(528) ack 2029994540
win 16940 urg 16940 <[bad opt]> (DF)
14:53:01.63 scannernet.30975 > target.556:
SFRP 2029978156:2029978684(528) ack 2029978156
win 556 urg 556 <[bad opt]> (DF)
```

Figure 11. Cooperative tcp stack analysis example.

We have a pattern we have never seen before and it occurs during transactions with multiple web servers from multiple domains. During the height of this technique, in October 1998, over twenty web-servers from a very large ISP were exhibiting this behavior.

After tracking this for several weeks, we were still leaning toward considering this benign, perhaps some error in the web-server code. However, two weeks later, probes were observed from the same address family that did not have any stimulus (no one visited a web page). These non-stimulus caused probes were targeting DNS and mail servers. At this point, the activity was considered hostile. Since multiple web-servers were performing these probes in concert, this was also considered a coordinated attack.

6. Target based analysis

Until now, every example has shown multiple attackers, multiple targets, and we have focused on the activity of the inbound packets and the analysis of that activity. Now let's consider a different analysis technique: examining the targets. One of the factors that helped us understand the fact that Reset scanners were working together was that they did not duplicate targets; each system probed was unique. Furthermore, many of the attackers would scan three hosts from one site and twelve from a second and this pattern would continue day after day.

Infrastructure systems such as DNS and email servers are a good starting place for target analysis. In a given week, a large number of the total attacks are usually against these types of systems. In figure 12, the traces show attacks that come from vastly different IP addresses. These IP addresses originate from Australia, Asia and the USA, but all include the same targets, and occurred over a single weekend. "Whoops" isn't really a name server or email server, though it was erroneously listed as one in a DNS table.

Also, please note that SourceA and SourceB have different IP address numbers. Since this is TCP, the exploit cannot work if they spoof the source address. One of the probe sets could be a decoy; it could be a multi-homed host, or it could be two systems working together. Please note the packet arrival times to see how related the first two scans appear to be and also the static source port. The third trace has a significant difference from the first two; the source port pattern indicates two processes. In the following example, we would assume that the first two traces are related and the third trace is a different actor.

One of the themes of this story is that the events of interest we classify as coordinated attacks are often detects that we had never seen before. Suddenly, we see it from (or to) multiple locations. To detect and classify a coordinated attack, it really helps to have a database of all traffic and techniques to complement your signatures. Without a database of traffic that covers a time window of at least a couple months, there is no way to determine whether this activity has been going on and simply hasn't been detected, or if it is a new pattern. Recently, we tested a pattern that had been detected by an analyst at another site. We were sure we had never seen it before. Wrong! What really stung us was that one of the attackers had spun this attack off of source port 7 (echo), something a good analyst should never miss. Oh well.

If you can only detect and examine traffic that matches your signature set, then how can you detect a new, or novel attack?

```
06:10:56.53 SourceA.10053 > NS1.111: S
1935318310:1935318310(0) win 242
06:32:42.15 SourceA.10053 > NS2.111: S
552822870:552822870(0) win 242
06:54:27.32 SourceA.10053 > MAIL1.111: S
944974642:944974642(0) win 242
07:16:12.73 SourceA.10053 > MAIL2.111: S
3045099303:3045099303(0) win 242
07:37:58.16 SourceA.10053 > Whoops.111: S
323776127:323776127(0) win 242

06:12:33.28 SourceB.10053 > NS1.domain: S
992750649:992750649(0) win 242
06:34:18.66 SourceB.10053 > NS2.domain: S
3455530061:3455530061(0) win 242
06:56:04.046 SourceB.10053 > MAIL1.domain: S
1895963699:1895963699(0) win 242
07:17:49.44 SourceB.10053 > MAIL2.domain: S
2485794595:2485794595(0) win 242
07:39:34.811723 SourceB.10053 > Whoops.domain:
S 3785701160:3785701160(0) win 242

08:01:20.23 SourceB.1025 > NS1.imap: S
1471781129:1471781129(0) win 512
08:23:05.64 SourceB.21053 > NS2.imap: S
4110489384:4110489384(0) win 512
08:24:50.96 SourceB.1026 > MAIL1.imap: S
1486592867:1486592867(0) win 512
08:23:05.64 SourceB.21055 > MAIL2.imap: S
1112489384:1112489384(0) win 512
08:44:50.96 SourceB.1028 > Whoops.imap: S
0486592777:0486592777(0) win 512
```

Figure 12. Target based analysis.

```
AttackerB.6667 -> 192.168.229.72.1437, 1
packet
AttackerB.6667 -> 192.168.229.72.1437, 2
packets
AttackerB.6667 -> 192.168.229.82.1437, 1
packet
AttackerB.6667 -> 192.168.229.82.1437, 2
packets
AttackerB.6667 -> 192.168.229.95.1437, 1
packet
AttackerB.6667 -> 192.168.229.95.1437, 2
packets
AttackerB.6667 -> 192.168.229.6.1437, 1
packet
AttackerB.6667 -> 192.168.229.6.1437, 1
packet
AttackerB.6667 -> 192.168.229.79.1437, 1
packet
AttackerB.6667 -> 192.168.229.79.1437, 2
```

```
packets
AttackerB.6667 -> 192.168.229.45.1437, 1
packet
AttackerB.6667 -> 192.168.229.45.1437, 2
packets

AttackerC.139 -> 192.168.229.28.1437, 1
packet
AttackerC.139 -> 192.168.229.28.1437, 1
packet
AttackerC.139 -> 192.168.229.28.1437, 1
packet
AttackerC.139 -> 192.168.229.122.1437, 1
packet
AttackerC.139 -> 192.168.229.122.1437, 1
packet
AttackerC.139 -> 192.168.229.122.1437, 1
packet
AttackerC.139 -> 192.168.229.122.1437, 1
packet
AttackerC.139 -> 192.168.229.28.1437, 1
packet
AttackerC.139 -> 192.168.229.28.1437, 1
packet
AttackerC.139 -> 192.168.229.28.1437, 1
packet
AttackerC.139 -> 192.168.229.75.1437, 1
packet
AttackerC.139 -> 192.168.229.75.1437, 1
packet
AttackerC.139 -> 192.168.229.75.1437, 1
packet
```

Figure 13.

Figure 13 shows the traffic from an event that took place over a four-day weekend. In this case, multiple addresses began to target a specific destination port. In the first trace, notice the one packet two packet pattern and the source port of 6667 (IRC). Attacker C has a different pattern or their IDS interprets it differently. For two months different IP addresses were probing this site on the same destination port. No other sites with which we share information have detected this activity.

7. Conclusions

The examples shown in this paper represent a change in the kinds of attacks and probes we track. Previously, it had been common for a single attacker to target multiple sites. Now we see indications of multiple attackers working together to target either single sites or multiple sites. We can use all of the analysis techniques we have learned to find differences or similarities in delivery mechanisms. These may help provide clues as to the number of discrete attackers involved, especially when we have data across a fairly large time window, such as a week or longer.

It should be noted that these techniques are starting to be widely used and the attacker community is building decoy techniques into commonly available tools. However, we are not aware of a widely available distributed scanner, or exploit delivery system. Additionally, these coordinated attacks display a significant amount of variability making them difficult to detect with signature-based algorithms.

There are three obvious purposes for coordinated attacks and probes: stealth, firepower, and intelligence gathering.

7.1. Stealth

By working from multiple IP addresses the attackers achieve a smaller per-IP signature and are more difficult to detect through conventional means. In addition, stealth is enhanced by the development of new hard-to-detect probing techniques such as Reset scans.

7.2. Firepower

By coordinating multiple attacking IP addresses, the attackers will be able to deliver more exploits to destination hosts in a smaller period of time. Furthermore, the defensive technique of blocking an attacker IP, also known as shunning, will be less effective. A single attacking entity can utilize multiple non-related Internet addresses for the attacks. This is especially true for denial of service attacks; most of these do not rely on a connection being made, so the probability of the address being spoofed is very high. Some of these coordinated probes and scans we detect today may be practice runs for future larger scale attacks. After a new exploit is discovered, there is often a limited "window of opportunity" for its use; usually until countermeasures are developed.

7.3. Intelligence gathering

As discussed in the coordinated traceroute example, by working from different IP addresses on different backbones against the same target, it is possible to obtain data that is impossible to obtain from a single source IP scan or probe. These data may include shortest route data, (i.e. packets from source A arrive faster than from source B), or even potential backdoors, (i.e. packets from source A can gain access to hosts that source B can't see). This type of data can be used to optimize future scans, probes, or attacks. It could also be used to isolate a target site by attacking the links it uses to communicate with the outside world.

The SFRP example shows how a network of servers can simply wait for the customer to come to them. The progress in TCP stack analysis is very impressive and we wouldn't be surprised to see this capability become integrated into commercial server software as one more method of gathering intelligence about the systems that visit the server.

8. Final words

Analysis of the network traffic collected by the SHADOW team indicates that new exploit delivery mechanisms are being developed and refined. These techniques employ multiple attackers and decoy hosts in an attempt to increase stealth, firepower, and reconnaissance.

Much of the network traffic discussed in this paper is definitely the result of coordinated attacks. However, a small portion can also be attributed to deception techniques and second order effects. Therefore, it is extremely important for the analyst to differentiate between the two possible causes of suspicious network traffic, and react accordingly. To this end, we have discussed the motivations for coordinating attacks, and also provided examples of each attack type. Methods for detecting this coordinated activity have been illustrated when possible.

Reference:

SHADOW is a freely available, public domain intrusion detection system. Information and software for the SHADOW System can be downloaded from the following website:

http://www.nswc.navy.mil/ISSEC/CID

Intrusion Detection and Intrusion Prevention on a Large Network. A Case Study.

Tom Dunigan, Network Research
Oak Ridge National Laboratory
Greg Hinkel, Computer & Network Security
Oak Ridge National Laboratory

Abstract

This paper describes the general requirements for an Intrusion Prevention and Detection System and the methods used to prevent and detect intrusions into Oak Ridge National Laboratory's network. In this paper we describe actual intrusions, how they were detected, and how they were handled. We also describe the monitoring tools we use for detecting intrusions.

Introduction

At Oak Ridge National Laboratory (ORNL), we have an open environment in which researchers around the world must collaborate with ORNL researchers. These users want and need easy access to each other's data, programs, and correspondence. Furthermore, many of the researchers have been accustomed to unfettered access to and from the Internet. Obviously, we also have data that should not be available to external users.

Our network consists of approximately 18,000 computers running a variety of operating systems, including UNIX, VMS, Windows, and MacOS. Our users abilities range from "untrained" desktop users to highly trained supercomputer programmers.

An open environment like ORNL's poses many security concerns. The dynamic nature of the work performed at ORNL introduces additional security concerns in that new project initiatives, with new users and new computers, begin almost daily. These new projects often create sudden increases in network activity from new and different computer systems, and the sudden increases make it difficult to weed out "new project" traffic from intrusion attempts. Also, many of our "users" are not physically located at ORNL. Trying to determine if a remote user is the "legitimate user" is not an easy task. The question, "Was login information sniffed by a hacker who is now logging in?," is quite difficult to answer.

A security plan is essential. Knowing what to look for takes time, experience, diligence, and a lot of luck. Our plan needed to answer the following questions.
- What is the threat?
- What can happen if an intrusion occurs?
- What should we watch for?
- What should we report?
  - What should our intrusion detection system report to us?
  - Should we report intrusions to someone and if so, to whom?
- What should we do if and when we suspect an intrusion?

Intrusion prevention is our goal. However, it was clear that we would not be able to completely prevent intrusions, so we decided to:
- try to reduce the number of possible intrusions, and
- quickly detect any intrusions that did occur.

A simple solution to intrusion prevention and detection was not possible at ORNL. Trying to reduce the number of intrusions would have to be accomplished by providing secure mechanisms for end users to access their computer systems and then educating those users and their system administrators about the proper use of those secure mechanisms. Additional hardware and software would be required for intrusion detection. Detecting intrusions in real time is preferable and in isolated cases is possible. However, to reduce the likelihood of terminating a legitimate connection and to be more effective at detecting intrusions, it was clear that we would have to log and analyze users' activities. There are commercial packages that satisfy some of our requirements; however, none would satisfy all of our requirements. Therefore, we had to implement a specialized program that used commercial packages in conjunction with solutions developed in-house.

At ORNL, we use a layered approach to network security because multiple layers make penetration more difficult while making detection a bit easier. We define our layers as follows:

1. firewall for limiting access,
2. external monitoring for detecting attacks,
3. internal monitoring for detecting attacks and reducing vulnerabilities,
4. system administration for reducing vulnerabilities, and
5. end users for reducing vulnerabilities.

The security staff must be knowledgeable security professionals and they must:

- know what to look for (i.e., what kinds of attacks might occur?);
- know what they are seeing (i.e., what does the data "on the wire" or in the log files represent?);
- know (or have an idea) what to do if their computers come under attack and know who to contact for additional information or assistance; and
- educate the users and system administrators about computer and network security issues, and keep them informed of current attack methods and counter measures.

We think it is important for the security staff to have a good rapport with users. Users and system administrators should trust the security professionals and look to them for advice; users should be able to depend on the security professionals to keep them abreast of current attack methods and countermeasures.

At ORNL, we need fast data collecting machines that are tightly controlled, with all unneeded services turned off. Encrypted communication is the only means of entry into these machines (except for console access). Our security staff is trained to use these encrypted channels correctly.

We also need plenty of disk space for log files because we planned to keep at least one month's worth of data online.

Policy Decisions

Q. What is the threat?
A. We generally consider the users on our network to be "trusted." Our main concern is people outside our network trying to get into our network. Many of our users log in through their ISP (Internet Service Provider); from a conference floor; or from a remote network (e.g., at a collaborator's site) using insecure applications, such as telnet, ftp, or POP. Therefore, we have determined that our biggest threat is from authorized remote users who access our machines and have their login information sniffed at the remote site.

Our second greatest threat is misconfigured or unpatched systems. We have several users that cannot (or do not want to) spend time/money to ensure the integrity of their machines, or they do not understand the threat and importance of keeping their machines secured. Our computers have been "hacked" because of "misconfigured" or unpatched systems. However, our decision to use a commercial security package, Internet Security Scanner (ISS), and to develop customized tools for checking for network vulnerabilities, have significantly reduced our vulnerabilities.

An internal scan may show no vulnerabilities one day, but that is no assurance that a vulnerability will not be present the next day. For example, we scanned our address space for "named" service and notified appropriate system administrators of potential vulnerabilities. The day after that scan, one of our users rebooted his machine from Windows 95 to Linux, which was running an unpatched "named." That night our network was scanned by a remote site, and that machine was compromised via a buffer overflow in "named."

Q. What can happen if an intrusion occurs?
A. Possible problems for us include:

1. loss of data;
2. modification of data, which can be more serious than loss of data;
3. misuse of equipment;
4. loss of employee time and/or CPU time;
5. time spent assessing damage and cleaning up; and
6. embarrassment to the company/project/individual.

Q. What should we watch for and what should our intrusion detection system report to us?
A. Because our biggest security threat is legitimate users having their login information sniffed at a remote site, we need to watch for unusual activity for each user. For example, if a user typically logs in from Knoxville and suddenly logs in from Peru, we need to be notified. Likewise, if a user typically uses a computer for editing, compiling, and running FORTRAN programs, and suddenly begins using IRC (Internet Relay Chat), we need to be notified. Following the activity patterns of users requires monitoring the commands they issue, which meant a network keystroke logger was needed.

Because port scanning is very popular and because we need to watch other network services (in addition to those that the keystroke logger picks up), it seemed prudent to detect incoming connection requests, which meant we also needed a "touch logger."

These monitors do not usually provide real-time notification, so we use a third party Intrusion Detection System (IDS) which does provide real-time notification. We also knew that there would be times when we would have to monitor specific services and/or hosts (for "special case" needs), so we added an additional machine for this purpose.

Q. What should we do if/when we suspect an intrusion?
A. Possible actions are:
1. remove compromised machine from the network,
2. setup additional monitoring,
3. deny access to effected machines and/or subnets,
4. deny access to specific users, and
5. notify essential personnel.

Q. Should we report intrusions (and attempts), and to whom should we report them?
A. We decided to report everything we determined to be "unfriendly activity." We report them to CIAC as well as to the registered administrator of the "attacking" subnet. We notify others as necessary, such as AUSCERT and EUROCERT. Our hope is that by notifying central security facilities, information about attacking sites could be disseminated to other "legitimate" facilities who could then watch more closely for activity from those sites. We have also received very favorable responses from ISPs, where, in many cases, accounts were terminated. Figure 1 shows the number of messages we sent to remote sites in 1998, as well as the number of intrusions that we had last year.

Hardware Configuration

At ORNL, we have several dedicated computer systems that collect network data coming from and going to external networks. They are all time-synchronized to ensure accurate "reconstruction" of each attack. Time synchronization is also necessary because with that information, personnel at the offending site can track the attacker much more easily.

These machines log successful and unsuccessful TCP connections, UDP packets, and user keystrokes with tools developed in-house. An additional computer logs selected connections and sessions with a third party IDS package. Another system assimilates the data, processes it, and generates human readable reports, which are mailed to security personnel several times a day. These reports show "interesting" traffic patterns, where "interesting" is defined as things that appear to be potentially unfriendly. A few examples follow:
- external machines connecting to TCP ports 111 (portmap) or 15 (netstat) or UDP port 31337 (the default for BackOrifice),
- external machines attempting to log into our central name servers,
- external hosts scanning internal hosts or ports,
- connections to/from local hosts that have recently been compromised,
- connections to/from hosts that have recently been the source of an attack, or
- hosts that generate the most network traffic.

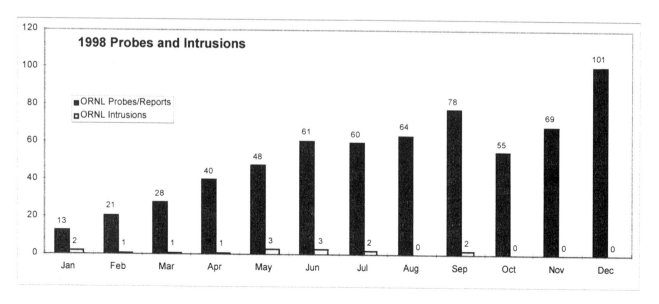

We have additional computers that can be used for "special case" monitoring when needed. Such special cases would include monitoring all traffic going to/from a given host or subnet (in the case of a hacked system), or it may include collecting all data related to a particular port (in the case of an ongoing port scan). These machines also can be configured to provide real-time alerts for specific activities.

Logging all TCP connections, whether successful or not, helps in the detection of port scans and also is valuable in determining where an attacker comes from and goes after gaining access to one of our machines. We also use this information to determine which of our computers respond to particular services. When an attacker runs a port scan against our computers, we collect the responses so that we can follow up on them (hopefully before the attacker does).

Our most useful intrusion detection tool is our "keystroke logger," which records session keystrokes. It is virtually impossible to detect intrusions without this tool. Because our users log in from around the world at all times of the day and night and all have different tasks, it is not possible to determine authorized sessions from unauthorized sessions by simply looking at the connections. Also, attackers often "clean up" system log files, so relying on end users and system administrators is not sufficient. Our reviews of users' keystrokes often indicates hacker activity.

Additional computers can be placed on selected subnets for special-case monitoring or for "replacement" of a hacked system. We do this to learn "back door" accounts that the attacker may have planted, as well as to learn more about the attacker's methods. Case 3 below shows an example of a modified telnet daemon that appears, to the attacker, to allow access to a recently compromised system for a given user. In that case, we held the attackers attention long enough to contact his ISP and determine his location.

Implementation

At ORNL, we use a layered approach to network security because multiple layers make penetration more difficult while making detection a bit easier. Our layers, both physical and administrative, are defined as follows:

1. a firewall,
2. external monitoring,
3. internal monitoring,
4. system administration, and
5. end users.

Our layered approach follows:

1. **A Firewall.**

A firewall is used to limit access to our network. Services, hosts, and subnets are selectively permitted or restricted from accessing our network. Occasionally, local hosts are restricted from accessing the Internet.

2. **External Monitoring.**
Several computers, as mentioned previously in "Hardware Configuration," are set up to monitor traffic coming from and going to our network. These machines detect probes and intrusion attempts and alert security personnel of such events.

3. **Internal Monitoring.**
We have several machines (honeypots) instrumented and alarmed to notify security personnel of particular events (e.g., a follow-up attack trying to exploit a vulnerability in a service that an attacker identified through a previous port scan). We also have our main WEB, mail, and DNS servers instrumented to notify security personnel of suspicious events, such as a remote user attempting to log into our name servers.

Using ISS, we scan our network for computers with known security vulnerabilities, and then reports are sent to the system administrator. Custom scans are developed to detect other vulnerabilities where ISS is insufficient. For example, scans for the latest "named" exploit were developed and used. The administrators for all machines identified as running "named" were notified, and they either patched or disabled "named." In another case, a teardrop check was developed to allow users to test their machines and verify vulnerabilities to a teardrop attack. Review of the latest CIAC and CERT advisories, as well as frequent checks of hacker resources such as bugtraq, provide critical knowledge of the "newest" attacks. These advisories and hacker resources are often the stimulation for development of a custom scan.

We also have a mechanism where we "bait" sniffer programs. The intent is to detect a sniffer program that may have been installed on a local machine but gone undetected. We inject packets onto the network that appear as a login session. Any sniffer should log the "session." We judiciously put different login "sessions" on various subnets, and we change them occasionally. If the attacker then tries to log in to one of the "baited" accounts, security personnel can determine where the attempted login came from but more importantly, can pinpoint on which subnet the sniffer was running and the time period it was running.

4. **System Administration.**
Good system administration is encouraged. A "scan me" web page was developed to allow system administrators to easily run ISS against their machines to determine vulnerabilities so that they could be patched quickly. System administrators are informed of current attack methods and vulnerabilities. They are encouraged to run md5 checksums on system files, and a "central" repository was established for master checksum lists. We encourage the use of TCP Wrappers for host-based access and for logging. Default routes are not set unless necessary. System administrators review system log files, including syslog and web server logs, and they notify security personnel of unusual activity. Administrators are encouraged to "know their users" and "know their machines."

5. **End Users.**
Ongoing efforts are made to educate the end users. They are instructed in selection of good passwords, on how clear text reusable passwords can be used against them, and about the importance of their account. A "central" web site was developed for security-related issues, making it easier for users (and system administrators) to locate necessary information and report unusual activity. We also provide guidelines for the "proper use" of .rhosts files and the "proper use" of ssh and s/key. End users are made aware of issues that may result in embarrassment to the company or to themselves, or issues that may harm their reputations or the company's reputation.

We look for signs of intrusion, such as hackers sharing information among themselves about their recent discoveries. Other things to look for (coming from external machines or from internal machines) include:
- probes/port scans;
- excessive pinging or pinging our broadcast addresses;
- top source addresses, destination addresses, and service ports;
- unauthorized access; and
- "changes," such as sudden increases in traffic by one machine.

Cases

Case 1 - Misconfigured System
ORNL's address space was scanned (by another government facility) for machines providing service on TCP port 1. This generally identifies SGI machines because they are the only vendor that enables this service by default. The port scan identified a machine at 11:23:19 and at 11:24:05; a user attempted to log into the machine via telnet. The attacker first tried "lp," which was password protected, then tried "demos," which was not password protected. The attacker grabbed the password file and the NIS password file then created a "hidden" directory (.a) and ftp'd their exploit and hack tools from several locations, including their "home base." The attacker exploited a bug in the "df" command and became root, started a sniffer program, and cleaned up the log files to remove their login records. The sniffer program was named "diag," and it logged to a file named /usr/spool/lp/.a/err. The attacker set a password on the "lp" account.

The port scan was detected by our "TCP connection logger." The "telnet" sessions were logged by our "keystroke logger." Access to the machine was disabled at the firewall. The system administrator was notified. All passwords were changed, and the operating system was reinstalled. This machine was on a switched Ethernet port, so the sniffer didn't log anything. After analysis of log files and files left by the attacker and in cooperation with remote sites (that were affected by the hack), it was determined that the attacker was in Russia.

Case 2 - Unpatched System
Our address space was scanned by a machine in Brazil beginning at 22:07. This was an "mscan" type scan. Beginning at 22:16, a second machine from Brazil did a "follow-up" scan of selected machines. At 23:35 a bug in "named" was exploited on one machine, resulting in a "root shell xterm" being sent to that second machine in Brazil. The attacker created the directory "/tmp/.a" and ftp'd their hack tools (a sniffer and a "smurf" program) into it. The attacker named the sniffer program "update" and the log file "blah.log" and installed a trojan /bin/login to allow rewt/lamer! to log in without being logged. The attacker also created an account "blah" without a password but did not clean up the system log files. The sniffer proved fruitful, and at 00:07, the attacker logged into another machine and tried to exploit known vulnerabilities to become root. This attempt was unsuccessful.

The port scan was detected by our "TCP connection logger." The login sessions were logged by our "keystroke logger," and access to the machines was disabled at the firewall. The system administrator was notified. All affected passwords were changed, and the operating system was reinstalled. We got no cooperation from Brazil and were not able to determine any further information about this attacker.

Case 3 - Sniffed password.

Our TCP connection logger indicated an unusually large increase in network traffic from one of our machines. The keystroke log indicated "inappropriate" activity on four machines. Analysis of the four machines revealed that an IRC "bot" was running. (An IRC bot is a program that allows a user to appear to be logged into IRC even after they have logged off. It has several features including allowing the user to keep their IRC nickname and channels so that no one else can take them.) There also were other hacker tools left on some of the systems. Network activity for the four machines was monitored for a couple hours before closing off access to those machines. Although the attacker attempted to exploit known vulnerabilities with these systems, he was unsuccessful. Review of the log files revealed all the remote sites visited by the attacker; those sites were notified of the activity. It was clear from our logs (and verified later) that an authorized user had his login information "sniffed." It was uncertain at first where it had been sniffed. The following day, unauthorized logins occurred on five other machines, using a different login name. The attacker was able to gain root access on two of the machines and installed a sniffer program on each machine. He changed passwords on some accounts and also installed an IRC "bot" on one of the machines.

Unfortunately, our keystroke logging machine had a disk failure during the critical time, and we were not able to log all of the activity. Fortunately, though, our other logging machines were running. Using them, along with system logs from some of the compromised machines, we were able to piece together the full attack. Like the previous user, it was clear that this user had his login information sniffed. Both authorized users were at the same remote location. We surmised (and later verified) that the accounts were "sniffed" at that location. We closed off access to the five computers and began reviewing log files and files left by the attacker. We contacted remote sites that were affected and requested information. Piecing this information together revealed the exact identity of the attacker, who was from a U.S. city. Anticipating a return visit to our machines, we replaced one of the hacked machines with a special-purpose machine, which appeared to grant access. It kept the attacker "busy" while the machine notified us. While the attacker was "on," we contacted the ISP from which he was coming. That ISP verified that the attacker was coming from the same location as the previous attacks. The attacker

returned several times later to see if his "holes" were still open.

The "unusual" network traffic was detected by our "TCP connection logger." The login sessions were recorded by our "keystroke logger." Access to the machines was disabled at the firewall. The system administrators were notified. All affected passwords were changed, and the operating systems were reinstalled on the machines that were "root" compromised.

Case Summary

Having multiple computer systems for intrusion detection allowed us to detect an intrusion, even when one of those monitoring systems was down. Diligent review of log files enabled us to detect the intrusions early. Quick response by security personnel contained the "damage" and permitted a short down time for the compromised systems. In all cases, we continue to monitor recently "hacked" machines and accounts for at least several weeks following an intrusion. This monitoring will often show other "hostile" sources that we can then either watch for or we can notify appropriate authorities. In at least one case, we detected unauthorized login attempts using login names and passwords that had been sniffed five months prior. Fortunately, those passwords had long since been changed.

Summary

An effective intrusion prevention and detection system includes limiting your vulnerabilities, knowing what methods attackers are using, educating your users, implementing hardware and software solutions that detect those vulnerabilities and attack methods. Knowing how to use the IDS and actually using it are critical. Day-to-day log review is boring at best; automating the review process is necessary. Diligent review of logs is paramount to detecting intrusions early and to limiting the damage. Effective computer and network security is very dynamic. Security staff must continually learn and experiment, developing and enhancing tools. Intrusion detection tools are only one part of an effective computer security plan. Trying to prevent the intrusions is of utmost importance and can be accomplished (or at least reduced) by educating end users, training system administrators, and running vulnerability checks on your machines. Cooperation from remote sites is necessary to close all holes.

References

William R. Cheswick and Steven M. Bellovin, "Firewalls and Internet Security," Addison-Wesley, 1994.

Vern Paxson, "Bro: A System for Detecting Network Intruders in Real-Time," Seventh USENIX Security Symposium Proceedings, pp. 31-51, January 1998.

"Network Intrusion Detector," Lawrence Livermore National Laboratory (UCRL-MA-116609 rev.3), November 1997.

Internet Security Systems, Inc., "Internet Security Scanner" and "RealSecure," http://iss.net, 1998.

Shadow, SANS Institute, http://www.nswc.navy.mil/ISSEC/CID, 1998.

Computer Incident Advisory Capability (CIAC), CIAC Bulletins, http://ciac.org, 1998.

Computer Emergency Response Team (CERT) Coordination Center, CERT Advisories, http://www.cert.org, 1998.

Rootshell, Exploit Information and Hacker Tools, http://rootshell.com, 1998.

BUGTRAQ, Bugtraq mailing list archives, http://www.geek-girl.com/bugtraq/index.html, 1998.

Computer Operations, Audit, and Security Technology (COAST), http://www.cs.purdue.edu/coast/coast.html, 1998.

An eye on network intruder-administrator shootouts

Luc Girardin
UBS, Ubilab

Abstract

Carefully logging network activity is essential to meet the requirements of high security and optimal resource availability. However, detecting break-in attempts within this activity is a difficult task. Making the distinction between misuse and normal use is hard, and identifying intrusions that use novel attacks is fundamentally difficult.

In this paper, we introduce a visual approach for analyzing network activity. This approach differs from anomaly and misuse detection because it considers human factors to support the exploration of network traffic. Our prototype application is based on an unsupervised neural network and consequently does not rely on any prior knowledge of the data being analyzed. We use self-organizing maps to project the network events on a space appropriate for visualization, and achieve their exploration using a map metaphor. The approach we present can be used to analyze past and present activities, as well as to show trends in the events.

To demonstrate the usability of our tools, we describe the investigation of a dataset containing common intrusion patterns. We also discuss some weaknesses of current intrusion detection systems and propose a new paradigm for monitoring network activity that enables the discovery of new, sophisticated, and structured attacks.

1. Introduction

The primary source of information that enables administrators to monitor their networks is the logging facilities provided by hubs, routers, firewalls, hosts, and network sniffers. Such facilities are often used to track real-time events and to archive the activity-history of the network. Careful logging is essential to the security [Geer et al., 1997], and provides the foundation for intrusion and anomaly detection. Intruders trying to break-in or spiteful employees attempting to gain unauthorized access are two important targets for intrusion detection systems. Audit logs can be used to detect abnormal behaviors to solve problems before occur. Logs are crucial to determine the cause of a failure, or the extent of damage after an attack and can, if monitored in real-time, be used to track failures and intrusions in progress. Another important use of audit logs is the analysis of how, when, and where resources are used, thus providing information on which to base planning decisions. Additionally, making potential intruders aware of the logging activity is a good deterrent, or can in the last resort provide evidence, which may be used to prosecute them.

Geographical maps have always provided a practical way to navigate our expanding world. From handwritten maps to satellite imaging, geography has played a major role in the analysis and in the expansion of human activity. They have become more than practical records of locations, they have given us a perception of space. People are easily able to explore cities and navigate through countries they have never visited before thanks to geographic tools. Despite the fact that maps must distort reality to portray meaningful relationships within a complex world [Monmonier, 1991], they are essential to our continuous expansion. Although the physical earth has been completely mapped, we usually still watch our activities in cyberspace through a keyhole. Maps of abstract spaces, such as the activity taking place in a network can help in getting a global view of what is going on, and in particular improve the way we protect ourselves from potential intruders.

Current intrusion detection systems are targeted toward unattended operations. The primary weakness of such systems is their inability to cope with new, sophisticated, and structured attacks. Such attacks represent the greatest threat to security. Our approach differs because it acknowledges the human ability to cope with complexity. It provides us with the possibility of using our tacit knowledge to make fuzzy decisions as to whether a pattern of activity is of harmless/dangerous or kindly/malicious nature, therefore giving a chance to detect unexpected attacks.

In this paper, we discuss our visual approach for monitoring network traffic in the context of intrusion detection. Visualizing the network activity provides us with new ways to explore, track, and analyze intruders. It makes the monitoring user-friendly and supports the mental representation by providing a frame of reference for the network activity. We describe our prototype application, which is based on the self-organizing map algorithm to perform topological clustering. We then explain how to use our network visualization tool to detect four different types of popular attacks.

2. Intrusion detection[1]

With the expansion of the Internet, electronic commerce and distributed computing, the amount of information transmitted through electronic networks is continuously increasing. Such possibilities have opened many new business horizons. However, they have also resulted in a considerable increase of illegal computer intrusions [Power, 1998]. While it is common to protect our networks the same way we lock our doors, it is no longer possible to widely monitor the activity taking place on our computers and networks. In fact, the rise in sophistication of intrusions and the ever-increasing network traffic and complexity make our current monitoring tools blind and impractical. Consequently, we cannot even be informed after a breach that our door has be smashed or our belongings stolen. Thus, all the symptoms disappear and we realize our errors through the consequences. The usual result is a decision to install better and more complicated locks on the doors, postponing the problem for a while, or to tighten the security policy, leading to a limitation in the way we can conduct our business.

An emerging trend that addresses these problems is the deployment of intrusion detection systems. These systems are aimed at detecting threatening situations which occur in spite of other security measures and follow two main paradigms: anomaly detection and misuse detection systems. They are intended to be used in conjunction with additional security measures enforcing the security policy. Like motion detectors in a building, they constitute a second line of defense sitting behind the locks on the doors and windows [Avolio, 1998].

Anomaly detection systems work by attempting to create a profile of what constitutes typical network activity.

---

[1] Readers already familiar with current anomaly and misuse detection approaches should skip to the next section.

This model is created by capturing observable behaviors in the network traffic in order to identify and extract characterizing and repeating patterns. Typically, such systems use rules to automate filtering by suppressing known-good behaviors and triggering appropriate alerts when required. To achieve this, the profile is compared against new patterns of activity that will trigger alarms if the difference with the model exceeds a certain threshold. One of the problems is to distinguish between normal and suspicious behaviors; a sophisticated intruder might still generate malicious activities that mimic normal behaviors. Also, because the profile is updated over time, there is still a possibility for an attacker to generate innocent traffic that might be useful in hiding a subsequent attack. Finally, one has to ensure that the extracted characteristics used to build the model will allow for the differentiation of normal and malicious activity. An attack might leave no identifiable clues that an intrusion detection system will pick-up [Amoroso, 1994]. Descriptions of such anomaly detection systems can be found in [Anderson et al., 1995, Frank, 1994, Hofmeyr et al., 1998, Lane et al., 1997, Lankewicz et al., 1997, Tan, 1997].

In misuse detection systems, events are compared against a database of known attack signatures. They are comparable to virus scanners and therefore exhibit the same problems. They will not be able to detect attacks they do not know about and therefore rely on the quality and completeness of their database of attacks. Thus they are not capable of recognizing future unforeseen and unexpected threats. Even worse, the detection system may not recognize the fingerprint of a slightly mutated generic attack. Another reproach to such systems is their limited scope of applicability; adding attack signatures that are specific to your organization is difficult and cumbersome. Because of the low rate of false positives such an approach exhibits and the low computational requirements, it is not surprising that it has led to many successful commercial products. To name a few, Cisco NetRanger, ISS RealSecure, and Security Dynamics KSM are among the most popular.

Another approach to the problem of detecting intruders is the installation of computerized burglar alarms that rely on an understanding of the network and what should not happen within it [Ranum, 1998]. While we believe that this could help to pinpoint intruders, this approach does not solve the issue of making a clear separation between usual and unexpected network events. Such alarm systems rely on the generation of a list of events that should not occur. This process is both time-consuming and prone to errors.

3. A new paradigm for intrusion detection

The intrusion and anomaly detection systems we mentioned previously, and other specialized applications [Couch ,et al., 1996, Hughes, 1996, Karam, 1994, Oetiker, 1998] usually provide us with reporting and monitoring capabilities. We like this possibility because it provides us with a condensed view of what is going on. However, most of the time this view will offer a simplistic interpretation and tends to ignore the complexity and context in which events are generated. Additionally, this view makes the ability to conduct interactive exploration a difficult task for the user. Our goal is to take advantage of our innate perceptual abilities by inducing the viewer to think about the substance, and not about the methodology.

From our perspective, we think that all these approaches fail to acknowledge the natural human ability to cope with complexity. After all, talented people who craft highly complex and unexpected attacks by mixing social and technical competence are the one we should fear the most. However, we acknowledge that the solutions presented before are well adapted to the popular brute force attacks, but we find them hopeless for the more serious threats. Thus, our motivation is to take into account our intrinsic capabilities using visual metaphor, which trigger our senses to make decisions. This gives the user the possibility to make fuzzy judgments whether something is normal/abnormal, important/benign, critical/isolated, etc.

In this work, we considered an approach that relies on visual metaphors and machine learning algorithms to accomplish unattended topological classification with interactive visualization to explore event logs. By presenting large amount of information in a condensed and coherent view, one can gain an overview of the global relationships within the data. Additionally, it provides a frame of reference to embed fine-grained tasks, along with a view that reveals the data at several levels of detail and encourages the eye to compare different pieces of information. Moreover, providing interactive visualization is a means of letting viewers conduct exploratory analysis, giving a chance to discover the unexpected.

In general, we believe there is a big difference between the rigidity and formalization required by traditional information systems, and the fluidity and intuition of the way we think and work as humans. Our work attempts to bridge that gap.

4. Overview

Network activity can usually be captured as a time ordered sequence of events. This operation can be performed by network sniffers, the Network Flight Recorder [Ranum et al., 1997], RMON and SNMP querying and trapping facilities, or using the logging mechanisms provided by firewalls and intrusion detection systems. Structured logs contain distinct and uniform entries characterizing each event or state by a given set of attributes.

Each entry found in structured logs can be seen as a vector representing a point in a high dimensional space. In this space, the distance between two points is proportional to their dissimilarity. This provides us with the ability to compute the extent to which two network patterns are similar.

Using these dissimilarities, we can use a dimensionality reduction process to map high dimensional points to a low dimensional representation. In our case, we rely on the self-organizing map algorithm [Kohonen, 1995], which provides us with a data reduction method to create a topologically ordered mapping. While such a process implies a loss of information, essential information is preserved and noise smoothed out. Many other techniques exist to perform the process of dimensionality reduction. Two popular approaches are principal components analysis and multidimensional scaling.

Creating a mapping is equivalent to the concept of building profiles of the network activity. A mapping can therefore be compared with some subsequent network events, as long as they are of similar nature and follow the initial distribution.

Appropriate visualization techniques can be used to graphically represent the output of such a mapping. Such visualizations provide for the visual comparison of a typical profile against new activity, thus highlighting divergences from the norm. The scheme we use to communicate this information provides the user with the overall frame of reference that visually highlights event correlation, and a set of interactive tools to conduct fine-grained exploration of the map.

To evaluate our approach, we use a dataset provided by the Information Exploration Shootout project [Grinstein, 1996, 1997]. This dataset contains four different attacks: IP spoofing, ftp password guessing, network scanning, and network hopping.

5. A multidimensional model

The attributes describing the characteristics of each entry in the logs form an *n*-dimensional space, where *n* is the number of attributes (see figure 1). Thus, each event has a unique spatial position depending on its specific characteristics. To create a context for the network activity, we must be able to compare one event to another using a similarity function. Such a function defines the extent to which two network events are related. Dissimilarities can be seen as distances in the metaphorical sense. Defining a similarity or distance function implies subjectivity and tacit knowledge should be used where available.

For our purpose, we mainly rely on the Euclidean metric, along with domain knowledge where available for weighting the different dimensions depending on their importance. However, our approach has one particularity in how categorical attributes are treated. This case is frequent with network protocols, where for example flags or types of service do not have any special order. In our case, we treat these attributes with one dimension for each categorical value, resulting in a very high-dimensional, but conceptually correct space.

6. Mapping the network activity

While we could rely on scatter plots or similar techniques to display information such as which hosts communicate with each other, we would like to provide the network administrator with a comprehensive picture of what is going on. These techniques are limited to a low number of dimensions that can be depicted simultaneously. A high-dimensional space like the one we described earlier cannot be directly portrayed to the user. In order to provide an overview of the network activity, we must reduce the dimensionality to create a representation of the relative similarities of events. By creating low-dimensional representation on a plane, the depiction on a screen or on paper can easily be achieved. We like to describe such representations as maps, with the particularity of conveying abstract relationships. Events that are similar are placed together while events with unrelated patterns are further apart.

In our previous paper [Girardin et al., 1998], we performed the dimensionality reduction process using two competing methods. The first was a method inspired from physics, the spring layout algorithm, while the other was the self-organizing map algorithm. During the

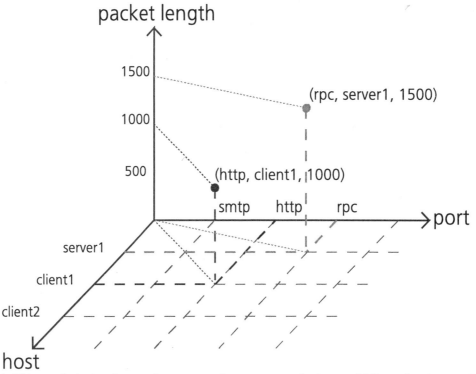

Figure 1. This graph depicts how each event may be seen as a point in a multidimensional space. Events are placed on each axis according to the values of their respective attributes. In this model, each attribute is equivalent to a single dimension. Of course, the datasets we are interested in contain many more dimensions.

present work, we did not rely on the spring layout algorithm due to its scalability issues. However, the spring layout algorithm might still be useful for obtaining more detailed information as this could be achieved by a coupling with the self-organizing map algorithm. Please refer to [Chalmers, 1996] for further information on the spring layout algorithm, and to [Girardin et al., 1998] for a description on how we use the two methods together.

We use an artificial neural network, the self-organizing map algorithm [Kohonen, 1995] to accomplish the dimensionality reduction process. Self-organizing maps are inspired from biology and are designed to behave, for example, like the somatotopic map of the motor nerves and the tonotopic map of the auditory region. The self-organizing map algorithm, is an unsupervised (self-organizing) neural network composed of an input layer and a competitive/output neural layer. For our purpose, the most interesting property of this network is that the feature map preserves the topology of stimuli according to their similarity. This algorithm does not depend on any prior knowledge of the network, and in this sense we can say that it exhibits self-organization.

The kind self-organizing maps we use are composed of a discrete two-dimensional grid of units (also referred to

as neurons within the artificial intelligence community). The algorithm is initiated by setting weights for each unit to random values. While feeding the network with events, the unit with a weight vector that matches the input pattern the best is sought. Then, the weight vector of this best match is slightly adjusted to resemble more closely the input pattern. Through iterations, the network will produce discrete maps that exhibit as best as possible the topology of the input space. Moreover, the network learns the distribution of the input patterns and will attempt to generalize it within a space of lower dimensionality.

The self-organizing map algorithm in the learning process stage can be summarized as follows (please refer to figure 2 for a graphical description):

1. Initialize the weight vectors;

2. Present a vector to the input layer;

3. Find the unit with the closest reference vector;

4. Modify the weight vectors of the neurons surrounding the winner; and

5. Repeat steps 2-5 until the number of required iterations has been performed.

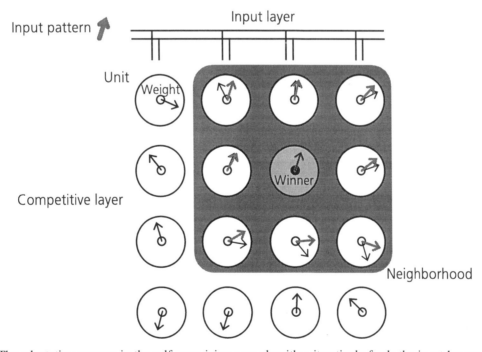

Figure 2. The adaptation process in the self-organizing map algorithm iteratively feeds the input layer with patterns. The initial configuration is random (black arrows). Then, the unit with a weight that best matches the input pattern, the winning node (gray unit), is sought in the competitive layer. Weights in the neighborhood (gray area) of the winner are now be slightly adjusted to resemble more closely the input pattern (gray arrows).

One problem with the adaptation process is that it is limited to continuous attributes. To cope with this limitation, we created a special kind of weight that holds a dynamically growing dictionary of weighted categorical values. Thus, each categorical weight is a vector in a subspace containing only the categories relevant to its associated unit.

The result of this process can be used to map any multi-dimensional dataset to units on the grid. Data points that are close in the high dimensional space will result in close units on the map. However, the dataset that has been used for the training and the one that is to be mapped must be of the same nature and, for optimal results should contain the same distribution as the data. For each entry, a measure of the mapping quality can be computed using a quantization error, which is the distance from one input data point to the best matching weight vector.

The self-organizing map algorithm outperforms other comparable methods [Li et al., 1995]. The computational time needed to create a map is proportional to the number of units in the map and to the number of input dimensions, but not to the size of the input dataset.

However, datasets containing complex relationships will certainly need more iterations to achieve convergence during the training stage.

There is still no theoretical proof about the convergence of the self-organizing map algorithm. Additionally, the different training parameters must be determined through empirical experimentation. Indeed, the number of iterations, the extent to which the weight vectors must be adapted, the size of the neighborhood, and the number of units composing the map must be specified manually. However, these issues are being tackled through growing self-organizing networks such as the one presented in [Fritzke, 1995].

7. Visualization of the self-organizing maps

The topology-preserving and dimensionality-reducing mapping performed by the self-organizing map algorithm is ideal for data visualization. We portray the units as squares within a grid and depict for each unit the following values (see figure 3):

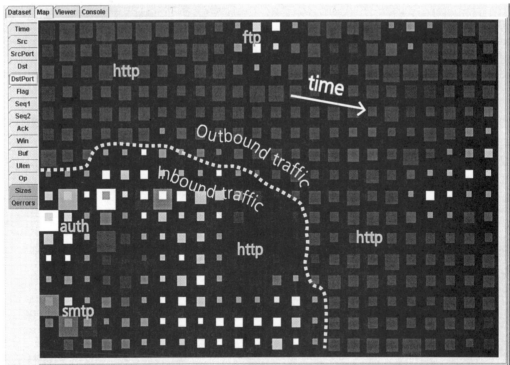

Figure 3. The user interface provides the possibility of showing the map colored by different attributes (panel on the left). In order to spot areas of similar nature across several attributes, the user can visually compare their distribution on the map to detect boundaries and correlated events. For example, we can see on this map that more connections are coming from the outside than from the inside. It also allows us to spot which are the main protocols flowing on the network. Additionally, because the outbound traffic is mainly composed of http requests, time becomes the prominent feature that gives order to this region.

- foreground color: the value of the weight for the selected attribute;

- size: the number of events mapped in the unit; and

- background color: the mean quantization error of all the entries resulting in the unit.

Our user interface lets network administrators select which feature (time, source and destination hosts and ports,...) they are interested in. The selection results in an appropriate coloring that can be used to spot area containing similar behaviors.

The size of each square is proportional to the number of network events that the unit contains. It allows for immediate identification of both the main and less frequent types of traffic.

The quantization error communicates the quality of the mapping. Usually, a high quantization error is the result of atypical and rare events. This may also be used in the context of anomaly detection where we would like to compare some network events to a previously built profile. The quantization error visually reflects how well these events match the typical activity. Therefore, there are no false positives; network administrators can decide how much they are willing to investigate these anomalies depending of their priorities and time.

Finally, selecting a unit in the map results in the display of the list of network events clustered in that location.

8. Exploration of an intrusion detection dataset

For our experiment, we use the network intrusion dataset provided for the Information Exploration Shootout project [Grinstein, 1996, 1997]. It consists of four different attacks provided in distinct files. Additionally, a baseline file that contains no attack is provided. The traffic was captured using the tcpdump tool and contains the following attributes for each network event:

- time stamp;

- source adresses, destination addresses and ports;

- flags like SYN, FIN, PUSH and RST (TCP only);

- data sequence number of the packet (TCP only);

- data sequence number of the data expected in return (TCP only),

- number of bytes of receive buffer space available (TCP only);

- indication of whether or not the data is urgent (TCP only); and

- packet length (UDP only).

Each file is roughly 50MB in size (30MB in comma separated format) and contains about 20 minutes of traffic captured on The MITRE Corp. network. These files are publicly available from http://iris.cs.uml.edu:8080/. Unfortunately, the different have been modified in a way which somewhat limits our ability to analyze them. The modifications include:

- all internal hosts addresses have been modified to share a unique address (ensuring the network topology is not revealed); and

- all external hosts have been assigned a fake address, which is not consistent across the different files.

Therefore, this dataset only offers limited information to clearly find out which hosts are communicating with each other. Moreover, it does not permit the use of the baseline as a profile for the files containing each attack. Otherwise, it would have been very easy to spot the traffic that deviates from the norm.

Through the analysis of the profile, we gained information about the typical traffic that flows within the MITRE network. Most of it is composed of http requests, more frequently outbound than inbound. The smtp protocol is also popular on their network and has the particularity of triggering ident queries every time a connection is initiated. Moreover, ident requests are most of the time not honored by the different mail servers and result in a reset of the connection. The activity described here can be also be seen in figure 3. We also found many connections from few external hosts to UDP port 7001. Additionally, some telnet, ftp, netbios related traffic was also spotted. Note that we only used this information to get a feeling of the nature of the network activity, and we did not use this profile for automatic comparison with the subsequent attacks.

The first attack involves the IP spoofing scheme used by Kevin Mitnick against Tsutomu Shimomura's computers on Christmas day, 1994 [Shimomura et al., 1996]. This attack was detected because some connections were left half-open, providing evidence of a SYN flooding denial of service scheme [Schuba et al., 1997]. The few connections that did not finish the three-way TCP handshake were unusual enough to be isolated on the map. The unusual number of connections initiated to the internal servers first captured our attention. Indeed, this was a clear indication that the mail and web servers had an outage. We also discovered many highly redundant packets and other strange behaviors, which were certainly symptomatic of an attempted IP spoofing scheme. Additionally, we found a network scan with connections every 5 seconds on unusually high UDP ports. Finally, we believe that the attack resulted in the ability of the intruder to gain telnet access, but we are unsure about this fact because of hidden internal network topology.

When exploring the second file, we found an unusually high number of FTP connections initiated on the internal network and directed towards 12 distinct hosts. There was a total of more than 60 suspicious connections that did not trigger any connection back through the ftp-data port, which makes us believe this was a password guessing attempt (and possibly a success). The attack started at 16:05 and ended at 16:20 (with a maximum of 10 connections per minute), which probably means that it had been automated or done by a good typist. This discovery includes 12 connections made within a 3 minute interval that was directed towards machines on the internal network that was possibly legitimate. Spotting this intrusion was aided by the corre-

lation amongst the following features:

- the time (hosts were probed one after another during a short interval, and most of the connections took place within a 5 minute time frame);

- the initiating host was always the same;

- the source ports were always very close to each other (a typical behavior of the TCP/IP stack of incrementally allocating the port numbers);

- the destination port was always ftp.

It was easy to discover a network scan contained in the third file (see figure 4). The scanning activity was made from and to the internal network. Hosts were probed through the echo port throughout the monitored period. At 15:26, certainly as a result of a host responding to the echo packet, a complete range of more than 40 ports were inspected. This activity had a one minute duration. Because many connections from a single source were initiated, their similarities resulted in one unit in the self-organizing map that clustered most of them (some were clustered in other close units).

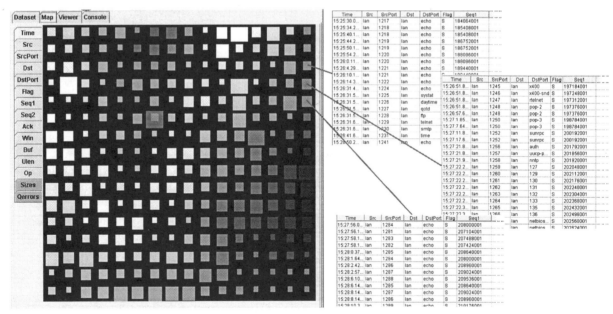

Figure 4. The activity resulting from the scanning attack has been mapped on three adjacent units. These units were inspected because of the distinctive nature of some of the attributes (time, hosts and ports, etc.). The upper unit contains the initial echo packets aimed at probing machines availability. The port scanning activity, which can mainly be found in the middle unit, probably followed the successfull probe of a host. The continuation of the network scan can be found in the lower unit.

The fourth attack was discovered because of a high correlation between some incoming and outgoing traffic. Indeed, some telnet packets going to the internal network were almost identical, both temporally and in term of size, to some rlogin packets directed towards an external host. This is clearly an indication of some network hopping activity. Network hopping is where one connection is used to initiated another connection to the outside, possibly in the hope of making tracing more difficult.

The computational time required by the self-organizing map algorithm for processing the above files on a 400 MHz workstation varied from 15 minutes to 2 hours, depending of the granularity of the map. Our prototype has been developed in Java and has not yet been optimized for speed. Furthermore, the algorithm is scalable for use on multiprocessor machines.

9. New directions

After having analyzed the network activity at the protocol level, we now feel that the information of such datasets is too poor to make complex patterns easily apparent. We think that using multiple sources of logs and finding ways to relate them could make our approach more effective. For instance, information from routers, firewalls, network sniffers, hosts, and networked applications can be grouped together and the causality of each event against others specified. We believe that such a scheme can greatly augment the value of the information and that unexpected behavior will be more easily detected.

In our experiments, we used the notion time as just another dimension. However, a more sophisticated model could be created to take advantage of the special properties and importance of this feature, such as the detection of periodicity in the network events. This could provide a way to discover cyclic behaviors, such as a network backup or database update taking place every night.

10. Conclusion

During this work, we have shown the use of a visual tool to explore and analyze network activity containing simple but popular attacks. Using self-organizing maps, the topological classification of the events is performed automatically and does not rely on any a priori knowledge about the content of the dataset. We use a map metaphor to provide the network administrator with a frame of reference and interactive facilities, enabling intuitive and effective interpretation of the information contained in these maps. Our system can be used to detect as many types of attacks that the event description model can possibly make explicit. We are confident that our tool will effectively support the discovery of unexpected, unforeseen, and hidden network behaviors. Additionally, our approach goes beyond intrusion detection and provides a global view of the activity under the administrator's supervision.

While the prototype we developed is still in its infancy, we have nonetheless shown that the visual paradigm for analyzing network activity is a powerful approach for anybody confronted with the monitoring of activity-based information.

Acknowledgements

We are indebted to a number of people who have contributed in this research. We are especially grateful to Karl Andersen, Dominique Brodbeck, Aline Chabloz, Hans-Peter Frei, Timothy Jones, Wendy Nather, Jon Rochlis, Václav Matyáš, Christian Zapf, and Kan Zhang for their interesting discussions, corrections, suggestions, developments, and support. Thanks also to Frederick Avolio for his insightful comments, suggestions and patience. Our gratitude also goes to Georges Grinstein for having made the network intrusion dataset available.

References

[Amoroso, 1994] Amoroso, Edward. "Fundamentals of computer security technology." Upper Saddle River: Prentice-Hall, 1994. ISBN: 0-13-108929-3.

[Anderson et al., 1995] Anderson, Debra; Lunt, Teresa F.; Javitz, Harold; Tamaru, Ann; Valdes, Alfonso. "Detecting Unusual Program Behavior Using the Statistical Components of NIDES." Menlo Pak: SRI International, 1995. Tech. Report SRI-CSL-95-06.

[Avolio, 1998] Avolio, Frederick M. "A multidimensional approach to internet security."; netWorker vol. 2.2, April 1998, pp. 15-22.

[Chalmers, 1996] Chalmers, Matthew. "A Linear Iteration Time Layout Algorithm for Visualising High-Dimensional Data." Proc. IEEE Visualization '96, San Francisco, California, USA, October 1996.

[Couch et al., 1996] Couch, Alva L. "Visualizing Huge Tracefiles with Xscal." Proc. 10th Systems Administration Conference (LISA'96), Chicago, IL, USA, September 29-October 4, 1996, pp. 51-58

[Frank, 1994] Frank, Jeremy. "Artificial Intelligence and Intrusion Detection: Current and Future Directions." Proc 17th National Computer Security Conference, 1994.

[Fritzke, 1995] Fritzke, Bernd. "Growing Grid – a self-organizing network with constant range and adaptation strength." Neural Processing Letters, vol. 2, no. 5, 1995, pp. 9-13.

[Geer et al., 1997] Geer, Dan (editor); Oppenheimer, David L.; Wagner; David A.; Crabb, Michele D. "System Security: A Management Perspective." Berkeley: The Usenix Association; 1997. ISBN: 1-880446-85-5.

[Girardin et al., 1998] Girardin, Luc; Brodbeck, Dominique. "A visual approach for monitoring logs." Proc. 12th Usenix System Administration conference, Boston, Massachusetts, USA, December 6-11, 1998, pp. 299-308.

[Grinstein, 1996] Grinstein, Georges (organizer). "Information Exploration Shootout or "Benchmarks for Information Exploration"." Proc. IEEE Visualization '96, San Francisco, California, USA, October 1996, pp. 449-450.

[Grinstein, 1997] Grinstein, Georges (organizer). "Information Exploration Shootout Project and Benchmark Data Sets: Evaluating how Visualization does in Analyzing Real-World Data Analysis Problems. "Proc. IEEE Visualization '97, Phoenix, Arizona, USA, October 20-21, 1997, pp. 511-513.

[Hofmeyr et al., 1998] Hofmeyr, Steven A.; Forrest, Stephanie; Somayaji, Anil. "Intrusion detection using sequences of system calls." Journal of Computer Security, 1998.

[Hughes, 1996] Hughes, Doug. "Using Visualization in System and Network Administration." Proc. 10th Systems Administration Conference (LISA'96), Chicago, IL, USA, September 29-October 4, 1996, pp. 59-66.

[Karam, 1994] Karam, Gerald M. "Visualization using Timelines." Proc. 1994 International Symposium on Software Testing and Analysis, Seattle, WA, USA, August 17-19, 1994.

[Kohonen, 1995] Kohonen, Teuvo. "Self-organizing maps." Berlin; Heidelberg; New-York: Springer; 1995. ISBN: 3-540-58600-8.

[Lane et al., 1997] Lane, Terran; Brodley, Carla. "An Application of Machine Learning to Anomaly Detection." 20th Annual National Information Systems Security Conference; Coast TR 97-03; 1997.

[Lankewicz et al., 1997] Lankewicz, Linda B.; Srikanth, Radhakrishnan; George, Roy. "Anomaly Detection using Signal Processing and Neural Nets." Proc. ONDCP International Technology Symposium, Chicago, USA, 1997.

[Li et al., 1995] Li, Sofianto; Vel, Olivier de, and Coomans, Danny. "Comparative analysis of dimensionality reduction methods," Learning from Data: Artificial Intelligence and Statistics V, New York: Springer-Verlag, 1995, pp. 323-331.

[Monmonier, 1991] Monmonier, Mark. "How to lie with maps." Chicago, London: The University of Chicago Press; 1991. ISBN 0-226-53414-6.

[Oetiker, 1998] Oetiker, Tobias. "MRTG – The Multi Router Traffic Grapher." Proc. 12th Usenix System Administration conference, Boston, Massachusetts, USA, December 6-11, 1998, pp. 141-147.

[Power, 1998] Power, Richard. "Current and Future Danger." San Francisco: Computer Security Institute; 1998.

[Ranum et al., 1997] Ranum, Markus J.; Landfield, Ken; Stolarchuk, Mike; Sienkiewicz, Mark; Lambeth, Andrew; Wall, Eric. "Implementing a Generalized Tool for Network Monitoring." Proc. 11th Usenix Systems Administration Conference, San Diego, California, USA, October 26-31, 1997, pp. 1-16.

[Ranum, 1998] Ranum, Marcus. "Intrusion Detection: Challenges and Myths." Network Flight Recorder, Inc; 1998.

[Schuba et al., 1997] Schuba, Christoph; Krsul, Ivan, Kuhn, Markus; Spafford, Eugene; Sundaram, Aurobindo; Zamboni, Diego. "Analysis of a Denial of Service Attack on TCP." IEEE Symposium on Security and Privacy; Oakland, CA; Coast TR 97-06; May, 1997.

[Shimomura et al., 1996] Shimomura, Tsutomu; Markoff, John. Take Down. New York: Hyperion; 1996. ISBN: 0-7868-8913-6.

[Tan, 1997] Tan, Kymie. The Application Of Neural Networks to UNIX Computer Security. 1997.

On Preventing Intrusions by Process Behavior Monitoring[1]

R. Sekar

*Department of Computer Science
Iowa State University, Ames, IA*
sekar@seclab.cs.iastate.edu

T. Bowen   M. Segal

*Bellcore
Morristown, NJ*
{bowen,ms}@bellcore.com

Abstract

Society's increasing reliance on networked information systems to support critical infrastructures has prompted interest in making the information systems *survivable*, so that they continue to perform critical functions even in the presence of vulnerabilities susceptible to malicious attacks. To enable vulnerable systems to survive attacks, it is necessary to detect attacks and isolate failures resulting from attacks before they damage the system by impacting functionality, performance or security. The key research problems in this context include:

- detecting in-progress attacks before they cause damage, as opposed to detecting attacks after they have succeeded,

- localizing and/or minimizing damage by isolating attacked components in real-time, and

- tracing the origin of attacks.

We address the detection problem by real-time event monitoring and comparison against events known to be unacceptable. Real-time detection differentiates our approach from previous works that focus on intrusion detection by post-attack evidence analysis. We address the isolation and tracing problems by supporting automatic initiation of reactions. Reactions are programs that we develop to respond to attacks. A reaction's primary goal is to isolate compromised components and prevent them from damaging other components. A reaction's secondary goal is to aid in tracing the origin of attack, e.g., by providing an illusion of success to the attackers (enticing them to continue the attack) while ensuring that the attack causes no damage.

Our approach to detecting attacks is based on specifying permissible process behaviors as logical assertions on sequences of system calls and conditions on the values of system call arguments. We compile the specifications into finite state automata for efficient runtime detection of deviations from the specified (and hence permissible) behavior. We seamlessly integrate detection and reaction by designing our specification language to also allow specification of reactions.

1. Introduction

Approaches to intrusion detection can be broadly divided into *anomaly detection* and *misuse detection*. Anomaly detection based approaches first create a profile that describes *normal behaviors* and then detect deviations from this profile [Fox90, Lunt88, Lunt92, Anderson95]. In contrast, *misuse detection* based approaches [Porras92, Ilgun93, Kumar94] define and look for precise sequences of events that damage the system. Anomaly detection approaches possess the advantage that learning to identify *normal behavior* can be automated, but they are prone to false positives, especially when permissible but previously unlearned behavior occurs. Misuse detection approaches are more precise and less prone to false positives. However, since misuse detection approaches require specification of damaging events, which is usually manual and based on previously known attacks, they are less effective against newly discovered vulnerabilities and attacks.

A *specification-based approach*, first proposed by Ko *et al.* [Ko94, Ko96], aims at overcoming the above drawback of misuse detection. Instead of describing the events occurring in known attacks, which may or may not occur in future attacks, a specification-based approach describes a program's *intended* behavior. Deviations from intended behavior can be flagged as intrusions, thus enabling detection of previously un-

[1] This project is supported by Defense Advanced Research Agency's Information Technology Office (DARPA-ITO) under the Information System Survivability Program, under contract number F30602-97-C-0244. The views and conclusions contained in this document are those of the authors and should not be interpreted as representing the official policies, either expressed or implied, of the Defense Advanced Research Projects Agency or the U. S. Government.

known attacks. Our approach uses manual production of specifications, which while having the drawback of requiring a human expert, has the advantage of minimizing false positives, especially those that arise when intended but infrequently exhibited behavior is observed. Thus, we can continue to retain the precision of misuse detection and can therefore initiate defensive actions as soon as any violations are detected.

An overview of our specification-based approach for improving survivability was presented in [Sekar98]. Our approach comprises a specification language, a compiler for the specification language, and a runtime execution environment. This paper provides a more in-depth treatment of our specification language, and outlines an approach for compiling the specifications into executable modules for efficient monitoring of program behaviors at runtime. While our approach applies in principle to any modern operating system, our implementation is specific to Linux.

The rest of this paper is organized as follows. In Section 2 we give a brief overview of our approach, in Section 3 discuss related work as it applies to our specification language, in Section 4 we present our language and practical examples of its use, and in Section 5 we describe language compilation.

2. Overview of Approach

We model the survivable system as a distributed system consisting of hosts interconnected by a network. The network and the hosts are assumed to be physically secure, but the network is interconnected to the public Internet. Since attackers do not have physical access to the hosts that they are attacking, all attacks must be launched remotely from the public network. Regardless of how the attack is delivered, any damage to a target host is effected via the system calls made by a process running on the target host.[2] Thus, it is possible in theory to detect all attacks by observing only the system calls made by processes executing on the hosts comprising the system, and to prevent damage by filtering out damage-causing system calls before they are executed. Basing our techniques on system call observation has an important advantage in its ability to defend existing software applications without modifying

their source code. We therefore develop a high-level specification language called Auditing Specification Language (ASL) for specifying normal and abnormal behaviors of processes as logical assertions on the sequences of system calls and system call argument values invoked by the process. ASL specifications are compiled into optimized programs for efficient detection of deviations from the specified behavior. When discrepancies are detected at runtime, automatic defensive actions, also described in ASL, to contain or isolate the damage are initiated. A simple defense is to terminate processes that deviate from specified behavior, but this approach may not be desirable since it may alert attackers that the attack has been detected. Instead, we may want to entrap attackers into continuing their activities so that we can observe and document their actions. This can be accomplished using *isolation techniques* that enable the compromised process to continue to run, while ensuring that the process cannot damage the rest of the system. As a result, the attackers may believe that they are succeeding, while in reality, they are simply wasting their time and resources. Our defensive reactions are also written in ASL, which enables a close yet flexible coupling between detection and reaction capabilities.

Our behavioral assertions are divided into two categories; similar to correctness properties of distributed systems:

- local correctness assertions involving the actions of a single process in isolation, and
- non-interference assertions that ensure that the concurrent actions of multiple processes do not interfere with one another

To illustrate the concept of local correctness, consider a privileged program with a buffer overflow vulnerability (such as the `fingerd` program exploited by the Internet worm) that allows an attacker to execute the data input to the program. Since the input data can be constructed to be a machine language program, the vulnerability allows execution of arbitrary programs with the authority of the attacked program, which in the case of fingerd is root. A popular attack to cause execution of a program using `execve()` to execute "/usr/bin," thus providing an interactive shell with root privilege, although other options are possible. The popular attack can be prevented by the specification shown below, which prevents the program from `execve`'ing arbitrary programs, while still permitting it to execute the program(s) that it may need to execute in order to provide its normal function

---

[2] This observation does not hold for some denial-of-service attacks such as ping-of-death that exploit errors in operating system kernel implementations. We monitor network packets to deal with this class of attacks, but this approach is not discussed further in this paper.

```
execve(f) | f != "/usr/ucb/finger"
    -> exit(-1)
```

As explained in Section 4, the example reads as follows. Whenever `fingerd` attempts an `execve()` system call, if the name of the file passed as the first argument to `execve()` is not `/usr/ucb/finger` then an `exit(-1)` is performed before the `execve()`.

To illustrate the concept of non-interference, consider an attack that exploits a race condition in a privileged program. The typical race condition exists because in an attempt to correctly manage file permissions in programs whose effective user and real user are different (for example setuid to root programs), programmers use two system calls, `access()` and `open()` when opening files. Both `access()` and `open()` check file permissions, but `access()` performs the check with respect to real user, while `open()` checks with respect to effective user. Therefore, to ensure that the privileged program does not open a file for which the real user does not have permission, the `access()`, `open()` pair is locally sufficient. However, the sequence is insufficient when interference is possible. Another process can change the underlying file in between `access()` and `open()`, so that the real user has permissions for the file checked by `access()`, but not for the file checked by `open()`. While this appears complicated, from a practical point of view the second process merely needs to execute two UNIX® commands, `rm` and `link`, to accomplish it. For correct permission checking, we need to ensure that `access()` and `open()` are executed without interference by other processes. This requires that the data read by `access()` is not modified by another process before the completion of the `open()`. We capture the non-interference requirement using the notion of an atomic sequence, which has the semantics that if any other process issues system calls that modify the data in the atomic sequence, we detect the modification as violation of the specification. In the example shown below, the notation "a..b" stands for the occurrence of an event a followed by event b.

```
nonatomic (f) in
  (access(f,mode) .. open(f)) -> exit(-1)
```

2.1. System Overview

UNIX is a registered trademark licensed exclusively through X/Open Company Ltd.

Our intrusion detection/prevention system consists of an offline and a runtime component as depicted in Figures 1 and 2.

The offline system generates detection engines based

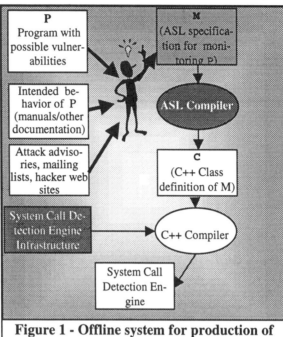

Figure 1 - Offline system for production of detection engines

on the ASL behavioral specifications, and the runtime system executes the generated engines. For each program P to be defended, a specification M is developed by a system security administrator who is familiar with intended behavior of the P (as can be determined from its manual pages or other documentation) as well as specific known vulnerabilities obtainable from sources such as attack advisories. The ASL compiler translates M into a C++ class definition, called C. C is then compiled by the C++ compiler and linked with a runtime infrastructure to produce a detection engine. The runtime infrastructure provides the mechanism for intercepting system calls; delivering them to the detection engine and providing functions the detection engine uses to take responsive actions.

Figure 2 shows how the detection engines generated by the offline component are used at runtime. When program P executes as process V_j, it is monitored using object O_j, which is an instantiation of C. For simplicity, we assume j is the process ID. System calls made by V_j are intercepted by the system call interceptor just before, and just after the system call's kernel level functionality is executed. At each interception, the system call information is passed to O_j through method invocation. The interception enables the system call detection engine's infrastructure and O_j to detect se-

---

quences of system calls requested by V_j which deviate from expectation, and to modify system call execution to prevent detected deviations from causing damage.

We implement the system call interceptor within the operating system kernel. Other alternatives include interception of system calls as they pass through the system call library, `libc`, or using the system call tracing and process control facilities of many UNIX variants. However, these approaches do not offer the same level of security as our kernel-based approach, since

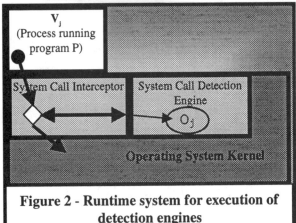

Figure 2 - Runtime system for execution of detection engines

they can be easily bypassed. It is also doubtful that either approach can be made as efficient as the kernel approach since the kernel approach alone allows interception and modification without process context switching.

2.2. Salient Features of Our Approach

- *Prevention.* The preventive ability makes it feasible to continue to allow the execution of programs that are known to contain exploitable vulnerabilities. Without preventive abilities, the potential of damage is so great that use of vulnerable programs must be prohibited until the program is repaired. The same reasoning even applies to programs from untrusted sources. Without assurance of damage prevention, the danger of damage from untrusted programs precludes their execution, but with damage prevention, even untrusted programs can be executed.

- *Programmability* enables a system administrator to respond quickly to a newly discovered vulnerability, without having to wait for a vendor-supplied patch.

- *Automated response.* Unlike previous approaches that focussed mainly on intrusion detection, our approach integrates detection and reaction within a uniform framework, since both are contained in the same specification. Automation reduces the

need for constant involvement of teams of human experts, thus providing a more cost-effective solution.

- *Deception.* Our approach allows the development of reactions that both isolate the attacked process to prevent damage, and deceive the attacker into believing that the attack is successful. Deception enables us to observe and document attacker behavior, either for apprehending attackers or to gain a better understanding of the system vulnerabilities.

- *Dynamically tunable monitoring.* Our technique allows the granularity of monitoring to be changed on the fly at runtime. We can use a low-level of monitoring under normal conditions, but can quickly increase the level of monitoring when errors or suspicious activities are detected.

3. Related Work

Use of a specification-based approach for intrusion detection was first proposed by Ko et al. [Ko94, Ko96]. Similar to their approach, we model the behavior of a process in terms of the system calls and their arguments. However, their approach analyzes logs of system calls to detect deviations from specification, and so are limited to post-attack detection. Our system intercepts system calls as they execute, so in addition to detecting deviations, we can *enforce* the specified behaviors at runtime to prevent damage. Runtime detection demands efficient execution of specifications, so our specification language design emphasizes efficiency. [Ko96] uses a specification language based on context-free grammars augmented with state variables, while our specification language is closer to regular languages augmented with state variables. Use of regular languages allows the compilation of specifications into an extended finite-state automaton (EFSA), which is a finite-state machine that is augmented with state variables. Such an EFSA permits efficient runtime checking, while using bounded resources (CPU or memory) that can be determined *a priori*. In addition, we believe that regular languages makes our specifications easier to understand and more concise. Although regular grammars are less expressive than context-free grammars, the difference is much less pronounced when these grammars are augmented with state variables.

Forrest *et al.* [Forrest97, Kosoresow97] developed intrusion detection techniques inspired by immune systems in animals. They characterize "self" for a UNIX process in terms of sequences of system calls that are made by the process under normal conditions. Intrusion is detected by monitoring for "foreign" system call sequences. Their research results are largely complementary to ours, in that their main focus is on *learning* normal behaviors of processes, whereas our focus is on *specifying* and *enforcing* these behaviors efficiently.

Goldberg *et al.* [Goldberg96] developed the Janus environment for confining helper applications (such as those launched by web-browsers) so that they are restricted in their use of system calls. Like our techniques, their techniques prevent unauthorized operations, such as attempts to modify a user's `.login` file. But their approach is more of a finer-grained access-control mechanism rather than an intrusion detection or prevention mechanism. The key distinction between the two mechanisms is as follows. Access control mechanisms restrict access rights for each process to the minimum rights required for the process's functionality, while intrusion detection verify that a process uses its access rights in the intended fashion. For instance, attacks based on race conditions and unexpected interactions among multiple processes manifest themselves as unintended use of access rights. Consequently, our specification language must be able to express sequencing relationships among multiple system calls made by one or more processes, whereas Janus only permits restriction of access to individual system calls made by a single process.

Our approach to isolation has some similarities with the approach used in the Deception Toolkit (DTK) [Cohen98]. In particular, when an intrusion is detected, our approach enables defenses that deceive the attacker with the illusion of success. The DTK employs a similar strategy. However, with DTK, deception depends upon enticing the attacker to use phony versions of the attacked service. The real service is no longer available at the DTK server, which contrasts with our approach, where standard server functionality is still present for legitimate uses.

As compared to our earlier work in [Sekar98], this paper presents a significantly improved version of ASL. It also outlines an approach for compiling the high-level specifications into finite-state automata that perform efficient runtime monitoring of process behavior. Improvements to ASL described in this paper are as follows. We have developed a more elegant approach for dealing with race conditions and other similar errors that result due to interference in data access by multiple processes. The pattern language for behavioral specification has also been improved by separating different classes of patterns. To further improve conciseness of specifications, the notion of event abstractions has been introduced. Another important improvement is the introduction of an interface definition component to ASL so as to decouple the ASL compiler from the specifics of the events monitored by the detection engine. As a result, we can now write ASL specifications that model system behaviors in terms of any observable events, as opposed to being limited to observation of system calls. Moreover, the ASL compiler need not be changed to deal with these new event types — we simply need to link the code produced by the ASL compiler with appropriate runtime infrastructure that can deliver these new events to the detection engine.

4. Auditing Specification Language (ASL)

We model the behavior of a process in terms of the system calls the process makes. We treat these system calls as *events*, which have the general form $e(a_1, ..., a_n)$, with e denoting the event name and $a_1, ..., a_n$ denoting the event arguments. Two events are associated with each system call, namely the entry to the system call and exit from the system call. We distinguish system call entry events from system call exit events by prefixing the $-symbol to exit events.

4.1. Interface Declarations

The interface between the detection engine and the monitored processes supports the conveyance of events from the process to the detection engine, and the conveyance of response functions from the detection engine to the monitored process. The functionality of the interfaces is realized via a set of interface functions that deliver events to the detection engine and provide mechanisms for invoking response actions. For generality, the functionality provided by the interface is specified in ASL via interface declarations. These declarations specify

- datatypes that can be exchanged over the interface
- events delivered over the interface in terms of their names, arguments and types
- external functions[3] provided by the interface that can be invoked by the detection code

We describe each of these components below.

4.1.1 ASL Data Types

Built-in types in ASL include `bit`, `byte`, `short`, `int`, `long`, `double`, and `string`. All of the integral types excluding `bit` and `byte` are either signed or unsigned. Their sizes coincide with the norm for the specific host for which the ASL specification is being

---

[3] We call the response function *external functions* to differentiate them from internal functions that are built into ASL.

applied. The string type is a variable length byte array prefixed with a 2-byte length field. ASL supports multi-dimensional arrays of built-in types.

Foreign types, correspond to data that can be exchanged on one or more of the interfaces, but whose representation is opaque to ASL. Foreign types are designed with the intent of modeling data within the virtual memory space of a monitored process. Depending on the particular implementation approach used in the detection engine, it may or may not be easy (or even possible) to access such data directly. To address this problem, we have developed *class* types that cannot be directly accessed in ASL, but can only be accessed using member functions defined on the type. Class types correspond to abstract data types. A sample class definition corresponding to a C-style string is:

```
class CString {
            string getVal() const;
            void setVal(string s);
}
```

A more complex definition suitable for manipulating data associated the stat system call is given below.

```
class StatBuf {
            int getDev()const;
            int getIno()const;
            int getMode()const;
            ⋮
            int getAtime()const;
            int getMtime()const;
            int getCtime()const;
}
```

Note that the return type of a member function could itself be a foreign type. Whether a member function changes the value of the object or not is given by the presence or absence of the const keyword in the declaration of the function. This fact is used by the ASL typechecker to ensure that expressions in ASL do not cause unexpected errors when evaluated at runtime.

Since ASL specifications may be compiled into detection engines that run within an operating system kernel, safety and reliability are especially important. Two important language mechanisms in ASL that promote safety and reliability are strong typing and the absence of pointer types.

4.1.2. External Functions

External functions are functions that are defined outside of the detection engines, but can be accessed from the detection engines. Semantically, they are no different from member functions associated with foreign types. In other words, member functions are simply external functions that use a different syntax.

The primary purpose of external functions is to invoke support functions needed by the detection engine or reaction operations provided by the system call interceptors. For instance, when an event for opening a file is received by a detection engine, the detection engine may need to resolve the symbolic links and references to "." and ".." in the file name to obtain a canonical name for file. The detection engine may use a support function declared as follows to find the canonical file name:

```
string realpath(CString s);
```

The detection engine may also need to check the file's access permissions, which may be done using a support function declared as follows:

```
StatBuf stat(const Cstring s);
```

In ASL system call names either represent an event (i.e., invocation of a system call by a monitored process) or are a component of a reaction taken by the detection engine (i.e., a statement in the a reaction program). We use the same syntax for system calls in both cases, since the context resolves any ambiguity.

4.2. Modules

The ASL specifications are structured as a collection of parameterized modules, each of which consists of a collection of *state variables* and *rules*. State information can be retained across multiple rules within a module via the state variables.

As an aid to programmability, modules may be parameterized. Parameterization enables specification of abstract behaviors that can be customized by providing values for these parameters. A typical use of parameterization is to allow a general-purpose module to be used in nearly identical situations that differ only in a few minor details. The process of generating a compilable module from a parameterized module is known as module *instantiation*.

Another important role of modules is that they provide a mechanism for dynamically altering the degree of monitoring, possibly in response to suspicious events. In particular, the action switch *ModuleName* can be used to start monitoring with respect to a module named *ModuleName*. It is also useful when a process uses the execve() system call to overlay itself with a new program. The switch action can then be used to perform monitoring that is appropriate for the new program. Finally, if a process is discovered to be compromised, we can alter the behavior of future system calls made by the process in such a fashion as to isolate the process from the system. This may also be accomplished by switching to a new specification.

4.3. Event Patterns

ASL *general event patterns* are used to specify valid or invalid behaviors. An *atomic pattern* is of the form $e(a_1,...,a_n)|C$, where e denotes an event and C is a boolean-valued expression on $a_1,...,a_n$. C may contain standard arithmetic, comparison and logical operations. C may also contain comparisons of the form $x = expr$ where x is new variable, with the semantics being that of binding the value of *expr* to x. A *primitive pattern* is obtained by combining atomic patterns with the disjunction operator $||$, and possibly preceding the entire expression with the complement operator '!'. As an example of a primitive pattern, consider:

```
!((open(f)|realpath(f)=/home/*/.plan)
   || (close(f))||(exit(f))
```

In this pattern, a shorthand notation /home/*/ is used to refer to any directory that is immediately contained within /home. The above primitive event pattern captures all system calls other than those for opening ".plan" files, closing files or terminating processes. (For illustrative purposes this example is simplified, it does not, for example, permit the opening of some necessary files, such as dynamically loaded libraries.)

General event patterns are obtained by combining primitive patterns using temporal operators. Such operators enable us to capture sequencing or timing relationships among system calls:

- *Sequential composition:* $p_1; p_2$ denotes the event pattern p_1 immediately followed by pattern p_2.

- *Alternation:* $p_1 || p_2$ denotes the occurrence of either p_1 or p_2.

- *Repetition:* $p\{n_1,n_2\}$ denotes at least n_1 repetitions and at most n_2 repetitions of p. $p\{n_1\}$ and $p\{,n_2\}$ are shorthand for $p\{n_1,\infty\}$ and $p\{0,n_2\}$ respectively. The notation $p*$ is shorthand for $p\{0,\infty\}$.

- *Real-time constraints:* p **within** $[t_1,t_2]$ denotes the occurrence of events corresponding to pattern p occurring over a time interval. The shorthand for [0,t] is [t], whereas the shorthand for [t,∞] is [t,].

- *Atomicity:* **nonatomic** d **in** p corresponds to an occurrence of pattern p within which the data item d is not accessed atomically.

For convenience, we define the operator ".." that can be applied only to primitive patterns. $p_1 .. p_2$ is equivalent to $p_1;(!(p_1 || p_2)*);p_2$, i.e., p_1 followed by p_2 with possibly other events occurring in between. The restriction that ".." be applied only to primitive patterns is imposed since the operator has unintuitive semantics on general event patterns.

We illustrate the use of temporal operators using several simple examples below. Note that in general, we wish to take reactive action when the behavior of a monitored process fails to satisfy certain properties. Hence, we typically develop patterns that are the negation of assertions describing normal behaviors.

- `e1;!e2*;e1` asserts that `e1` must occur twice with no intervening `e2`. This corresponds to the negation of the property that `e1` must always be followed by `e2` before a second occurrence of `e1`.

- `(e1;!e2*) within [t,]` captures violation of property that `e1` is followed by `e2` within time t

- `e1;!e2*;e3` captures violation of property where `e2` must always occur between `e1` and `e3`

- `e{k} within [t]` captures violation of property that `e` occurs less than `k` times within time t

4.4. Event Abstractions

An event abstraction is a convenience mechanism allowing programmer definition of abstract events comprising arbitrary event patterns. Event abstractions allow the programmer to name and treat complex event patterns as if they were primitive events. To illustrate the use of event abstractions, note that many UNIX system calls have overlapping functionality. When we write behavioral specifications, it is cumbersome to write several variants of the specification based on the exact system calls used by a particular program. For convenience, we group similar system calls so that all of the calls in one group can be viewed as implementations of a higher level abstract system call. For instance, the `creat()` and `open()` system calls can both be used to open new files, so we define the abstract event `writeOpen` which captures this commonality. Then, a single behavioral specification using `writeOpen` can be used to monitor processes that open new files using either `creat()` or `open()`.

```
event writeOpen(path) =
 open(path, flags) |
    flags&(O_WRONLY|O_APPEND|O_TRUNC) ||
 open(path, flags, mode) |
    flags&(O_WRONLY|O_APPEND|O_TRUNC) ||
 creat(path, mode);
```

Code Example 1 - Definition of `writeOpen()` Abstract Class

Different levels of abstraction may be desired in different contexts, and hence there may be overlaps among different user-defined abstract events. For instance, we may have an abstract event that corresponds to readOpen, and another that corresponds to any open, regardless of whether it is for reading or writing. For simplicity, we restrict the definition of abstract events to be primitive event patterns.

4.5. Rules

A rule is of the form *pat* → *action*, where *pat* is a pattern of the form described above, and *action* is a sequence of responsive steps to be initiated when an event matching the pattern occurs. Actions may be empty, variable assignment, function invocation, or switch. Function invocation causes the specified function to be executed by the runtime infrastructure, and thus may be used by the detection engine for purposes such as reading or writing data in the monitored process, or executing arbitrary system calls in the monitored process. The switch *SpecName* action enables switching to the behavioral specification named *SpecName* for monitoring.

5. Example Behavior Specifications

In this section we illustrate ASL using several example specifications.

5.1. Finger Daemon

The following specification restricts the finger daemon[4] so that it can open only specific files for reading, cannot open any file for writing, cannot execute any file, and cannot initiate a connection to any host. If any specified behavior is attempted, the system call associated with the attempt does not execute. Instead, an error code is returned or the process terminated. For events whose arguments are not of interest, it is not necessary to specify the arguments. We make use of a support function, inTree, which determines whether a file resides within a directory or its descendents. The ex-

---

[4] The specification pertains to the GNU finger program, and in particular, the finger daemon running as the master server. Note that GNU finger is implemented differently from the BSD finger daemon, and does not need to execve the finger program.

ample shows only a subset of those system calls that must be disallowed for an adequate defense.

```
open(file, mode) |
   ((f = realpath(file)) &&
   ((f != "/etc/utmp") &&
    (f != "/etc/passwd") &&
    !inTree(f,"/usr/spool/finger")) ||
   (mode != O_RDONLY))
-> fail(-1,EACCESS)
execve || connect || chmod || chown
   || chgrp || create || truncate
   || sendto || mkdir
-> exit(-1);
```

Code Example 2 - ASL Specification for Monitoring `fingerd`

5.2. Race Conditions

We illustrate two approaches to protect against race condition attacks. Our first approach monitors for an access() followed by an open() and ensures that both use identical conditions for checking permission. Identical in this case means that the effective user at the time of open() is the same as the real user at the time of access().

Rprog1 defines two state variables and an event abstraction for use in the rules defined subsequently. The event abstraction simplifies the structure of the rules. In the first rule, the comparisons in acc1 event definition bind the temporary variable ruid. Whenever the monitored process performs an open() following an access() on the same file, we temporarily set the effective user ID of the monitored process to the value of the real user ID before the open() executes. Before doing this, we save the current value of the effective user ID in the state variable savedEuid, and set a flag changedEuid to record that we have temporarily changed the effective user ID. When open() completes, we use the values stored in the state variables to restore the original effective user ID.

```
int savedEuid;
bit changedEuid;

event acc1(name, ruid) =
 access(name, mode)|(ruid = getuid());

acc1(name, ruid)..open(name1, flags)|
   (name = name1)
-> changedEuid = 1;
   savedEuid = geteuid();
   setreuid(-1,ruid);

$open(f, f1)|(changedEuid = 1)
-> changedEuid = 0;
   setreuid(-1,changedEuid);
```

Code Example 3 - ASL Specification `rProg1` for a Race Condition Vulnerability

The second defense against the race vulnerability uses the concept of atomic sequences. The race vulnerability exists because two system calls access() and open() must be used to accomplish what is essentially a single function, that is, opening a file with respect to real user's permissions. We can execute a sequence of system calls as if they were all a single system call by placing them in an atomic sequence as follows:

```
nonatomic (f) in
    (access(f,md) .. writeOpen(f))
  -> fail(-1,EACCESS)
```

An atomic sequence is a sequence of system calls executed by process P whose execution appears not to be interleaved with the system calls of any other concurrently executing process. Atomic sequences are similar to transactions in databases. Atomic sequences depend on the definition of read and write sets for all system calls. We also note that runtime checking of atomicity requires coordination among the monitors for different processes, since it depends not only on the system calls performed by a process being monitored, but also the calls made by other process.

5.3. Program from Untrusted Source

To ensure that a program from an untrusted source does not damage the host executing it, we want to ensure that the program can read only world readable files, can write only within the /tmp directory, cannot execute any programs, and cannot perform network operations.

```
open(file, mode) |
  [(!inTree(realpath(file), "/tmp") &&
   (mode & (O_WRONLY|O_APPEND|
            O_CREAT | O_TRUNC)))||
   !accessible(realpath(file), mode,
                "nobody"))
-> fail(-1,EACCESS);

exec || connect || bind || chmod ||
  chown || chgrp || create ||
  truncate || sendto || mkdir
-> exit(-1);
```

Code Example 4 - ASL Specification sandbox for Untrusted Programs

5.4. Using Specification for Isolation

When we detect an attack on process V_j, we can use the switch action to switch to a specification that contains ASL rules to isolate V_j. The isolation specification contains rules that modify the behavior of system calls made by V_j in such a way that V_j is prevented from executing operations that can damage the survivable system. For example, the isolation specification can perform one or more of the following:

- return faked return value. When a system call that can potentially damage the system is invoked by the isolated process, we can prevent the system call from being completed, and instead return a faked (but legitimate) return value.

- log the activity for later analysis.

- reduce limits on resources that the isolated process can consume.

- restrict access to files. We can use the setuid() system call to change the effective user ID of the process to that of a user with very few access rights and we can use the chroot() system call to change the root directory of the compromised process.

To illustrate this idea, consider the modification to the previous specification for the finger daemon which implements isolation. In particular, we introduce the rule:

```
execve ->
  chroot("/altroot"); setuid(-1);
  nice(100); switch genericIsolate;
```

This rule changes the root of the monitored process to a decoy file system (called altroot), changes the user ID to nobody, reduces the priority of the process, and finally switches to a new monitoring specification called genericIsolate.

```
module genericIsolate
  connect
     -> sleep(60); fail(-1,ETIMEDOUT);
  bind
     -> sleep(5); fail(-1,EADDRINUSE);
  recv
     -> sleep(1);
  open
     -> sleep(1);
end
```

Code Example 5 – ASL Specification for Damage Prevention

As shown, genericIsolate gives only a few of the rules that would be needed for isolation. Since the isolated process is operating in a decoy file system, file system operations are allowed. However, network operations are restricted. Most operations are slowed down using sleep(), so that the CPU and resource usage of the attacked host are reduced, but the attacker will probably attribute the delay to normal host or network congestion.

6. Compilation of ASL

The main task in translating an ASL specification into a C++ class definition is to translate the patterns into an extended finite-state automaton (EFSA). An EFSA is similar to a finite-state automaton, with the following differences:

- In addition to the control state of an FSA, an EFSA can make use of a fixed set of state variables.

- The EFSA makes transitions based on events, event arguments and conditions on event arguments and state variables. The transitions may assign new values to state variables.

An EFSA may be deterministic (DEFSA) or nondeterministic (NEFSA). For the sake of efficiency, we always prefer to generate a DEFSA rather than a NEFSA. However, this is not always possible as conversion of NEFSA into a DEFSA can cause unacceptable explosion in space requirements. For traditional FSA, every nondeterministic automaton can be converted into an equivalent deterministic automaton with at most an exponential increase in the number of (control) states. For performance critical applications (e.g., lexical analysis phase of a compiler), this increase in state space is quite acceptable, especially because the worst case behavior is unusual. For EFSA, the explosion in size is exponential in the product of the number of control states and the range of values that can be assumed by each of the auxiliary state variables. For instance, a deterministic EFSA that is equivalent to a nondeterministic EFSA with one integer (32-bit) state variable and N control states can have $2^{N*2^{32}}$ states! This problem leaves us with two choices:

- restrict the class of ASL patterns so that they can be compiled into DEFSA, or

- do not convert an NEFSA into an EFSA, and simulate the NEFSA at runtime.

Note that at runtime, the transitions of an EFSA are represented in code, whereas its current state (which includes the control state and the state variables) is stored in a data structure. Since we plan to combine all patterns in one ASL specification into a single EFSA, there is only one instance of the transition relation at runtime. To support nondeterminism, we permit multiple instances of the dynamic state of the EFSA. These multiple instances capture all of the states the NEFSA could have reached after examining its input up to this point.

If an EFSA needs to make a two-way nondeterministic transition on an event e, we perform a "fork" operation on the EFSA, i.e., replicate its current state. The replica follows one of the non-deterministic choices, while the parent follows the other choice. This approach can lead to an unbounded increase in the number of instances of

EFSA, but unbounded growth should happen only when certain unusually repetitive sequences of system calls are observed at runtime, and hence is not a serious issue in practice. We are currently working on techniques that can avoid unbounded growth by restricting the class of patterns permitted in ASL.

The starting points for our algorithm for generating EFSA from ASL patterns are the seminal papers by Brzozowski [Brzozowski64] and Berry and Sethi [Berry86]. However, these papers address regular expressions and classical FSA, whereas we must address conditions on event arguments and state variables that can be complex data structures. Our earlier work on first-order term-matching [Sekar95] provides the starting point for addressing this aspect. By combining and extending these two techniques, we developed an algorithm for generating EFSA from a restricted class of ASL specifications. A detailed description of this algorithm is beyond the scope of this paper, so we only provide a description of how we map an NEFSA into C++ code.

At code generation time, the EFSA generated from ASL specifications is turned into a C++ class. Specifically, one class is generated from each ASL specification. This class has one member function for each event, and these member functions have the same number and types of arguments as the event. When the runtime infrastructure intercepts an event, it delivers it to the appropriate detection engine by invoking the corresponding member. For instance, the runtime infrastructure invokes the open_entry method when a monitored program enters an open system call, and the open_exit method when the process is about to exit this system call.

The transitions in the EFSA are translated into code as follows. We maintain a list of active EFSA instances at runtime. When an event is delivered, we go through the list of EFSA instances and for each of them, make a transition based on its current state and the newly delivered event. If multiple transitions exist out of the current EFSA state for this event, then copies of the EFSA are made (using the fork operation mentioned earlier), so that there is one EFSA to make each of these transitions. If there is no transition for an EFSA instance, then it is "killed" and any resources used for the instance are released.

7. Conclusions and Future Work

In this paper we presented an approach for intrusion detection that is based on specifying the valid behaviors of processes in terms of system call sequences together with constraints on the argument values that the processes can make. We described our specification language and illustrated it with several examples. Based on these examples, we are optimistic that concise and clear specifications of security-related behaviors can be developed with relative ease in the ASL language. These examples also indicate that the approach can successfully prevent (or at least quickly detect) attacks. Additional preliminary evidence in this context was presented in [Sekar98] where we examined the attack advisories from CERT®over the past five years and concluded that most of them can be detected by our approach.

We are continuing to refine and experiment with our specification language. We are also developing algorithms for compiling ASL specifications into deterministic EFSA, rather than non-deterministic EFSA. In parallel, we are also in the process of developing medium to large-scale experiments designed to assess the performance impact of our online monitoring approach. Our preliminary indications are that indeed we can do such monitoring using our current, kernel-level interception approach easily, especially since our EFSA enable efficient checking of specification assertions at runtime.

References

[Anderson95] D. Anderson, T. Lunt, H. Javitz, A. Tamaru, and A. Valdes, Next-generation Intrusion Detection Expert System (NIDES): A Summary, *SRI-CSL-95-07, SRI International*, 1995.

[Aslam96] T. Aslam, I. Krsul and E. Spafford, A Taxonomy of Security Faults, *National Computer Security Conference*, 1996.

[Berry86] G. Berry and R. Sethi, From Regular Expressions to Deterministic Automata, *Theoretical Computer Science* 48 pp. 117-126, 1986.

[Bishop96] M. Bishop and M. Dilger , Checking for Race Conditions in File Access. *Computing Systems* 9(2), pp. 131-152, 1996.

[Brzozowski64] J.A. Brzozowski, Derivatives of Regular Expressions, *Journal of ACM* Vol. 11, No.4, pp. 481-494, 1964.

[Cai98] Y. Cai. A Specification-Based Approach for Intrusion Detection. *M.S. Thesis, Department of Computer Science, Iowa State University*, Dec 1998.

[CERT98] CERT Coordination Center Advisories 1988--1998, http://www.cert.org/advisories/index.html.

[Cheswick92] W.R. Cheswick, An evening with berferd, in which a cracker is lured, endured and studied, *Winter USENIX Conference*, 1992.

[Cohen98] Fred Cohen and Associates, The Deception Toolkit Home Page, http://www.all.net/dtk/dtk.html.

[Connet72] J. Connet et al., Software Defenses in Real-Time Control Systems, *IEEE Fault-Tolerant Comp. Sys.*, 1972.

[Denning87] D. Denning, An Intrusion Detection Model, *IEEE Trans. on Software Engineering*, Feb 1987.

[Forrest97] S. Forrest, S. Hofmeyr and A. Somayaji, Computer Immunology, *Comm. of ACM* 40(10), 1997.

[Fox90] K. Fox, R. Henning, J. Reed and R. Simonian, A Neural Network Approach Towards Intrusion Detection, *National Computer Security Conference*, 1990.

[Goldberg96] I. Goldberg, D. Wagner, R. Thomas, and E. Brewer, A Secure Environment for Untrusted Helper Applications, *USENIX Security Symposium*, 1996.

[Hlady95] M. Hlady, R. Kovacevic, J. J. Li. et al., An Approach to Automatic Detection of Software Failures, Proc. *IEEE 6th International Symposium on Software Reliability Engineering*, 1995.

[Ilgun93] K. Ilgun, A real-time intrusion detection system for UNIX, *IEEE Symp. on Security and Privacy*, 1993.

[Ko94] C. Ko, G. Fink and K. Levitt, Automated detection of vulnerabilities in privileged programs by execution monitoring, *Computer Security Application Conference*, 1994.

[Ko96] C. Ko, Execution Monitoring of Security-Critical Programs in a Distributed System: A Specification-Based Approach, *Ph.D. Thesis, Computer Science, University of California at Davis*, 1996.

[Kosoresow97] A. Kosoresow and S. Hofmeyr, Intrusion detection via system call traces, *IEEE Software '97*.

[Kumar94] S. Kumar and E. Spafford, A Pattern-Matching Model for Intrusion Detection, *National Computer Security Conference*, 1994.

CERT® is a registered trademark and service mark of Carnegie Mellon University.

[Landwehr94] C. Landwehr, A. Bull, J. McDermott and W. Choi, A Taxonomy of Computer Program Security Flaws, *ACM Computing Surveys 26(3),* 1994.

[Lunt92] T. Lunt et al., A Real-Time Intrusion Detection Expert System (IDES) - Final Report, *SRI-CSL-92-05, SRI International,* 1992.

[Lunt93] T. Lunt, A survey of Intrusion Detection Techniques, *Computers and Security,* 12(4), June 1993.

[Mukherjee94] B. Mukherjee, L. Todd Heberlein, Karl N. Levitt. Network Intrusion Detection, *IEEE Network,* pp.26-41, May/June 1994.

[Porras92] P. Porras and R. Kemmerer, Penetration State Transition Analysis - A Rule Based Intrusion Detection Approach, *Computer Security Applications Conference,* 1992.

[Sekar95] R. Sekar, I.V. Ramakrishnan and R. Ramesh, Adaptive Pattern Matching, *SIAM Journal of Computing,* 1995.

[Sekar98] R. Sekar, Y. Cai and M. Segal, A Specification-Based approach for Building Survivable Systems, 21st National Information Systems Security Conference.

[Spafford91] E. H. Spafford. The Internet Worm Incident, *Technical Report CSD-TR-993,* Purdue University, West Lafayette, IN, September 19, 1991.

[Vankamamidi98] R. Vankamamidi. ASL: A specification language for intrusion detection and network monitoring. *M.S. Thesis, Department of Computer Science, Iowa State University,* Dec 1998.

[Yang98] G. Yang. A Real-time Packet Filtering Module for Network Intrusion Detection System, *M.S. Thesis, Department of Computer Science, Iowa State University,* Jul 1998.

Intrusion Detection through Dynamic Software Measurement

Sebastian Elbaum
John C. Munson
Computer Science Department
University of Idaho
Moscow, ID 83844-1010
{elbaum, jmunson}@cs.uidaho.edu

Abstract

The thrust of this paper is to present a new real-time approach to detect aberrant modes of system behavior induced by abnormal and unauthorized system activities. The theoretical foundation for the research program is based on the study of the software internal behavior. As a software system is executing, it will express a set of its many functionalities as sequential events. Each of these functionalities has a characteristic set of modules that it will execute. In addition, these module sets will execute with clearly defined and measurable execution profiles. These profiles change as the executed functionalities change. Over time, the normal behavior of the system will be defined by profiles. An attempt to violate the security of the system will result in behavior that is outside the normal activity of the system and thus result in a perturbation in the normal profiles. We will show, through the real-time analysis of the Linux kernel, that we can detect very subtle shifts in the behavior of a system.

INTRODUCTION

The literature and media abound with reports of successful violations of computer system security by both external attackers and internal users [6,9]. Very recently, we experienced such an attack by a hacker on one of our Linux based computers at the University of Idaho. These breaches occur through physical attacks, social engineering attacks, and attacks on the system software. It is this later category of attack that is the focus of this paper. During an attack, the intruder subverts or bypasses the security mechanisms of the system in order to gain unauthorized access to the system or to increase their current access privileges. These attacks are successful when the attacker is able to cause the system software to execute in a manner that is typically inconsistent with the software specification and thus leads to a breach in security [1].

Intrusion detection systems monitor traces of user activity to determine if an intrusion has occurred. The traces of activity can be collated from audit trails or logs [3,14,21], network monitoring [12,17] or a combination of both. Once the data regarding a relevant aspect of the behavior of the system is collected, the classification stage starts.

Although taxonomies that are more complex exist [5,9], intrusion detection classification techniques can be broadly catalogued in the two main groups: *misuse intrusion detection* [15,16] and *anomaly intrusion detection* [3,13,20]. The first type of classification technique searches for occurrences of known attacks with a particular "signature" and the second type searches for departures from normality. Some of the newest intrusion detection tools incorporate both approaches [2,7,20].

The intent of this paper is to report on our work on the software engineering approach of dynamic software measurement to assist in the detection of intruders. Dynamic software measurement provides a framework to analyze the *internal* behavior of a system as it executes and makes transitions among its various modules governed by the structure of the program call graph. What is novel about our approach to dynamic intrusion detection is that we instrument the target system so that we can obtain measurements to profile the module activity on the system in real time. This paper reports on our investigations in intrusion detection with an instrumented Linux kernel. The objective of this research program has been to study the nominal behavior of the kernel software under a typical task load and then measure the direct effect of the application of a suite of known intrusion scenarios in the presence of the nominal activity.

As we will see, program modules are distinctly associated with certain functionalities and operations that the program is capable of performing. As each operation is executed, a subset of software modules is executed which creates a particular and distinct *signature* of transition events [19]. As we come to understand the nominal behavior of a system as it is executing its customary activities we can *profile* this nominal system behavior quite accurately. Departures from the nominal system profile represent potential invidious activity on the system. Some unwanted activity may be understood from previous assaults on the system. We can store profiles and recognize these activities from our historical data. What historical data cannot do is to permit us to recognize new assaults. An effective security tool would be designed to recognize assaults *as they occur* thorough the understanding and comparison of the current behavior against nominal system activity.

SOFTWARE ARCHITECTURAL MAPPING

Software systems are constructed to perform a set of operations for their customers, the users. An example of such an operation might be the activity of adding a new user to a computer system [1]. At the software level, these operations must be reduced to a well-defined set of functions. These functions represent the decomposition of operations into sub-problems that may be implemented on computer systems. The operation of adding a new user to the system might involve the functional activities of

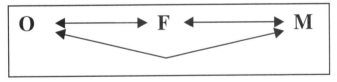

Figure 1. Software Mapping

changing to current directory to a password file, updating the password file, establishing user authorizations, and creating a new file for the new user. During the software design process, the basic functions are mapped by system designers to specific software program modules. These modules will implement the functionality. This software

mapping from operation to functionality to modules is represented in Figure 1.

From the standpoint of computer security, not all operations are equal. Some user operations may have little or no impact on computer security considerations. Other operations, such as, system maintenance activities, have a much greater impact on security. System maintenance activities being performed by systems administrators would be considered nominal system behavior. System maintenance activities being performed by dial-up users, on the other hand, would *not* be considered nominal system behavior. In order to formalize this decomposition process, a formal description of these relationships will be established [18].

Mapping Operations to Functionalities

Assume that the software system S was designed to implement a specific set of mutually exclusive functionalities F. Thus, if the system is executing a function $f \in F$ then it cannot be expressing elements of any other functionality in F. Each of these functions in F was designed to implement a set of software specifications based on a user's requirements. From a user's perspective, this software system will implement a specific set of operations, O. This mapping from the set of user perceived operations, O, to a set of specific program functionalities is one of the major functions in the software specification process. It is possible, then, to define a relation IMPLEMENTS over $O \times F$ such that IMPLEMENTS(o, f) is true if functionality f is used in the specification of an operation, o.

From a computer security standpoint, we can envision operations as the set of services available to a user (e.g., login, open a file, write to a device) and functionality as the set of internal operations that implement a particular operation (e.g., user-id validation, ACL lookup, labeling). When viewed from this perspective, it is apparent that user operations that may appear to be non-security relevant may actually be implemented with security relevant functionalities (sendmail is a classic example of this, an inoffensive operation of send mail can be transformed into an attack if the functionalities that deal with buffers can be overloaded).

Mapping Functionalities to Modules

The software design process is strictly a matter of assigning functionalities in F to specific program modules $m \in M$ the set of program modules of system S. The design process may be thought of as the process of defining a set of relations, ASSIGNS over $F \times M$ such that ASSIGNS(f, m) is true if functionality f is expressed in module m.

Mapping Modules to Operations

We can see that there is a distinct relationship between any given operation, o, and a given set of program modules. That is, if the user performs an particular operation then this operation will manifest itself in certain modules receiving control. We can tell, inversely, which program operations are being executed by observing the pattern of modules executing, i.e. the module profile. In a sense, then, the mapping of operations to modules and the mapping of modules to operations is reflexive.

It is a most unfortunate accident of most software design efforts that there are really two distinct set of operations. On the one hand, there is a set of explicit operations O_E. These are the intended operations that appear in the Software Requirements Specification documents. On the other hand, there is also a set of implicit operations, O_I, that represent unadvertised features of the software that have been implemented through designer carelessness or ignorance. These are not documented, nor well known except by a group of knowledgeable and/or patient system specialists, called hackers.

The set of implicit operations, O_I, is not well known for most systems. We are obliged to find out what they are the hard way. Hackers and other interested citizens will find them and exploit them. What is known is the set of operations O_E and the mappings of the operations onto the set of modules, M. For each of the explicit operations there is an associated module profile. That is, if an explicit operation is executed, then a well defined set of modules will execute in a very predictable fashion. We can use this fact to develop a reasonable profile of the system when it is executing a set of operations from the set of explicit operations. We can use this nominal system behavior to serve as a stable platform against which we may measure intrusive activity. That is, when

we observe a distribution of module profiles that is not representative of the operations in O_E then we may assume that we are observing one or more operations from the set O_I; we are being attacked.

THE PROFILES OF SOFTWARE DYNAMICS

When the software is subjected to a series of unique and distinct functional expressions, there will be a different behavior for each of the user's operations. Each operation will implement a different set of functions that will in turn, invoke possibly different sets of program modules.

Operational Profile

As a user performs the various operations on a system, he/she will cause each operation to occur in a series of steps or transitions. The transition from one operation to another may be described as a stochastic process. In which case we may define an indexed collection of random variables $\{X_t\}$, where the index t runs through a set of non-negative integers, $t = 0,1,2,\ldots$ representing the individual transitions or intervals of the process. At any particular interval the user is found to be expressing exactly one of the system's a operations. The fact of the execution occurring in a particular operation is a *state* of the user. During any interval the user is found performing exactly one of a finite number of mutually exclusive and exhaustive states that may be labeled $0,1,2,\ldots,a$. In this representation of the system, there is a stochastic process $\{X_t\}$, where the random variables are observed at intervals $t = 0,1,2,\ldots$ and where each random variable may take on any one of the $(a+1)$ integers, from the state space $O = \{0,1,2,\ldots,a\}$.

Each user may potentially bring his/her own distinct behavior to the system. Thus, each user will have his/her own characteristic operational profile. It is a characteristic, then, of each user to induce a probability function $p_i = \Pr[X = i]$ on the set of operations, O. In that these operations are mutually exclusive, the induced probability function is a multinomial distribution.

Functional Profile

As the system progresses through the steps in the software lifecycle, the user requirements specifications, the set O, must be mapped on a specific set of functionalities, F, by system designers. This set F is in fact the design specifications for the system. As per our earlier discussion, each operation is implemented by one for more functionalities. The transition from one functionality to another may be also be described as a stochastic process. In which case we may define a new indexed collection of random variables $\{Y_t\}$, as before representing the individual transitions events among particular functionalities. At any particular interval a given operation is found to be expressing exactly one of the system's $b+1$ functionalities. During any interval the user is found performing exactly one of a finite number of mutually exclusive and exhaustive states that may be labeled $0,1,2,\ldots,b$. In this representation of the system, there is a stochastic process $\{Y_t\}$, where the random variables are observed at intervals $t = 0,1,2,\ldots$ and where each random variable may take on any one of the $(b+1)$ integers, from the state space $F = \{0,1,2,\ldots,b\}$.

When a program is executing a given operation, say o_k, it will distribute its activity across the set of functionalities, $F^{(o_k)}$. At any arbitrary interval, n, during the expression of o_k the program will be executing a functionality $f_i \in F^{(o_k)}$ with a probability, $\Pr[Y_n = i \mid X = k]$. From this conditional probability distribution for all operations we may derive the *functional profile* for the design specifications as a function of a user operational profile to wit:

$$\Pr[Y = i] = \sum_j \Pr[X = j]\Pr[Y = i \mid X = j].$$

Alternatively,

$$w_i = \sum_j p_j \Pr[Y = i \mid X = j].$$

Module Profile

The next logical step is to study the most internal behavior of a software system, the module level. Each of the functionalities is implemented in one or more program modules. The transition from one module to another may be also be described as a

stochastic process, in which case we may define a third indexed collection of random variables $\{Z_t\}$, as before representing the individual transitions events among the set of program modules. At any particular interval a given functionality is found to be executing exactly one of the system's c modules. The fact of the execution occurring in a particular module is a *state* of the system. During any interval the system is found executing exactly one of a finite number of mutually exclusive and exhaustive states (program modules) that may be labeled $0,1,2,\ldots,c$. In this representation of the system, there is a stochastic process $\{Z_t\}$, where the random variables are observed at *epochs* $t = 0,1,2,\ldots$ and where each random variable may take on any one of the $(c+1)$ integers, from the state space $M = \{0,1,2,\ldots,c\}$.

Each functionality j has a distinct set of modules M_{f_j} that it may cause to execute. At any arbitrary interval, n, during the expression of f_j the program will be executing a module $m_i \in M_{f_j}$ with a probability, $\Pr[Z_n = i \mid Y = j]$. From this condition probability distribution for all functionalities we may derive the *module profile* for the system as a function of a the system functional profile as follows:

$$\Pr[Z = i] = \sum_j \Pr[Y = j]\Pr[Z = i \mid Y = j].$$

Again,

$$r_i = \sum_j w_j \Pr[Z = i \mid Y = j].$$

The module profile, **r**, ultimately depends on the operational profile, **p**. We can see this by substituting for w_j in the equation above.

$$r_i = \sum_j \sum_k p_k \Pr[Y = j \mid X = k]\Pr[Z = i \mid Y = j]$$

Each distinct operational scenario creates its own distinct module profile. Operational profile characteristics can be inferred from the module profile. It is this fact that we wish to exploit in the detection of unwanted or intrusive events.

Interestingly enough, for all software systems at the application level, there is a distinguished module, the main program module that will always receive execution control from the operating system. If we denote this main program as module 0 then, $\Pr[Z_0 = 0] = 1$ and $\Pr[Z_0 = i] = 0$ for $i = 1, 2, \ldots, c$. Further, for epoch 1, $\Pr[Z_1 = 0] = 0$, in that control will have been transferred from the main program module to another function module. The sequence of possible transitions from one program module to another may be represented as a call graph as shown in Figure 2.

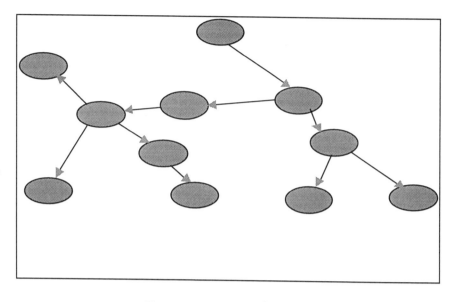

Figure 2. Program Call Graph

The granularity of the term epoch is now of interest. An epoch begins with the onset of execution in a particular module and ends when control is passed to another module. The measurable event for modeling purposes is this transition among the program modules. We will count the number of calls from a module and the number of returns to that module. Each of these transitions to a different program module from the one currently executing will represent an incremental change in the epoch number.

In practice: Execution Profile

In reality, few, if any systems are understood at the functional or operation level. We are continually confronted with systems whose functionality is not completely understood. While we have developed methodologies to recapture the essential functionalities [10,18], the majority of the time we will not know the precise behavior of the system that we are working with. To this end we will develop a more relaxed form of profile called the execution profile of a system. The execution profile reflects the internal system behavior based only on the understanding of the modular activity. Although it is not as powerful as the family of profiles presented before, it is simpler and allows obtaining basic profile information under environments with poor specifications and other constraints.

When a user is exercising a system, the software will be driven through a sequence of transitions from one module to the next, $S = \langle m_{ab}, m_{bc}, m_{cd}, \ldots \rangle$ where m_{ab} represents a transition from module a to module b. Over a fixed number of epochs, each progressive sequence will exhibit a particular *execution profile*. It represents a sample drawn from a pool of nominal system behavior. Thus, the series of sequence, $\mathbf{S} = \langle S_i, S_{i+1}, S_{i+2}, \ldots \rangle$, above will generate a family of execution profiles $\langle \mathbf{p}_i, \mathbf{p}_{i+1}, \mathbf{p}_{i+2}, \ldots \rangle$. What becomes clear after a period of observation is that the range of behavior exhibited by a system and expressed in sequences of execution profiles is highly constrained. Certain standard behaviors are demonstrated by the system doing what it normally does. The activities of an intruder will create significant disturbances in the nominal system behavior.

The whole notion of intrusion detection would be greatly facilitated if we knew what the functionalities of the system were. It would also be very convenient if we were to have a precise description of the set of operations for the software. Indeed, if these elements of software behavior were known and precisely specified, we probably would not have to worry about security faults in the behavior that present opportunities for hackers. In the absence of these specifications, we will assume that we cannot observe operational profiles nor functional profiles directly. Instead we must observe the distribution of activity among the program modules to make inferences about the behavior of the system.

METHODOLOGY

Objectives

The main objective of our intrusion detection methodology is to trap in real-time any behavior that is considered abnormal. We want to observe the software modules and their behavior to determine with a certain level of confidence the existence of an intrusion. The two fundamental aspects used to determine an intrusion are the execution of a set of modules that define 1.) An implicit operation and 2.) A set of explicit operations in abnormal sequences or quantities.

This intrusion detection approach observes not only the external events produced by the system (such us the popular "logs audit trails") but also the internal behavior of the software. The main advantages of observing and analyzing the internal behavior of the system instead of its external events are: 1.) Internal behavior disorders can be detected much earlier (external events might be visible much after the disorder started) 2.) It is more sensitive to anomalies because it makes observations at a system's component level. 3.) Higher level events can be derived from the lower level information provided by the internal analysis.

In order to accomplish internal system behavior monitoring, we have developed a suite of profiler techniques that allows us to track the component interactions at the module level as stated before. These interactions constitute fingerprints of systems behavior that are represented in the execution profile. Each user and application generate a unique behavior that can be characterized through this technique. Normal behaviors can be established and, while the system is running, its behavior can be compared to the one defined as nominal. If the current behavior statistically differs from the normal then a flag must be raised because there is a probability that the system is under attack.

The phases of detection

Detection instrumentation must really be installed at five different levels of software: the system kernel, the network layer, the file-system, the shell, and the end user application. At the kernel level, the operating system will generate and display a normal level of activity as shown in its nominal execution profile. When this profile shifts to an off-nominal profile, something new and potential intrusive is occurring on the system. At the network level, the generation, assembly and transport of data packages can be characterized by a profile. When package generation is abnormally increased or decreased, when the assembly produces enormous packages or when the send or receive process takes unusual steps then something abnormal and potentially dangerous is occurring at the network level. At the file system level, each user accesses different files, in different locations, with different frequencies that describe certain patterns that can be represented in a profile. At the shell level, each user generates a standard profile representing the normal activities that are customary for that person. Finally, each application generates profiles of characteristic nominal behavior for each activity [2].

In any of these levels, when a user profile begins to differ from a nominal profile by a pre-established amount, an alarm is activated. Two things might be wrong. An intruder has gained entry to the system and is masquerading as an existing user. Alternatively, a current user is acting abnormally (possibly, in anticipation of an eminent departure from the company) and means us harm. Although a complete intrusion detection system would take into consideration all five levels, at this experimental stage, we are focusing strictly on the kernel level. We are interested in the kernel because it has the most complex requirements in terms of timing constraints allowing us to evaluate the worst case performance burden. We are focusing in the application domain because the other levels can be considered subsets of the application level with some special characteristics. Since each one of these levels provides a different perspective for the system, we expect that the integration of these levels will provide us with a more integral view of the whole system security. At this point, we are only equipped to deal with them individually.

EXPERIMENTING WITH THE LINUX KERNEL

In this paper, we are introducing for the first time a simplified and preliminary version of the internal behavior analysis of the Linux kernel. It is now possible to instrument any application written in C with the CLIC tool [8], even time constrained

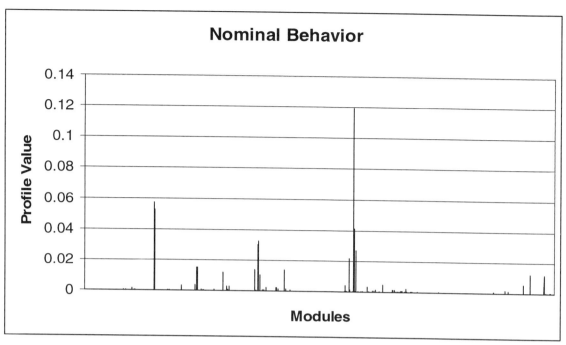

Figure 3. Nominal Activity

software such as a kernel. We have chosen to instrument the Linux kernel as an example of a security relevant real-time application. The CLIC tool was employed to insert the necessary hooks into 2500 C modules of the kernel. Then the Linux kernel was recompiled. We were then able to profile the nominal activities of the kernel under four distinct application environments. First, we profiled the kernel when there was no user activity, the system was idle. Next, we profiled the kernel when there were a number of compute-bound scientific programs running. We then profiled the system with a number of I/O intensive activities, such as edit functions, running. Finally, we obtain profiles for the system running a large number of relative small tasks including a variety of networked activities. From these various exercises of the Linux kernel, we were able to establish a baseline profile for its nominal functionality under a host of legitimate user activities. Figure 3 shows an execution profile with normal system activity. On the x-axis are the 2500 instrumented modules and on the y-axis the percentage of execution that each module received. The execution is measured in terms of epochs as it was explained in the profile section.

Over a period of time we can clearly establish reasonable boundaries for the nominal user

activities on a given Linux system. We would clearly like to be able to raise the alarm when off-nominal activity occurs. Off-nominal behavior will be classified into one of two mutually exclusive categories. First, is the case when we can match the signature of the activity with a known system assault [3,12]. Second, is when we do not recognize the nature of the activity. This new observation represents new system behavior. This may or may not represent an assault. In either event, a security tool must signal an alarm. The system administrator will be notified that either a known assault is in progress or that a novel activity is now running and should be examined further.

It was next of interest to examine the behavior of the kernel in response to a series of assault scenarios. In this investigation, we have explored several intrusion scenarios and their effect on the Linux kernel.

Each activity running on the Linux kernel will cause the kernel to execute in a particular manner. By controlling for the effect of nominal system activity from any other activity we generate a *signature* profile for each one of them. In figures 4,5 and 6, we show the output of this differential comparison process for three intrusion scenarios we have investigated. The y-axis represents the impact

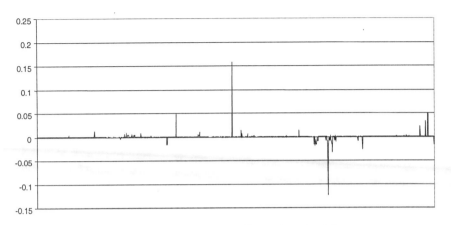

Figure 4. Intrusion Scenario: Synk4

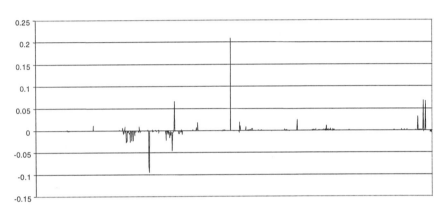

Figure 5. Intrusion Scenario: The Octopus

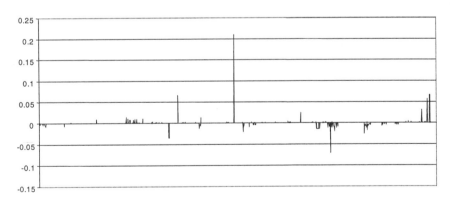

Figure 6. Intrusion Scenario: Boink

executing. Conversely, a negative value on the y-axis represents increased kernel module activity due to the intrusion.

The first attack scenario is produced by the program synk4. Synk4 floods the system ports with different types of requests. The system can be halted by overloading and IP addresses can be spoofed by this application.

The second intrusion scenario is produced by Octopus. Octopus is usually used to generate a denial of service attack opening many connections to a remote host. The host is overwhelmed by the number of request and halts.

The last attack scenario is given by boink. Boink exploits the overlapping IP fragment bug present in most Linux kernels.

What is astonishing and is clearly revealed on inspection of the intrusion scenarios we present is that the signatures of each of these activities are very different. These distinct scenarios have their own recognizable signatures that differ sharply from the nominal activity profile. We are currently developing signatures for the full gamut of known intrusions. This will permit us to recognize the full spectrum of known attacks involving the Linux kernel. It will also permit us to

of each intrusion activity on the nominal kernel activity. A positive value on the y-axis means that the system resources have decreased on the specific kernel module while the attack scenario was

identify new and potentially invidious assaults that we have yet to witness.

CONCLUDING REMARKS

We have presented a novel methodology for intrusion detection in real time that uses dynamic measurement techniques to analyze the internal software behavior. After a series of experiments, which were presented in this paper, we have shown that internal behavior analysis has an enormous potential as an effective means to detect abnormal activities that might constitute threats to a system. Through the real time analysis of the internal program activities we can detect very subtle shifts in the behavior of a system. In addition, based on the initial experiments, we can presume that each attack has a particular internal behavior signature that can be recognized.

At this experimental stage, we have not addressed many issues. A more complete procedure and formalism for the determination of the normal profile is necessary. We haven't established a mechanism to reduce and filter the "noise" generated by multiple users and applications, although the multiple stage detection might provide some answers to that. Last, we are currently starting to assess the performance and the detection rates provided by this methodology and there is still a lot of work ahead of us in this arena.

In order to validate our methodology, we have created an environment to allow experimentation and characterization of different profiles. The environment will provide a means to facilitate the study and evaluation of the comparison strategies and provide the experimentation platform to run attacks on. That a system has functioned securely in its past is *not* a clear indication that it will function securely in the future. The continuing evaluation of profiles over the life of a system can provide substantial information as to the changing nature of the program's execution environment. This, in turn, will foster the notion that software security assessment is as dynamic as the operating environment of the program.

Though we have specifically chosen to focus our energies on the investigation of intrusions against the Linux kernel, the methodology we have presented in this paper is not restricted to kernel type activities. The kernel was our first choice because it is a complicated real time embedded application. If the technology can be shown to work in this complex environment, it will easily port to applications outside of the kernel. Any software system is a potential candidate for this methodology.

REFERENCES

[1] J. Alves-Foss, D. Frincke and J. Munson. Measuring Security: A Methodological Approach, *International Workshop on Enterprise Security*, Stanford, CA, June 1996.

[2] D. Anderson, T. Frivold and A. Valdez: Next-generation intrusion detection expert system (NIDES). Technical Report, Computer Science Laboratory, SRI International, Menlo Park, CA, SRI-CSL-95-07, May 1995.

[3] D.Anderson, T.F. Lunt, H. Javitz, A. Tamaru and A. Valdes: Detecting Unusual Program Behavior Using the Statistical Component of the Next-generation Intrusion Detection Expert System (NIDES), SRI-CSL-95-06, *SRI International, Menlo Park*, CA, May 1995.

[4] M. Bishop: A standard audit log format. *Proc. of the 18th National Information Systems Security Conference*, pp. 136-145, October 1995.

[5] M.Bishop: A Taxonomy of UNIX and Network Security Vulnerabilities," M. Bishop, Technical Report 95-10, *Department of Computer Science, University of California at Davis*, May 1995.

[6] CERT coordination Center http://www.cert.org/advisories

[7] D. Denning: An intrusion-detection model. *IEEE Transactions on Software Engineering*, Vol.13, No:2, pp.222-232, February 1987.

[8] S.G.Elbaum, J.C.Munson and M.Harrison. CLIC: a Tool for the Measurement of Software System Dynamics. *Software Engineering Testing Lab technical report TR-98-04*, University of Idaho, 1998.

[9] Fathom Group - Intrusion Detection http://www.cs.uidaho.edu/~elbaum/fathom.html

[10] G. Hall."Usage Patterns: Extracting System Functionality from Observed Profiles". Dissertation. *University of Idaho. Computer Science Department.* 1997.

[11] L.R. Halme and R.K.Bauer: AINT misbehaving - a taxonomy of anti-intrusion techniques. *Proc. of the 18th National Information Systems Security Conference*, pp. 163-172, October 1995.

[12] J. Hochberg, K. Jackson, C. Stallings, J.F.McClary, D. DuBois and J. Ford: NADIR: An automated system for detecting network intrusion and misuse. *Computers & Security*, Vol.12, No:3, pp.235-248, May 1993.

[13] H.S. Javitz and A. Valdes: The SRI IDES statistical anomaly detector. *Proc. of the IEEE Symposium on Research in Security and Privacy*, pp.316-326, May 1991.

[14] A.P.Kosoresow and S.A.Hofmeyr, "Intrusion Detection via System Call Traces", *IEEE Software*, Septemeber/October 1997, pp. 35-42.

[15] S. Kumar and E.H. Spafford: A pattern matching model for misuse intrusion detection. *Proc. of the 17th National Computer Security Conference*, pp. 11-21, October 1994.

[16] S. Kumar and E.H. Spafford: A Software Architecture to Support Misuse Intrusion Detection, *Proc. 18th National Information Systems Security Conference*, pp.194-204, 1995.

[17] B. Mukherjee, L.T. Heberlein and K.N. Levitt: Network intrusion detection. *IEEE Network*, Vol.8, No:3, pp.26-41, May/June 1994.

[18] J.C.Munson, A Functional Approach to Software Reliability Modeling. In Boisvert, ed., *Quality of Numerical Software, Assessment and Enhancement*, Chapman & Hall, London, 1997. ISBN 0-412- 80530-8.

[19] J.C.Munson, "A Software Blackbox Recorder." *Proceedings of the 1996 IEEE Aerospace Applications Conference*, IEEE Computer Society Press, Los Alamitos, CA, November, pp. 309-320, 1996.

[20] A.P. Porras and G.P. Neumann: EMERALD: Event Monitoring Enabling Responses to Anomalous Live Disturbances. *National Information Systems Security Conference*, 1997.

[21] M. Sobirey, Richter and H. Konig. The intrusion detection system AID. Architecture, and experiences in automated audit analysis. *Proc. of the International Conference on Communications and Multimedia Security*, pp. 278-290, September 1996.

Learning Program Behavior Profiles for Intrusion Detection*

Anup K. Ghosh, Aaron Schwartzbard & Michael Schatz
Reliable Software Technologies Corporation
21515 Ridgetop Circle, #250, Sterling, VA 20166
phone: (703) 404-9293, fax: (703) 404-9295
email: anup.ghosh@computer.org
www.rstcorp.com

Abstract

Profiling the behavior of programs can be a useful reference for detecting potential intrusions against systems. This paper presents three anomaly detection techniques for profiling program behavior that evolve from memorization to generalization. The goal of monitoring program behavior is to be able to detect potential intrusions by noting irregularities in program behavior. The techniques start from a simple equality matching algorithm for determining anomalous behavior, and evolve to a feed-forward backpropagation neural network for learning program behavior, and finally to an Elman network for recognizing recurrent features in program execution traces. In order to detect future attacks against systems, intrusion detection systems must be able to generalize from past observed behavior. The goal of this research is to employ machine learning techniques that can generalize from past observed behavior to the problem of intrusion detection. The performance of these systems is compared by testing them with data provided by the DARPA Intrusion Detection Evaluation program.

1 Introduction

Intrusion detection tools seek to detect attacks against computer systems by monitoring the behavior of users, networks, or computer systems. In-trusion detection techniques are the last line of defense against computer attacks behind secure network architecture design, secure program design, carefully configured network services, firewalls, penetration audits, and personnel screening. Attacks against computer systems are still largely successful despite the plethora of intrusion prevention techniques available. For instance, insider attacks and malicious mobile code have been able to penetrate most security defenses. Largely, however, most computer security attacks are made possible by poorly configured software or by buggy software.

Some of the first intrusion detection activities were performed by system administrators who examined audit logs of user and system events recorded by computer hosts. Activities such as super user login attempts, FTP transfers of sensitive files, or failed file accesses were flags for potential intrusive activity. Soon thereafter, expert systems were used to automatically detect potential attacks by scanning audit logs for signs of intrusive behavior or for departures from normal behavior. The Intrusion Detection Expert System (IDES) developed at SRI performed intrusion detection by creating statistical profiles for users and noting unusual departures from normal profiles [16]. IDES keeps statistics for each user according to specific intrusion detection measures, such as the number of files created and deleted each day. These statistics form the statistical profile of each user. The profiles are periodically updated to include the most recent changes to the user's profile. Therefore, this technique is adaptive with changing user profiles. However, it is also susceptible to a user slowly changing his or her profile to include possibly intrusive activities.

More recently, network-based intrusion detection tools have gained popularity among researchers and even in commercial tools. Network-based intrusion

---

*This work is sponsored under the Defense Advanced Research Projects Agency (DARPA) Contract DAAH01-98-C-R145. THE VIEWS AND CONCLUSIONS CONTAINED IN THIS DOCUMENT ARE THOSE OF THE AUTHORS AND SHOULD NOT BE INTERPRETED AS REPRESENTING THE OFFICIAL POLICIES, EITHER EXPRESSED OR IMPLIED, OF THE DEFENSE ADVANCED RESEARCH PROJECTS AGENCY OR THE U.S. GOVERNMENT.

detection tools will typically search network data for signatures of known computer attacks. For example, network probing attacks, which map out the network topology of a site, can often be detected by their characteristic "pings" to the range of network services across many machines.

Today, there are generally two types of intrusion detection systems: anomaly detection and misuse detection. Anomaly detection approaches attempt to detect intrusions by noting significant departures from normal behavior [7, 5, 20, 18, 15, 17, 16]. Misuse detection techniques attempt to model attacks on a system as specific patterns, then systematically scan the system for occurrences of these patterns [22, 14, 10, 9, 19]. This process involves a specific encoding of previous behaviors and actions that were deemed intrusive or malicious.

It is important to establish the key differences between anomaly detection and misuse detection approaches. The most significant advantage of misuse detection approaches is that known attacks can be detected fairly reliably and with a low false positive rate. However, the key drawback of misuse detection approaches is that they cannot detect novel attacks against systems that leave different signatures. So while the false positive rate can be made extremely low, the rate of missed attacks (false negatives) can be extremely high depending on the ingenuity of the attackers. As a result, misuse detection approaches provide little defense against novel attacks, until they can learn to generalize from known signatures of attacks.

Anomaly detection techniques, on the other hand, directly address the problem of detecting novel attacks against systems. This is possible because anomaly detection techniques do not scan for specific patterns, but instead compare current activities against models of past behavior. One clear drawback of anomaly detection is its inability to identify the specific type of attack that is occurring. However, probably the most significant disadvantage of anomaly detection approaches is the high rates of false alarm. Because any significant deviation from the baseline can be flagged as an intrusion, it is likely that non-intrusive behavior that falls outside the normal range will also be labeled as an intrusion — resulting in a false positive. Another drawback of anomaly detection approaches is that if an attack occurs during the training period for establishing the baseline data, then this intrusive behavior will be established as part of the normal baseline.

In spite of the potential drawbacks of anomaly detection, having the ability to detect novel attacks makes anomaly detection a requisite if future, unknown, and novel attacks against computer systems are to be detected.

In this paper, we consider three techniques for intrusion detection that are based on anomaly detection. Our primary goal in this work is to be able to detect novel attacks against systems, *i.e.*, attacks that have not been seen before by our intrusion detection system. Our secondary goal is to reduce the false positive rate, *i.e.*, the rate at which our system classifies normal behavior as intrusions. Our approach is to learn the normal behavior of programs (using different techniques) and then flag significant departures from normal behavior as possible intrusions. This approach is designed to achieve our primary goal of detecting novel attacks.

To achieve our secondary goal of reducing the false positive rate, our approach is to generalize from past observed behavior to inputs the system did not encounter during training. To this end, we have developed three algorithms that range in their ability from being able to simply memorize past events to being able to classify inputs previously unseen based on a similarity measure, to being able to recognize recurrent patterns. Before developing the three algorithms, we first present related work in program-based intrusion detection.

2 Analyzing Program Behavior for Anomaly Detection

Analyzing program behavior profiles for intrusion detection has recently emerged as a viable alternative to user-based approaches to intrusion detection (see [7, 21, 12, 5, 3, 6, 14] for other program-based approaches). Program behavior profiles are built by capturing system calls made by the program under analysis under normal operational conditions. If the captured behavior represents a compact and adequate signature of normal behavior, then the profile can be used to detect deviations from normal behavior such as those that occur when a program is being misused for intrusion.

One of the first groups to develop program-based intrusion detection was Stephanie Forrest's research group out of the University of New Mexico. Their work in [5, 6] established an analogy between the human immune system and intrusion detection. The approach consisted of using short sequences of system calls (called a string or N-gram) from the target program to the operating system to form a signature for normal behavior. A database of system calls is built for each monitored program by capturing system calls made by the program under normal usage conditions. The Linux program strace was used in their work to capture system calls.

Once constructed, the database essentially serves as the repository for self behavior against which all subsequent online behavior will be judged. If a string formed during the online operation of the program does not match a string in the normal database, a mismatch is recorded. If the number of mismatches detected are a significant percentage of all strings captured during the online session, then an intrusion is registered. The application of this technique was shown viable for Unix programs sendmail, lpr, and ftpd.

It was later recognized by a research group out of Columbia University [14] and by another research project at UNM [12] that program anomalies were temporally located in clusters. Thus, averaging the number of anomalies over the entire execution trace as performed in the UNM's earlier work could potentially "wash out" the intrusive behavior among normal variation in program behavior. Hence, the notion of fixed-length frames in which anomalies were to be counted was used in both groups' subsequent work.

The Columbia group applied a rule learning program (RIPPER [2]) to the data to extract rules for predicting whether a sequence of system calls is normal or abnormal. Because the rules made by RIPPER can be erroneous, a post-processing algorithm is used to scan the predictions made by RIPPER to determine if an intrusion has occurred or not. The post-processing algorithm uses the notion of temporal locality to filter spurious prediction errors from intrusions which should leave temporally co-located abnormal predictions. The results in [14] verified that system calls can be used to detect intrusions, even with different intrusion detection algorithms.

Subsequent work performed by the UNM group and reported in [12], applied fixed-length frames to the equality matching approach developed earlier in [6]. However, their work was further distinguished by their analysis of the structure of system calls made by the program. The empirical analysis found recurrent patterns of system calls in execution traces of any given program. For instance most programs have a prefix, a main portion, and a suffix. Within these portions, system calls tended to be repeated in a regular fashion. As a result, they hypothesized that a deterministic finite automaton (DFA) could be constructed to represent this behavior using a macro language. For each program, they manually selected macros that matched the pattern they believed to represent the normal behavior. Anomalies were then detected by applying the macros against the observed behavior and noting mismatches. However, because their technique involves creating DFAs heuristically and by hand, the technique will not scale well to real systems. Furthermore, an exact DFA representation of the program behavior could lead to a state explosion problem.

In a similar vein as the work of [12] in creating finite state automata, a group from Iowa State is implementing a program-based intrusion detection approach that analyzes system calls using state machine models of program behavior [21]. However, their approach is not concerned with detecting anomalies, as much as detecting violations of specified behavior. As a result, the approach of the Iowa State group requires the development of specification models for acceptable program behavior, where the work of [12, 14, 5, 6] used models of program behavior derived from empirical training. An auditing specification language (ASL) is used to develop a representation of expected or allowed program behavior based on specification models of programs; violations of this model are used to detect potential intrusions and isolate the program in question from privileged resources. This approach is similar to sandbox models of programs that constrain program behavior based on policies or models of acceptable program behavior [8, 11].

In this paper, we build upon the work of the UNM group in creating normal program behavior profiles from system calls and performing anomaly detection from these profiles. We present an evolution of techniques that begin from a table lookup equality matching approach (similar to the UNM work in [5]) to machine learning approaches that can generalize from past observed behavior. Our goal in applying the equality matching technique was to verify the feasibility and performance of the technique on a much larger scale than previously performed. Our approach was simply to improve on the equality matching technique where it was obvious improvements could be made.

In the equality matching approach, we use fixed-size frames to capture temporally co-located events similar to [14, 12]. However, unlike the approach in [12], our technique automatically builds profiles for programs and performs anomaly detection. No heuristics or hand coding of macros are necessary to do anomaly detection. We have been able to scale up our program-based anomaly detection approach significantly over previous studies [12, 14, 5] to monitor over 150 programs as part of the 1998 DARPA Intrusion Detection Evaluation program[1]. Hence the results presented here represent the first significant study of applying an equality matching technique for system calls to a realistic system in a comprehensive intrusion detection study.

One of the key drawbacks in using an equality matching approach in its current form is the inability to generalize from past observed behavior. Thus, if the normal program behavior is not adequately captured, future unseen normal behavior will be classified as anomalous, thus contributing to the false positive rate. Desiring the ability to reduce the false positive rate while still providing the ability to detect novel attacks consistently, we investigated machine learning approaches for learning program behavior. Neural networks were the best fit for learning associations between observed inputs and desired outputs. We implemented a standard back-propagation neural network (a feedforward multi-perceptron network) to be able to generalize from previously seen inputs to map future unseen inputs into normal or anomalous outputs. We tested our backpropagation networks against the same corpus of data provided by the DARPA evaluation program. The results show both the benefits and pitfalls of using backpropagation networks for this purpose.

While working with neural networks, we re-visited the input domain for our networks in order to develop a proper encoding function to the network. We noticed recurrent patterns of system calls in the execution traces of the programs similar to what Kosoresow et al. noted in [12]. Unlike the approach developed by Kosoresow et al., however, we were interested in automatically learning the behavior of the program that would be able to exploit the recurrent features in the data. Furthermore, we desired

our learning algorithm to be able to generalize to recognize future, previously unseen behavior — unlike the equality matching algorithm. These requirements led us to the development of Elman networks. Elman networks use the sequential characteristics of the input data to learn to recognize sequentially related (or in our case temporally co-located) features of variable length. Hence, we applied the Elman networks to the DARPA evaluation data for anomaly detection.

The study presented in the rest of this paper is able to provide a side-by-side comparison of three different algorithms for anomaly detection that represent evolutions from pure memorization to generalization based on the recurrent characteristics of system calls made by programs. The results are significant because the data on which the algorithms are evaluated represents a significant corpus of scientifically controlled data by which the false positive rate of a given intrusion detection algorithm can be simultaneously measured against the correct detection rate. Hence, we are able to scientifically validate our approaches against a good set of data. In the rest of this paper, we describe the algorithms and the results from their implementation.

3 Equality Matching: A Simple Anomaly Detection Approach

The first approach we implemented built on the work of Forrest et al. [5, 12, 6]. But rather than using the strace(1) program on Linux for capturing system calls, we used Sun Microsystem's Basic Security Module (BSM) auditing facility for Solaris. This approach is practical because no special software need be written to capture system calls. The BSM events serve as an adequate representation of the behavior of the program for our purposes because any privileged calls that might be made by a program are captured by BSM. Furthermore, a program can only abuse system resources if it is making system calls. Our study also finds that out of approximately 200 different BSM events that can be recorded, programs typically make only 10 to 20 different BSM events. Therefore, capturing BSM events also serves as a compact representation of program behavior, while still leaving ample room to detect deviant behavior (through odd BSM events or odd sequences of BSM events). Finally, the BSM events we recorded for program executions showed

---

[1]See www.ll.mit.edu/IST/ideval/index.html for a summary of the program.

regular patterns of behavior such as a common beginning and ending sequence, as well as recurrent strings of system calls. Any anomaly detection algorithm will perform better when the entity it is monitoring has well-defined regular patterns of behavior. For all these reasons, in addition to the simplicity of the algorithm and the early success of the UNM group, we applied this algorithm with improvements to a large set of data to benchmark its success.

The equality matching algorithm is simple but effective. Sequences of BSM events are captured during online usage and compared against those stored in the database built from the normal program behavior profile. If the sequence of BSM events captured during online usage is not found in the database, then an anomaly counter is incremented. This technique is predicated on the ability to capture the normal behavior of a program in a database. If the normal behavior of a program is not adequately captured, then the false alarm rate is likely to be high. On the other hand, if the normal behavior profile built for a program includes intrusive behavior, then future instances of the intrusive behavior are likely to go undetected.

The data is partitioned into fixed-size windows in order to exploit a property of attacks that tends to leave its signature in temporally co-located events. That is, attacks tend to cause anomalous behavior to be recorded in clusters. Thus, rather than averaging the number of anomalous events recorded over the entire execution trace (which might wash out an attack in the noise), a much smaller size window of events is used for counting anomalous events.

Several counters are kept at varying levels of granularity ranging from a counter for each fixed window of system calls to a counter for the number of windows that are anomalous. Thresholds are applied at each level to determine at which point anomalous behavior is propagated up to the next level. Ultimately, if enough windows of system calls in a program are deemed anomalous, the program behavior during a particular session is deemed anomalous, and an intrusion detection flag is raised.

The equality matching algorithm was evaluated by MIT's Lincoln Laboratory under the DARPA 1998 Intrusion Detection Evaluation program. Unlabeled sessions were sent by Lincoln Labs and processed by our intrusion detection algorithm. These sessions had an unspecified number of attacks of the following four types: denial of service (DoS), probe, user to root (u2r), and remote to local (r2l). A user to root attack is defined as an attack that elevates the privilege of a user with local account privileges. Remote to local attacks grant a remote user with no account privileges to local user account privileges. Because this approach is mainly suited to u2r and r2l types of attacks, and because there were a statistically insignificant amount of DoS and probe attacks in the BSM data, we present results only from the u2r and r2l attacks.

Attack Type	Instances	Detections	Percent Detected
u2r	22	19	86.4
r2l	3	2	66.7
Total	25	21	84%

Table 1: **Performance of table look up intrusion detection algorithm against user to root (u2r) and remote to local (r2l) attacks.**

Table 1 shows the performance of the equality matching algorithm for detecting attacks at a particular threshold of sensitivity. If the threshold is set too low, then the false alarm rate will be low, but detection rate will be low, too. Similarly, a threshold set too high may end up detecting most intrusions, but suffer from a high false alarm rate. False alarm rates are not shown for these attacks because our algorithm will not label a particular attack — it only notes when an attack (any attack) is occurring. As a result, false positives cannot be tracked to particular attack types.

While the table is useful for quickly determining how many attacks of a particular type were detected, a more useful measure of the performance of the method can be obtained from Receiver Operating Characteristic (ROC) curves.

A measure of the overall effectiveness of a given intrusion detection system can be provided by the ROC curve. An ROC curve is a parametric curve that is generated by varying the threshold of the *intrusive measure*, which is a tunable parameter, and computing the probability of detection and the probability of false alarm at each operating point. The curve is a plot of the likelihood that an intrusion is detected, against the likelihood that a non-intrusion is misclassified (*i.e.*, a false positive) for a particular parameter, such as a tunable threshold. The ROC curve can be used to determine the performance of the system for different operating points

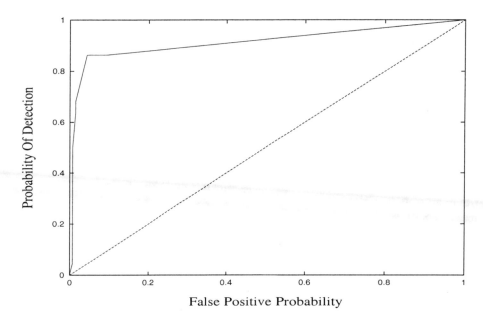

Figure 1: Performance of the equality matching technique as a function of false positive percentage (horizontal axis) and the correct detection percentage (vertical axis). This graph shows both the worst possible ROC curve (*i.e.*, $y = x$) as well as the ROC curve generated from actual data using the equality matching algorithm.

such as configurable thresholds, or for comparing the performance of different intrusion detection algorithms for given operating points.

Figure 1 shows performance of the equality matching algorithm as a ROC curve. To better understand this performance measure, consider an intrusion detection oracle that scores a session with a value of one if and only if it is an intrusion, and a value of zero otherwise. The resulting ROC curve would actually not be a curve, but rather, a single point at the location (0,1) since it is would detect intrusions with a likelihood of 1/1, and it would misclassify non-intrusions with a likelihood of 0/1. Further, as the threshold varied between zero and one (exclusive), there would be no change in the way sessions are classified, so the parametric value would remain at that one point. This can be called the *oracle point*. However, at the thresholds of 1 and 0 (inclusive), the (0,0) and (1,1) points remain fixed. Connecting these points and computing the area under the curve gives an area of 1, or a power of 100%.

At the other end of the spectrum, consider the curve that defines the worst possible intrusion detection system. The ROC curve for the worst case scenario is the $y = x$ line shown in Figure 1. Assume a system that randomly assigns a value between zero

and one for every session. Starting from a threshold of zero, we derive the (1,1) point because all sessions would be classified as intrusions. As the session threshold increases, the likelihood of both correctly classifying an intrusion and incorrectly classifying a non-intrusion decrease at the same rate until the session threshold is 1 (corresponding to the point (0,0)). The power of this system is 50%, corresponding to the area under this curve of 0.5. If an intrusion detection system were to perform even worse than this curve, one would simply invert each classification to do better. Therefore, the $y = x$ plot represents the benchmark by which all intrusion detection systems should do better.

The results in Figure 1 for the equality matching algorithm represent an optimal tuning of the window (or frame) size to 20 and an N-gram size to six. These parameter values were found to be optimal through experimental analysis. The $y = x$ curve is shown as the benchmark for the worst case scenario. The equality matching method was able to detect 68.2% of all intrusions with a false positive rate of 1.4%. Higher detection rates could be achieved at the expense of more false positives. At a detection rate of 86.4%, the false positive rate rose to 4.3%. Similar curves are generated and compared for the two other intrusion detection approaches.

4 The Backpropagation Network

The goal in using neural networks for intrusion detection is to be able to generalize from incomplete data and to be able to classify online data as being normal or anomalous. Applying machine learning to intrusion detection has been developed elsewhere as well [4, 1, 13]. Lane and Brodley's work uses machine learning to distinguish between normal and anomalous behavior. However, their work is different from ours in that they build *user* profiles based on sequences of each individual's normal user commands and attempt to detect intruders based on deviations from the established user profile. Similarly, Endler's work [4] used neural networks to learn the behavior of users based on BSM events recorded from user actions. Rather than building profiles on a per-user basis, our work builds profiles of *software behavior* and attempts to distinguish between normal software behavior and malicious software behavior. The advantages of our approach are that vagaries of individual behavior are abstracted because program behavior rather than individual usage is studied. This can be of benefit for defeating a user who slowly changes his or her behavior to foil a user profiling system. It can also protect the privacy interests of users from a surveillance system that monitors a user's every move.

The goal in using artificial neural networks (ANNs) for intrusion detection is to be able to generalize from incomplete data and to be able to classify online data as being normal or intrusive. An artificial neural network is composed of simple processing units, or *nodes*, and connections between them. The connection between any two units has some *weight*, which is used to determine how much one unit will affect the other. A subset of the units of the network acts as *input nodes*, and another subset acts as *output nodes*. By assigning a value, or *activation*, to each input node, and allowing the activations to propagate through the network, a neural network performs a functional mapping from one set of values (assigned to the input nodes) to another set of values (retrieved from the output nodes). The mapping itself is stored in the weights of the network.

In this work, a classical feed-forward multi-layer perceptron network was implemented: a backpropagation neural network. The backpropagation network has been used successfully in other intrusion detection studies [7, 1]. The backpropagation network, or backprop, is a standard feed-forward network. Input is submitted to the network and the activations for each level of neurons are cascaded forward.

In order to train the networks, it is necessary to expose them to normal data and anomalous data. Randomly generated data were used to train the network to distinguish between normal and anomalous data. The randomly generated data, which were spread throughout the input space, caused the network to generalize that all data were anomalous by default. The normal data, which tended to be localized in the input space, caused the network to recognize a particular area of the input space as non-anomalous.

During training, many networks were trained for each program, and the network that performed the best was selected. The remaining networks were discarded. Training involved exposing the networks to four weeks of labeled data, and performing the backprop algorithm to adjust weights. An epoch of training consisted of one pass over the training data. For each network, the training proceeded until the total error made during an epoch stopped decreasing, or 1,000 epochs had been reached. Since the optimal number of hidden nodes for a program was not known before training, for each program, networks were trained with 10, 15, 20, 25, 30, 35, 40, 50, and 60 hidden nodes. Before training, network weights were initialized randomly. However, initial weights can have a large, but unpredictable, effect on the performance of a trained network. In order to avoid poor performance due to bad initial weights, for each program, for each number of hidden nodes, 10 networks were initialized differently, and trained. Therefore, for each program, 90 networks were trained. To select which of the 90 to keep, each was tested on two weeks of data which were not part of the four weeks of data used for training. The network that classified data most accurately was kept.

After training and selection, a set of neural networks was ready to be used. However, a neural network can only classify a single string (a sequence of BSM events) as anomalous or normal, and our intention was to classify entire sessions (which are usually composed of executions of multiple programs) as anomalous or normal. Furthermore, our previous experiments showed that it is important to capture the temporal locality of anomalous events in order to recognize intrusive behavior. As a result, we desired an algorithm that provides some memory of

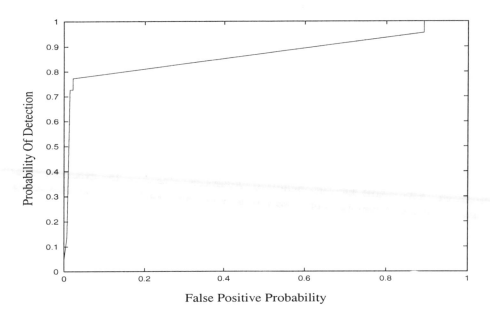

Figure 2: Performance of the backpropagation network expressed in a ROC curve. The horizontal axis represents the percentage of false positives while the vertical axis represents the percentage of correct detections for different operating thresholds of the technique.

recent events.

The leaky bucket algorithm fit this purpose well. The leaky bucket algorithm keeps a memory of recent events by accumulating the neural network's output, while slowly leaking its value. Thus, when the network computes closely related anomalies, the leaky bucket algorithm will quickly accumulate a large value in its counter. Similarly, as the network computes a normal output, the bucket will "leak" away its anomaly counter back down to zero. As a result, the leaky bucket emphasizes anomalies that are closely temporally co-located and diminishes the values of those that are sparsely located.

Strings of BSM events are passed to a neural network in the order they occurred during program execution. The output of a neural network—that is, the classification of the input string—is then placed into a leaky bucket. During each timestep, the level of the bucket is decreased by a fixed amount. If the level in the bucket rises above some threshold at any point during execution of the program, the program is flagged as anomalous. The advantage of using a leaky bucket algorithm is that it allows occasional anomalous behavior, which is to be expected during normal system operation, but it is quite sensitive to large numbers of temporally co-located anomalies, which one would expect if a program were really being misused. If a session contains a single anomalous program, the session is flagged as anomalous.

The performance of the IDS should by judged in terms of both the ability to detect intrusions, and by false positives—incorrect classification of normal behavior as intrusions. We used ROC curves to compare intrusion detection ability of the backpropagation network to false positives. The results from the backpropagation network are shown in Figure 2. The test data consisted of 139 non-intrusive sessions, and 22 intrusive sessions. Different leak rates from the leaky bucket algorithm produce different ROC curves. A leak rate of 0 results in all prior timesteps being retained in memory. A leak rate of 1 results in all timesteps but the current one being forgotten. We varied the leak rate from 0 to 1.

In Figure 2, the ROC curve is shown for a leak rate of 0.7. The curve and performance is similar to the equality matching algorithm results shown in Figure 1. A detection rate of 77.3% can be achieved with a false positive rate of 2.2%.

Purely feed-forward network topologies possess a major limiting characteristic. That characteristic is that the output produced by any input is independent of prior inputs. While this characteristic is appropriate for tasks which require processing of independent inputs, it is not optimal when the inputs are sequential elements of a *stream* of data. In the next section, we discuss an alternative network that can recognize recurrent features in the input.

5 Elman Networks

In this section, we motivate the reasons for using recurrent networks, then describe the Elman recurrent network used for anomaly detection. Results from applying the Elman network to the DARPA data are presented in comparison to the previous techniques.

The BSM events produced by a single program during a single execution can be considered to be a stream of events. That is, each event is part of an ordered series. A given portion of a program will typically generate similar sequences of BSM events during different executions. Since there is a limited number of ways in which a transition (or branch) from one portion of the program to another can occur, it is often possible to determine what sequence of events will follow the current sequence of events.

By using a feed-forward topology (with backpropagation learning rules), as described in the preceding section, we *train* ANNs to recognize whether small, fixed-sized sequences of events are characteristic of the programs in which they occur. For each sequence, an ANN produces an output value that represents how anomalous the sequence is (based on the training data). In addition, the leaky bucket algorithm used to classify the program behavior ensures that two highly anomalous sequences have a larger impact on the classification of a program if they are close together than if they are far apart. However, as determined by investigation of raw BSM data, the large-scale structure of a stream of BSM data has features that cannot be captured within individual sequences of lengths being used in our experiments.

In order to accommodate the large-scale structure of BSM features during a given execution trace, two options are apparent: 1) increase the size of individual sequences so that large-scale structures of the stream are represented within individual strings, or 2) use a system which maintains some degree of state between inputs. The first option will fail because in order to capture large-scale structures, individual sequences would necessarily be very large. As sequence sizes grow, so do the network and the

difficulty in accurate classification.

The second alternative—to maintain state information between sequences—is more appealing. It allows the system to retain the generality of small sequences. It simply adds information concerning prior sequences. One possible way to maintain state information is through the use of a deterministic finite automaton (DFA). This approach was applied manually by a UNM group [12]. However, DFAs have several drawbacks. The primary drawback is the lack of flexibility. If the BSM stream briefly enters a state not represented in the DFA, the DFA cannot recover to recognize that the state was a slight aberration of the sort one would expect to encounter even during normal runs of a program. Thus, the DFA would need to be completely specified to represent all possible allowable sequences of BSM events, or a heuristic-based approach similar to the UNM approach would need to be adopted with its perils [12]. If the DFA is completely specified such that it represents enough states that no normal execution of a program produces states outside of the machine, then the machine will have represented so many of the target program's possible states that recognizing anomalous behavior may be difficult. Beyond the lack of flexibility of DFAs, it should be recognized that determining what constitutes a *state* of a program (and should be represented in the DFA) can be a difficult task. While neither of these issues is insurmountable, ANNs address each of them quite naturally.

We originally employed ANNs because of their ability to *learn* and *generalize*. Through the learning process, they develop the ability to classify inputs from exposure to a set of *training inputs* and application of well defined *learning rules*, rather than through an explicit human-supplied enumeration of classification rules. Because of their ability to generalize, ANNs can produce reasonable classifications for novel inputs (assuming the network has been trained well). Further, since the inputs to any node of the ANN used for this work could be any real-valued number, no sequence of BSM events could produce an encoding that would fall outside of the domain representable by the ANN.

In order to maintain state information between inputs, we required a recurrent ANN topology. A recurrent topology (as opposed to a purely feed-forward topology) is one in which cycles are formed by the connections. The cycles act as delay loops—causing information to be retained indefinitely. New

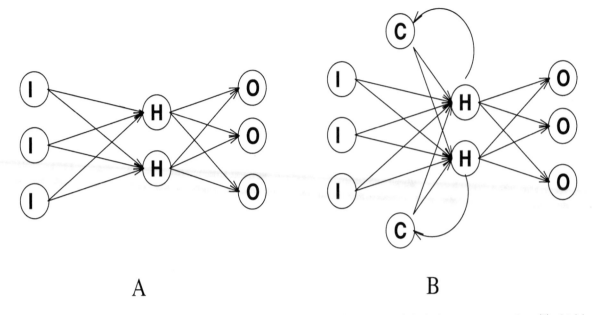

A   B

Figure 3: In each of the examples above, the nodes of the ANNs are labeled as input nodes (I), hidden nodes (H), output nodes (O), or context nodes (C). Each arc is unidirectional, with direction indicated by the arrow at the end of the arc. A) A standard feed-forward topology. B) An Elman network.

input interacts with the cycles, both the activations propagating through the network and the activations in the cycle are affected. Thus, the input can affect the state, and the state can affect the classification of any input.

One well known recurrent topology is that of an Elman network, developed by Jeffrey Elman. An Elman network is illustrated in Figure 3. The Elman topology is based on a feed-forward topology—it has an *input layer*, an *output layer*, and one or more *hidden layers*. Additionally, an Elman network has a set of *context nodes*. Each context node receives input from a single hidden node and sends its output to each node in the layer of its corresponding hidden node. Since the context nodes depend only on the activations of the hidden nodes from the previous input, the context nodes retain state information between inputs.

Because an Elman network retains information concerning previous inputs, the method used to train purely feed-forward ANNs to perform anomaly detection (see Section 4) will not suffice. We employ Elman nets to perform classification of short sequences of events as they occur in a larger stream of events. Therefore, we train our Elman networks to *predict* the next sequence that will occur at any point in time. The nth input, I_n, is presented to the network to produce some output, O_n. The out-

put O_n is then compared to I_{n+1}. The difference between O_n and I_{n+1} (that is, the sum of the absolute values of the differences of the corresponding elements of O_n and I_{n+1}) is the measure of anomaly of each sequence of events. We continue to use the leaky bucket algorithm that causes anomalies to have a larger effect when they occur closer together than when they occur farther apart. However, the classification of a sequence of events will now be affected by events prior to the earliest event occurring within the sequence.

We implemented an Elman net and applied it for anomaly detection against the same set of DARPA evaluation data. Despite being the least extensively tuned of the three methods employed, the Elman nets produced the best results overall. The performance of the Elman nets in comparison to the equality matching (table lookup) technique and the backpropagation network is shown in Figure 4. The Elman ROC curve is the left-most curve that quickly reaches 100% detection. With a leak rate of 0.7, the Elman networks were able to detect 77.3% of all intrusions with no false positives — a very significant improvement over the other algorithms. Further, the Elman nets were able to detect 100.0% of all intrusions with significantly fewer false positives than either of the other two systems.

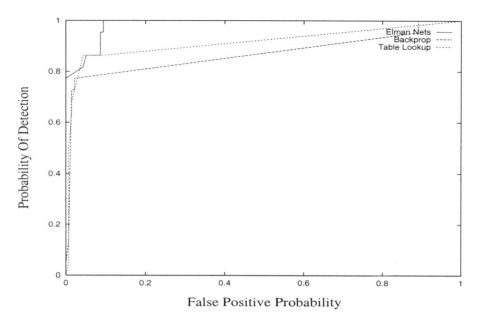

Figure 4: Performance of three anomaly detection algorithms expressed as ROC curves against the DARPA evaluation data. The horizontal axis represents the percentage of false positives while the vertical axis represents the percentage of correct detections for different operating thresholds of the technique. The Elman network performs the best overall.

6   Conclusions

This paper presented three different anomaly detection algorithms for detecting potential intrusions by using program behavior profiles. The algorithms range from pure memorization using an equality matching approach to the ability to generalize, to the ability to recognize recurrent features in the input. The results show that though the equality matching approach worked fairly well, the performance can be significantly improved (particularly in reducing the false positive rate) by using Elman networks.

References

[1] J. Cannady. Artificial neural networks for misuse detection. In *Proceedings of the 1998 National Information Systems Security Conference (NISSC'98)*, pages 443–456, October 5-8 1998. Arlington, VA.

[2] W.W. Cohen. Fast effective rule induction. In *Machine Learning: Proceedings of the Twelfth International Conference*. Morgan Kaufmann, 1995.

[3] P. D'haeseleer, S. Forrest, and P. Helman. An immunological approach to change detection: Algorithms, analysis and implications. In *IEEE Symposium on Security and Privacy*, 1996.

[4] D. Endler. Intrusion detection: Applying machine learning to solaris audit data. In *Proceedings of the 1998 Annual Computer Security Applications Conference (ACSAC'98)*, pages 268–279, Los Alamitos, CA, December 1998. IEEE Computer Society, IEEE Computer Society Press. Scottsdale, AZ.

[5] S. Forrest, S.A. Hofmeyr, and A. Somayaji. Computer immunology. *Communications of the ACM*, 40(10):88–96, October 1997.

[6] S. Forrest, S.A. Hofmeyr, A. Somayaji, and T.A. Longstaff. A sense of self for unix processes. In *Proceedings of the 1996 IEEE Symposium on Security and Privacy*, pages 120–128. IEEE, May 1996.

[7] A.K. Ghosh, J. Wanken, and F. Charron. Detecting anomalous and unknown intrusions against programs. In *Proceedings of the 1998 Annual Computer Security Applications Conference (ACSAC'98)*, December 1998.

[8] I. Goldberg, D. Wagner, R. Thomas, and E.A. Brewer. A secure environment for untrusted helper applications: Confining the

wiley hacker. In *Proceedings of the 1996 Usenix Security Symposium*. USENIX, July 22-25 1996.

[9] K. Ilgun. Ustat: A real-time intrusion detection system for unix. Master's thesis, Computer Science Dept, UCSB, July 1992.

[10] K. Ilgun, R.A. Kemmerer, and P.A. Porras. State transition analysis: A rule-based intrusion detection system. *IEEE Transactions on Software Engineering*, 21(3), March 1995.

[11] C. Ko, G. Fink, and K. Levitt. Automated detection of vulnerabilities in privileged programs by execution monitoring. In *10th Annual Computer Security Application Conference*, pages 134-144, December 1994. Orlando, FL.

[12] A.P. Kosoresow and S.A. Hofmeyr. Intrusion detection via system call traces. *Software*, 14(5):35-42, September-October 1997. IEEE Computer Society.

[13] T. Lane and C.E. Brodley. An application of machine learning to anomaly detection. In *Proceedings of the 20th National Information Systems Security Conference*, pages 366-377, October 1997.

[14] W. Lee, S. Stolfo, and P.K. Chan. Learning patterns from unix process execution traces for intrusion detection. In *Proceedings of AAAI97 Workshop on AI Methods in Fraud and Risk Management*, 1997.

[15] T.F. Lunt. Ides: an intelligent system for detecting intruders. In *Proceedings of the Symposium: Computer Security, Threat and Countermeasures*, November 1990. Rome, Italy.

[16] T.F. Lunt. A survey of intrusion detection techniques. *Computers and Security*, 12:405-418, 1993.

[17] T.F. Lunt and R. Jagannathan. A prototype real-time intrusion-detection system. In *Proceedings of the 1988 IEEE Symposium on Security and Privacy*, April 1988.

[18] T.F. Lunt, A. Tamaru, F. Gilham, R. Jagannthan, C. Jalali, H.S. Javitz, A. Valdos, P.G. Neumann, and T.D. Garvey. A real-time intrusion-detection expert system (ides). Technical Report, Computer Science Laboratory, SRI Internationnal, February 1992.

[19] P.A. Porras and R.A. Kemmerer. Penetration state transition analysis - a rule-based intrusion detection approach. In *Eighth Annual Computer Security Applications Conference*, pages 220-229. IEEE Computer Society Press, November 1992.

[20] P.A. Porras and P.G. Neumann. Emerald: Event monitoring enabling responses to anomalous live disturbances. In *Proceedings of the 20th National Information Systems Security Conference*, pages 353-365, October 1997.

[21] R. Sekar, Y. Cai, and M. Segal. A specification-based approach for building survivable systems. In *Proceedings of the 1998 National Information Systems Security Conference (NISSC'98)*, pages 338-347, October 1998.

[22] G. Vigna and R.A. Kemmerer. Netstat: A network-based intrusion detection approach. In *Proceedings of the 1998 Annual Computer Security Applications Conference (ACSAC'98)*, pages 25-34, Los Alamitos, CA, December 1998. IEEE Computer Society, IEEE Computer Society Press. Scottsdale, AZ.

Automated Intrusion Detection Using NFR: Methods and Experie

Wenke Lee   Christopher T. Park   Salvatore J. Stolfo

Computer Science Department, Columbia University
500 West 120th Street, New York, NY 10027
{wenke,cpark,sal}@cs.columbia.edu

Abstract

There is often the need to update an installed Intrusion Detection System (IDS) due to new attack methods or upgraded computing environments. Since many current IDSs are constructed by manual encoding of expert security knowledge, changes to IDSs are expensive and require a large amount of programming and debugging. We describe a data mining framework for adaptively building Intrusion Detection (ID) models specifically for use with Network Flight Recorder (NFR). The central idea is to utilize auditing programs to extract an extensive set of features that describe each network connection or host session, and apply data mining programs to learn rules that accurately capture the behavior of intrusions and normal activities. These rules can be used for misuse detection and anomaly detection. Detection models are then incorporated into NFR through a machine translator, which produces a working detection model in the form of N-Code, NFR's powerful filtering language.

1 Introduction

With the increase of Internet connectivity, there is the ever increasing risk of attackers illicitly gaining access to computers over the network. Intrusion detection is often used as another wall to protect computer systems, in addition to the standard methods of security measures such as user authentication (e.g. user passwords or biometrics), avoiding programming errors, and information protection (e.g., encryption). Intrusion detection techniques can be categorized into *anomaly detection* and *misuse detection*. While accuracy is the essential requirement, its extensibility and adaptability are also critical design criteria in today's network computing environment. There are multiple "penetration points" for intrusions to take place in a network system. For exam-

ple, at the network level, carefully crafted "malicious" IP packets can crash a victim host; at the host level, vulnerabilities in system software can be exploited to yield an illegal root shell. Since activities at different penetration points are normally recorded in different audit data sources, an IDS often needs to be extended to incorporate (additional) modules that are specialized for certain components (e.g., hosts, subnets, etc.) of a network systems. The large traffic volume in security related mailing lists and Web sites suggests that new system security holes and intrusion methods are continuously being discovered. Therefore, it is imperative that IDSs be updated frequently and rapidly.

Currently building an effective IDS is an enormous knowledge engineering task. System builders largely rely on their intuition and experience to select the statistical measures for anomaly detection [6]. Many IDSs only handle one particular audit data source, and updating these systems is expensive and slow. Some of the recent research and commercial IDSs have begun to provide built-in mechanisms for customization and extension. The Network Flight Recorder (NFR) [8] is one such extensible system that combines data collection, analysis, and storage within a single platform. We discuss NFR in more depth in Section 2.2. Such systems would normally be located between a firewall and an Internet connection, an area aptly named the DMZ. Analysis in NFR is accomplished by scripts based on a language called N-code, NFR's flexible language for traffic analysis. Information is displayed in NFR to a web-based interface with Java support. NFR also has a real time alerting capability and a storage subsystem that allows data to be stored, rotated, and archived to other external devices [8]. However, this does not eliminate the need for experts to first analyze and categorize attack scenarios and system vulnerabilities, and hand-code the corresponding rules and patterns in N-code for misuse detection. Because of the manual and ad hoc nature of the development process, current IDSs including NFR have limited extensibility and adaptability. Our goal is to substantially reduce this effort by automating:

1) the task of building intrusion detection through data-mining.

2) generating the N-code for NFR to detect intrusions via a machine translator.

While using such methods, system builders and administrators will still have to maintain and fine-tune the respective IDS. However a large amount of their work will be automated, thus effectively reducing time and manpower in fielding an effective IDS.

2   Techniques for Intrusion Detection

There are two major categories of techniques that are used by most IDS's:

- Anomaly detection attempts to determine whether deviation from an established normal behavior profile can be flagged as an intrusion [4]. A profile typically consists of a number of statistical measures on system activities, for example, the *CPU usage* and the *saturation of bandwidth at a given time period*. Deviation from a profile can be computed as the weighted sum of the deviations of the constituent statistical measures. Profiles can be updated periodically (aged) so that shifts of normal behavior are accounted. The key advantages of anomaly detection systems is that they can detect unknown intrusions since they require no *a priori* knowledge about specific intrusions. However, defining and maintaining "normal" profiles is a nontrivial and error-prone task.

- Misuse detection refers to techniques that use patterns of known intrusions (for example, *more than three consecutive failed logins within 2 minutes* can be classified as a penetration attempt). The sequence of attack actions, the conditions that compromise a system's security, as well as the evidence (e.g., damage) left behind by intrusions can be represented by a number of general pattern matching models. The key advantage of misuse detection systems is that once the patterns of known intrusions are stored, future instances of these intrusions can be detected effectively and efficiently. However, newly invented attacks will likely go undetected.

In Section 3.1, we discuss the data-mining algorithms that can be used to build both anomaly and misuse detection models.

3   Systematic Framework

Our framework consists of data-mining programs for learning detections models, a translator for converting learned rules to real-time models, and NFR for capturing network traffic and applying the real-time N-code modules for ID.

3.1   Data-Mining Algorithms

Data mining generally refers to the process of (automatically) extracting models from large stores of data [3]. The recent rapid development in data mining has made available a wide variety of algorithms, drawn from the fields of statistics, pattern recognition, machine learning, and databases. Several types of algorithms are particularly useful for mining audit data.

Classification : maps a data item into one of several pre-defined categories. These algorithms normally output "classifiers", for example, in the form of decision trees or rules. An ideal application in intrusion detection will be to gather sufficient "normal" and "abnormal" audit data for a user or program, then apply a classification algorithm to learn a classifier that can label or predict new unseen audit data as belonging to the normal class or the abnormal class. We use the package RIPPER [2] as our classification rule-learner.

Link analysis : determines relations between fields in database records. Correlations of system features in audit data can serve as the basis for constructing normal usage profiles. A programmer would have "emacs" highly associated with "C" files, for example. Observed deviations from these automatically learned associations may suggest an attack. We use the association rules algorithms [1] for this particular type of analysis.

Sequence analysis : models sequential patterns. These algorithms can discover what (time-based) sequence of audit events frequently occur together. These frequent event patterns provide guidelines for incorporating temporal statistical measures into

duration	the length (in seconds) of the connection
protocol_type	type of protocol being used (e.g. tcp, udp, icmp, etc.)
protocol	if the protocol is privileged (≤ 1024) or not
flag	normally SF (successfully connected and terminated according to the protocols), but can be an error status such as REJ, S0, S1, etc.
urgent	is the "urgent" flag used in any of the data
wrong_size_rate	if packet is fragmented, how many are "wrong" fragments per second

Table 1: Within Connection

count	the count of such connections
rej_count	the count of connections to a service that get the flag "REJ" (i.e. a packet that has a flag SYN which is met by an RST packet from the receiving end)
S01_count	the count of connections to a service that receive an ACK on a SYN packet that they never sent
diff_hosts	the count of unique (different) destination hosts
diff_rate	diff_hosts / count

Table 2: Same Service

intrusion detection models. We use the frequent episodes algorithms [7] for this analysis.

A framework has been developed, first proposed in [4], of applying data mining techniques to build intrusion detection models. This framework consists of programs for learning classifiers as well as a support environment that enables system builders to interactively and iteratively drive the process of constructing and evaluating improved detection models. The end product of this process is a set of concise and intuitive rules (that can be easily inspected and edited by security experts when needed) that can detect intrusions. The rules are then subsequently ported over to N-code as sub-routines or independent functions.

3.2 Mining Data to Construct Attributes

In order for data-mining programs to compute effective intrusion detection models, we must first process and summarize packet-level network traffic data into "connection" records. We initially start out with the raw audit data (commonly `tcpdump` binary output) of the designated network we wish to monitor. This is then subsequently preprocessed into individual packets/events in ASCII format. As the packets are summarized according to their separate connections, we record their within-connection features which may be deemed as "traditional attributes" of a connection record. Refer to to Table 1 for examples of these attributes. We use the mined

patterns from network connection records as guidelines to construct temporal statistical attributes for building classification models [5]. We performed pattern mining and comparisons using intrusion data of several well-known attacks, e.g., port-scan, ping-sweep, etc., as well normal connection records. Each of the unique intrusion patterns are used as guidelines for adding additional features into the connection records to build better classification models. These temporal and statistical attributes are shown in Table 2, and Table 3. *Same Destination* attributes deal with all connections to a particular host, and is not concerned with the number of ports or services being accessed; it only keeps track of the connections for the specified host. *Same Service* attributes deal with all connections to a particular port or service being sent throughout the network; it keeps track of the connections for the specified service. An N-code filter has been written for each of these attributes.

With the addition of these specific attributes to the standard features of connections, "rules" of intrusion detection models can be produced in NFR by machine learning via RIPPER.

3.3 Learning Detection Rules

We apply RIPPER to the connection records to generate the classification rules for the intrusions. Like other rule learning systems, it is used for classifications problems.

count	the count of such connections
rej_count	the count of connections that get the flag"REJ" met by a particular host
S01_count	the count of connections that send a SYN packet but never get the ACK packet (S0), or receive an ACK on SYN that they never have sent (s1)
diff_services	the count of unique (different) services
diff_srv_rate	diff_services / count

Table 3: Same Destination

Figure 1: Example tcpdump File

```
...
12:22:18.336681 im.a.hacker.com.2019 > your.machine.org.talk: udp 28 (frag 242:36@0+)
12:22:18.336681 im.a.hacker.com > your.machine.org: (frag 242:4@24)
12:22:18.356681 im.a.hacker.com.2019 > your.machine.org.talk: udp 28 (frag 242:36@0+)
12:22:18.356681 im.a.hacker.com > your.machine.org: (frag 242:4@24)
12:22:18.376681 im.a.hacker.com.2019 > your.machine.org.talk: udp 28 (frag 242:36@0+)
12:22:18.376681 im.a.hacker.com > your.machine.org: (frag 242:4@24)
...
```

A "training" period is initially required for RIPPER to gather the necessary data on the network to compute models. The purpose is two-fold:

1) establishing "normal" traffic patterns and variants that the network may encounter to establish anomaly detection,

2) introducing known intrusion methods and attack scripts into the network in order to inductively learn the classification models of intrusions

Here we provide example rules used to detect known attacks. In particular, we illustrate how to detect and recognize an attack which is categorized as *denial-of-service*.

Let us suppose that a hacker launches "teardrop" from machine im.a.hacker.com and is attempting to bring down the server your.machine.org. Teardrop transmits a number of overlapping fragmented UDP packets to a specified host. Fig. 1 shows the tcpdump data of such an attack.

Here, the data is first processed into connection records with the attributes described in section 3.2 along with the class label "teardrop". RIPPER is then applied to these records to produce a teardrop rule shown to Table 4, for monitoring the teardrop intrusion.

While this may seem intuitive to a system builder, it is important to distinguish that our data mining programs has *automated* the process of generating such heuristics. Our system would then call upon the machine translator to compile the teardrop rule, and generate the appropriate N-code that filters out all network traffic except for the information concerning this particular type of attack.

3.4 Network Flight Recorder

NFR is a powerful software package that monitors and provides information concerning network traffic. It also analyzes the traffic and generates statistics that can then be displayed in a graphical format. We primarily chose NFR for the following reasons:

1) it does not interfere with network activity, necessary for accurate data analysis

2) it possesses a language flexible and portable enough to be programmed on an internal basis, rather than hard-coded in the monitoring application

3) it has real-time alert capability

NFR runs primarily on a packet-sniffing engine that is responsible for filtering and reassembling. While packets are passed through the NFR daemon, they are checked against a list of filters for evaluation. The filters, written in "N-code", (an interpreted programming

Rule	Translation
if (protocol = UDP and wrong_size_rate ≥ 3)	(the current connection has succession of fragmented packets coming in at a rate over 3 packets/sec and the fragmentation is "wrong")

Table 4: Tear Drop Rule

language) perform the various functions and tasks that are activated by the incoming packets. [8]

In Appendix we have an example of the wrong_size_rate attribute concerning UDP packets.

3.5 Generation of N-Code Filters

As discussed earlier, the attributes of connection records are implemented as subroutines that may be called upon to check the rules that were generated by machine-learning.

Observe that a RIPPER rule simply consists of a sequence of attribute value tests. With each attribute implemented as an N-code filter, a rule can be automatically translated into an N-code filter that consists of a sequence of function calls to the N-code filters. For example, the "teardrop" RIPPER rule is translated into a "teardrop" N-code filter, as shown in Figure 2.

4 Experiments

Our network for intrusion detection research runs primarily on six hosts connected to a T1 subnet of a larger domain of a university LAN. NFR 1.6, runs on a Solaris X86 machine where all data recorded is contained on an external 6.0 GB SCSI HD. While a training period of 2-3 days has been allotted for this network, it is important to establish that training periods were continuously being conducted to fine-tune the accuracy of the detection. Traffic is relatively light in saturation, rarely ever going over 60-70 Megabits/sec.

The types of intrusions that we are primarily concerned with fall into 4 main categories:

1) denial-of-service (e.g., ping-of-death, SYN flood, smurf, teardrop, etc.)

2) unauthorized access from a remote machine (e.g. via guessing password)

3) unauthorized access to local superuser privileges by a local unprivileged user (e.g., various buffer overflow attacks)

4) surveillance and probing (e.g., port-scan, IPscan, etc)

We are gathering training data on these attacks, producing RIPPER rules, and converting the rules into NFR N-code filters.

4.1 Details

A connection filter is used to generate and store a record for each network connection. These connection records are kept in a global array, and are ordered by their timestamps (that is, the start time of the connections). This array is used for temporal and statistical analysis on the connections and for feature construction.

A connection record consists of a timestamp, the source and destination hostnames, the port numbers, the "traditional" attributes, and the temporal and statistical attributes.

4.2 Issues

The biggest issues we face are optimizing the connection filter, and excluding certain types of connections that may occur within the LAN that are proven to be harmless, but may overload the buffer allocated by the connection filter with the number of packets being generated.

Connections within a network may remain open for long periods of time and create large amounts of packet traffic. This can occur, for example, when exporting X window system and browser applications to a remote host. We consider all traffic generated by such remote applications to be part of one connection; consequently, keyboard, mouse, and display update operations can easily overflow the single connection's buffer. Currently our only workaround is to forbid such exported applications.

```
filter teardrop_rule(ip.src, conn_id, ip.protocol) {
 if (wrong_size_rate (conn_id) >= 3 && ip.protocol ==17)
          {
          $message = cat("This is a TEARDROP!* sent from ", ip.src'')
    }
  echo ($message);
          }
```

Figure 2: Automatically Generated N-code Filter for "teardrop"

To minimize dropped packets, NFR filters should reduce the volume of incoming packet traffic before forwarding to a backend; *en masse* recording is best done in the NFR engine itself. Our present connection filter consumes a substantial portion of the NFR host CPU, subsequently increasing the number of dropped packets from the engine.

Finally, an online IDS such as ours cannot afford the luxury of deferring the analysis of packet traffic; this analysis must be done in real-time and consumes additional CPU over offline methods. However, we hope to continuously improve the efficency of our filters by considering the computational cost of the attributes and prioritizing the rules that are being called.

5   Conclusions and Future Work

In this paper, we have outlined a data mining framework for building ID models. We describe how models produced via on-line analysis of audit data that can be automatically translated into NFR, a real-time IDS. Our experiences thus far show that our approaches are very effective.

We plan to port our system to the latest 2.0.3 commercial release of NFR, to take advantage of its new features, such as it's new functions and capabilities in N-code, a faster packet-sniffing engine, and the provision of a mini-Web Server which eliminates the need for an independent Web daemon to be running. Preliminary steps have already been taken to detect simple intrusions (ie portscan, ping-of-death, synflood) and while these rules derived from the attributes have proven to be successful, we would like to implement more complex attributes for sophisticated methods of intrusions.

6   Acknowledgments

We are very grateful to the NFR engineering team who have continuously provided us with support concerning the NFR software. We would like to also thank Matthew Miller from Columbia University for his help and encouragement.

References

[1] R. Agrawal, T. Imielinski, and A. Swami. Mining association rules between sets of items in large databases. In *Proceedings of the ACM SIGMOD Conference on Management of Data*, pages 207–216, 1993.

[2] W. W. Cohen. Fast effective rule induction. In *Machine Learning: the 12th International Conference*, Lake Taho, CA, 1995. Morgan Kaufmann.

[3] U. Fayyad, G. Piatetsky-Shapiro, and P. Smyth. The KDD process of extracting useful knowledge from volumes of data. *Communications of the ACM*, 39(11):27–34, November 1996.

[4] W. Lee and S. J. Stolfo. Data mining approaches for intrusion detection. In *Proceedings of the 7th USENIX Security Symposium*, San Antonio, TX, January 1998.

[5] W. Lee and S. J. Stolfo. A data mining framework for building intrusion detection models. In *1999 IEEE Symposium on Security and Privacy.*, Oakland, CA, May 1999.

[6] Teresa F. Lunt. Detecting intruders in computer systems. In *Proceedings of the 1993 Conference on Auditing and Computer Technology*, 1993.

[7] H. Mannila, H. Toivonen, and A. I. Verkamo. Discovering frequent episodes in sequences. In *Proceedings of the 1st International Conference on*

Knowledge Discovery in Databases and Data Mining, Montreal, Canada, August 1995.

[8] Inc. Network Flight Recorder. Network flight recorder. http://www.nfr.net, 1997.

Appendix

```
#    UDP wrong_size_rate Detection contains two filters:
#    First is the udpfrag filter which keeps an array indexed by
#    cat (ip.dst, "-", ip.src)
#    which keeps track of how many fragmented udp packets have been sent
#    between src and dst.
#
#  Second is the wrong_size_rate filter wich checks udpFrags every second to check
#  to see if hostpair has had more than m udpfrags where m is ALERT_NUM.

ALERT_NUM = 1;   # The number of frags in TEAR_FREQ seconds that should
                 # trigger an alert.

TEAR_FREQ = 1;   # The frequency (in seconds) to check the frag count.

# This filter will be triggered by only udp packets
filter udpFragFilter udp () {
    # byte(packet.blob, 14) is the first byte of the ip header
    #    inside the ethernet frame
    # so: byte(packet.blob, 20) is the 7th byte of the ip header.
    # We only want to continue if more fragments bit is set.

    # The 18th and 19th bytes of the packet are the 5th and 6th bytes of
    # the ip header.  This is the Identification, which is only used if there
    # is fragmentation.  Thus, if it is zero, then there is no fragmentation,
    # and we don't need to look at the packet.
    if (short(packet.blob, 18) == 0) {
        return;
    }

    #    record system.time,
    #        $sport, $dport,
    #        ip.src, ip.dst
    #        to ipfrags_recorder

    $message = cat (ip.src, ":", $sport, " sent ",
                    ip.dst, ":", $dport,
                    " a fragmented UDP packet.");
    echo ($message);
    # assemble the index into udpFrags
    $index = cat (host(ip.dst), ":", $dport);

    # No one should be sending fragments whose size is not evenly
    # measurable in bytes!!

    if (ip.len % 8 != 0) {
        if (udpFrags[ [$myIndex, "badCount"] ] == NULL)
            udpFrags[ [$myIndex, "badCount"] ] = 1;
        else
        udpFrags[ [$myIndex, "badCount"] ] =
                udpFrags[ [$myIndex, "badCount"] ] + 1;
```

```
#   Get together important info about the packet:
#   We want to know the length of the packet, and we want the
#   3-bit flags and 13-bit offset.  These are bytes 6 and 7
#   of the IP header, or 20 - 21 of the ethernet packet.

$pktInfo["ip.len"] = ip.len;
$pktInfo["fragShort"] = short(packet.blob, 20);

# We need 2 pkts to be able to check the offset correctedness.
# If this is the first fragmented packet, we need to keep track
# of the "fragShort" in order to be able to compute the offset in
# subsequent packets, so we'll record it.

if (udpFrags[$myIndex] == NULL) {
    udpFrags[$myIndex] = listadd(udpFrags[$myIndex], $pktInfo);
    udpFrags[ [$myIndex, "firstShort"] ] = $pktInfo["fragShort"];
    return;
} else { # now we know it's a subsequent packet.
    udpFrags[$myIndex] = listadd(udpFrags[$myIndex], $pktInfo);
    $fragList = udpFrags[$myIndex];

    $n = listlen($fraglist);
    while ($n > 0) {
        $pkt1 = elem($fraglist, $n - 1);
        $pkt1Short = $pkt1["fragShort"];
        $pkt1Size = $pkt1["ip.len"];
        $pkt2 = elem($fraglist, $n);
        $pkt2Short = $pkt2["fragShort"];
        $pkt2Size = $pkt2Short["ip.len"];

        # Here we figure out the fragmentation offsets by subtracting
        # the "firstShort".  This eliminates the values of the 3-bit
        # flags, which we aren't concerned with at this point.

        $offset1 = $pkt1Short - udpFrags[ [$myIndex, "firstShort"] ];
        $offset2 = $pkt2Short - udpFrags[ [$myIndex, "firstShort"] ];

        # Here's where we test the offsets and increment
        # the count of udpFrags if they don't line up.
        if (($offset1 + $pkt1Size) != $offset2)) {
            if (udpFrags[ [$myIndex, "badCount"] ] == NULL)
                udpFrags[ [$myIndex, "badCount"] ] = 1;
            else
                udpFrags[ [$myIndex, "badCount"] ] =
                    udpFrags[ [$myIndex, "badCount"] ] + 1;
        } else # we're fine!!
            return;
        $n = $n - 1;
    } # close while
} # close else
} # close func.

# Here we free up udpFrags.
func purge_udpFrags timeout (sec: (TEAR_FREQ + 1), repeat) {
```

```
    # if there aren't any entries, then exit
    if (!udpFrags) {
        return;
    }

    # empty all the entries.
    foreach $myIndex inside (udpFrags) {
        udpFrags[$myIndex] = NULL;
    }
}


# This is the main filter to check for the teardrop attach using the rule:
#       if ((udpFrags in TEAR_FREQ) >= ALERT_NUM)

$myIndex=$conn_Id
filter wrong_size_rate timeout (sec:1, repeat) {

    if (!udpFrags) {
        return;
    }

    foreach $myIndex inside (udpFrags) {
        # Here we give the alarm
        if (udpFrags[ [$myIndex, "badCount"] ] >= ALERT_NUM) {
            $message = cat ("*Wrong_Size_Rate*: ", ip.src, " sent ", $index,
                            " more than ", ALERT_NUM,
                            " wrongly fragmented UDP packets in ",
                            TEAR_FREQ, "seconds.");
            echo ($message);
        }
    }
  # Here we call our function to clear udpFrags.
    purge_udpFrags();
}
```

EXPERIENCE WITH EMERALD TO DATE

Peter G. Neumann and Phillip A. Porras
Computer Science Laboratory
SRI International, Menlo Park CA 94025-3493
Neumann@CSL.sri.com and Porras@CSL.sri.com
1-650-859-2375 and 1-650-859-3232

1st USENIX Workshop on Intrusion Detection and Network Monitoring
Santa Clara, California, 11-12 April 1999

Abstract

After summarizing the EMERALD architecture and the evolutionary process from which EMERALD has evolved, this paper focuses on our experience to date in designing, implementing, and applying EMERALD to various types of anomalies and misuse. The discussion addresses the fundamental importance of good software engineering practice and the importance of the system architecture – in attaining detectability, interoperability, general applicability, and future evolvability. It also considers the importance of correlation among distributed and hierarchical instances of EMERALD, and needs for additional detection and analysis components.

1. Introduction

EMERALD (Event Monitoring Enabling Responses to Anomalous Live Disturbances) [6, 8, 9] is an environment for anomaly and misuse detection and subsequent analysis of the behavior of systems and networks. EMERALD is being developed under DARPA/ITO Contract number F30602-96-C-0294 and applied under DARPA/ISO Contract number F30602-98-C-0059. EMERALD has farsighted goals for real-time detection, analysis, and response for a broad range of threats other than just security.

Anomaly detection involves the recognition of deviations from expected normal behavior, whereas misuse detection involves the detection of various types of misuse. The term "intrusion detection" is often used to encompass both, but unfortunately suggests only the *detection of intrusions* rather than the broader scope of EMERALD.

2. EMERALD

EMERALD targets both external and internal threat agents that attempt to misuse system or network resources. It is an advanced highly software-engineered environment that combines signature-based and statistical analysis components with a resolver that interprets analysis results, all of which can be used iteratively and hierarchically. Its modules are designed to be independently useful, dynamically deployable, easily configurable, reusable, and broadly interoperable. Its design scales well to very large enterprises. The objectives include achieving innovative analytic abilities, rapid integration into current network environments, and much greater flexibility of surveillance whenever network configurations change.

EMERALD employs a building-block architectural strategy using independently tunable distributed surveillance monitors that can detect and respond to malicious activity on local targets, and can interoperate to form an analysis hierarchy. The basic architectural structure is shown in Figure 1. The figure shows the three main types of existing analysis units (profiler engines, signature engines, and resolver) surrounding the target-specific resource objects. It also shows the possible integration of third-party modules, including inputs derived from other sources, and outputs sent to other analysis platforms or administrators and emergency response centers. This architecture is explained in the following text.

A key aspect of this approach is the introduction of EMERALD monitors. An EMERALD monitor is dynamically deployed within an administrative domain to provide localized real-time analysis of infrastructure (e.g., routers or gateways) and ser-

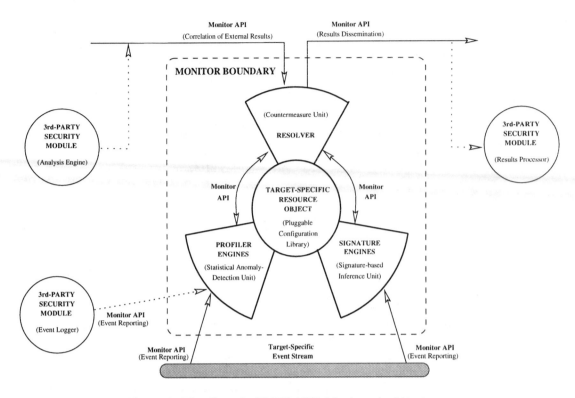

Figure 1: The Generic EMERALD Monitor Architecture

vice (privileged subsystems with network interfaces). An EMERALD monitor may interact with its environment passively (reading activity logs or network packets) or actively (via probing that supplements normal event gathering). As monitors produce analytical results, they are able to disseminate these results asynchronously to other client monitors. Client monitors may operate at the domain layer, correlating results from service-layer monitors, or at the enterprise layer, correlating results produced across domains.

Under the EMERALD framework, a layered analysis hierarchy may be formed to support the recognition of more global threats to interdomain connectivity, including coordinated attempts to infiltrate or destroy connectivity across an enterprise.

Equally important, EMERALD does not require the adoption of this analysis hierarchy. Monitors themselves stand alone as self-contained analysis modules, with a well-defined interface for sharing and receiving event data and analytical results among other third-party security services. An EMERALD monitor is capable of performing both signature analysis and statistical profile-based anomaly detection on a target event stream. In addition, each

monitor includes an instance of the EMERALD resolver, a countermeasure decision engine capable of fusing the alerts from its associated analysis engines and invoking response handlers to counter malicious activity. The statistical subsystem tracks subject activity via one of four types of statistical variables called measures: categorical (e.g., discrete types), continuous (e.g., numerical quantities), traffic intensity (e.g., volume over time), and event distribution (e.g., a meta-measure of other measures) [9]. EMERALD's signature analysis subsystem employs a variant of the P-BEST (Production-Based Expert System Tool) expert system [6] that allows administrators to instantiate a rule set customized to detect known "problem activity" occurring on the analysis target. Results from both the statistical and signature engines are then forwarded to the monitor's resolver – which acts as the coordinator of the monitor's external reporting system and the implementor of the monitor's response policy.

Fundamental to EMERALD's design is the abstraction of analysis semantics from the monitor's code base. Under the EMERALD monitor architecture, all analysis-target-specific information is contained within each resource object, specifying items from a pluggable configuration library. The resource object encapsulates all the analysis semantics necessary to instantiate a single service monitor, which can then be distributed to an appropriate observation point in the network. Resource-object elements customize the monitor for the analysis target, containing data and methods, such as the event collection methods, analytical module parameters, valid response methods, response policy, and subscription list of external modules with which the monitor exchanges alarm information. This enables a spectrum of configurations from lightweight distributed monitors to heavy-duty centralized analysis platforms.

In a given environment, service monitors may be independently distributed to analyze the activity of multiple network services (e.g., FTP, SMTP, HTTP) or network element (router, firewall). Resource objects are being developed for each analysis target. As each EMERALD monitor is deployed to its target, it is instantiated with an appropriate resource object (e.g., an FTP resource object for FTP monitoring, and a BSM resource object for BSM Solaris kernel analysis). The monitor code base itself is analysis target-independent. As EMERALD monitors are redeployed from one target to another, the only thing that is modified is the content of the resource object.

See the paper by Lindqvist and Porras [6] for discussion of the analysis of FTP (which currently exists for SunOS, FreeBSD, and Linux) and BSM (on Solaris). In particular, that paper gives specific examples of rules for failed authentication, buffer overflows, and SYN flooding attacks.

Resource objects lend themselves to the key project objectives of reusability and fast integration to new environments. The project is developing a library populated with resource objects that have been built to analyze various service and network elements. Installers of EMERALD will be given our monitor code base, which they do not have to touch. They can then download appropriate resource objects associated with their analysis targets, modify them as desired, and instantiate the monitors with the downloaded resource objects.

The project is also working toward new techniques in alarm correlation and management of analytic services. The concept of composable surveillance will allow EMERALD to aggregate analyses from independent monitors in an effort to isolate commonalities or trends in alarm sequences that may indicate a more global threat. Such aggregate analyses are classified under four general categories: commonality detection, multiperspective reinforcement, alarm interrelationships, and sequential trends.

Briefly, commonality detection involves the search for common alarm indicators produced across independent event analyses. In such cases, the results from one monitor's analyses may occur under a threshold that warrants individual response, but in combination with results from other monitors may warrant a global response. This approach can address low-rate distributed attacks and cooperative attacks, as well as widespread contamination effects. Multiperspective analysis refers to efforts to independently analyze the same target from multiple perspectives (e.g., an analysis of a Web server's audit logs in conjunction with Web network traffic). Alarm interrelationships refer to EMERALD's ability to have a monitor model an interrelationship (cause and effect) between the occurrence of alarms across independent analysis targets. For example, an alarm regarding activity observed on one host or domain may give rise to a warning indicator for a different threat against a second host or domain. Last, sequential trends in alarms seek to detect patterns in alarms raised within or across domains. These patterns of aggressive activity may warrant a more global response to counteract than can be achieved by a local service monitor.

The EMERALD project represents an effort to combine research from distributed high-volume event correlation with over a decade of intrusion-detection research and engineering experience. It represents a comprehensive attempt to develop an architecture that inherits well-developed analytical techniques for detecting intrusions, and casts them in a framework that is highly reusable, interoperable, and scalable in large network infrastructures. Its inherent generality and flexibility in terms of what is being monitored and how the analytical tools can be customized for the task suggest that EMERALD can be readily extended for monitoring other forms of malicious and nonmalicious "problem activities" within a variety of closed and networked environments.

3. Experience Gained

This section summarizes our experience in the EMERALD development thus far.

Earlier Experience

EMERALD has drawn on our earlier experience in developing and using IDES (Intrusion Detection Expert System [7]) and its successor NIDES (Next-Generation IDES [1, 2, 3, 4]. Particularly for those people who are not aware of our earlier work, we summarize a few conclusions.

- From IDES, we attained considerable flexibility and runtime efficiency in the use of P-BEST [7]), which we have now adapted into EMERALD's pluggable analysis-engine framework as a self-sufficient component. The P-BEST approach proved to be very useful, and rules are relatively easy to write. P-BEST was adapted by Alan Whitehurst from its previous incarnation in MIDAS [10]. IDES also gave us the second generation of our statistical algorithms, begun in 1983 in an earlier project [5].

- From the NIDES development [1], several observations influenced the EMERALD effort. (1) Much of the available audit data (e.g., from C2 Unix and BSM) was not naturally well suited for our analytical purposes, and different sources of data would have been desirable. Greater abstraction would have been useful. (2) Although we did experiment with some higher-level audit data (from database management systems in relatively closed environments), attempting to detect misuse was less fruitful because the security policies of the DBMSs generally permitted what was closer to acceptable behavior. (3) We recognized that the NIDES statistical detection system as then configured would not scale well to distributed and networked environments, for two reasons. First, the measures needed to be treated in their entirety, rather than subsetted – as would be desirable for lightweight instances. Second, the results were not in a form that could be used recursively at a higher-layer instance. (4) We recognized the importance of the administrator interface, and observed that its complexities are unavoidable if flexibility in detection and response is required. However, we initially spent too much effort on developing our own GUI tools, until we decided to rely on some newly developed generic tools. In retrospect, we believe we would have progressed faster if we had had more emphasis on software engineering and on in-house applications.

- From the NIDES Safeguard effort [2], we observed that profiling functionality proved to be more effective than profiling individual users. That approach resulted in far fewer profiles, each of which tended to be much more stable. The resulting false-positive and false-negative rates were reduced considerably. We concluded that statistical analyses could be very effective in dealing with systems and subsystems such as servers and routers. (As a consequence, EMERALD subsequently broadened the statistics algorithms to improve handling of network protocols, by having a master profile of client usage against which a single service can be compared. For example, anonymous FTP sessions can simultaneously be profiled against the master profile for anonymous sessions.)

These observations have had a significant impact on the EMERALD architecture and its implementation, particularly in moving to a distributed and networked target environment.

EMERALD Experience

The underlying generic analysis-engine infrastructure uniformly wraps the signature analysis, statistical engine, resolver, and any future engines we might wish to integrate. The infrastructure provides the common EMERALD API, event-queue management, error-reporting services, secondary storage management (primarily for the statistical component), and internal configuration control. The statistical and P-BEST components are integrated as libraries. The infrastructure was assembled first for the EMERALD statistics component (estat), but proved its generality when we attempt to integrate P-BEST as the EMERALD expert system (eXpert). The integration of P-BEST inference engines required some linkage code to bind with the underlying EMERALD libraries, and is now automatically generated as part of the compilation process.

After more than two years developing EMERALD, our experience thus far is summarized as follows.

- Generality of approach. We have attempted to solve some difficult problems rather generally, and have typically avoided optimizing our approach to any domain-specific assumptions. In particular, the decoupling of generic and target-specific concepts simplifies reusability of components and extensibility, and enhances integration with other data sources, analysis engines, and response capabilities. The hierarchically iterative nature permits analyses with broader scope across networks and distributed systems. Although the advantages of such a farsighted approach may not be evident until EMERALD is more widely used and extended to new application areas, we firmly believe that this approach can be very instructive to us and to other groups, from the perspective of research and development potential – and can have major long-term advantages. (Platform-specific optimizations are of course possible, if they are deemed necessary.)

- Software engineering. We believe that our strong emphasis on good software engineering practice in EMERALD has already had substantial payoffs, particularly in enabling us to rapidly incorporate different analytic engines into the generic framework. (The modularization and integration of the P-BEST expert system component is discussed below.) This emphasis clearly improves the general evolvability of the system, and also has significant benefits with respect to interoperability – within EMERALD, with independently developed analysis engines, with analysis data from arbitrary sources, and in terms of the distribution of analysis results. The software-engineering emphasis also helps facilitate the iterative use of EMERALD analytic engines by making the layered instances of the system symmetric. These benefits remain to be demonstrated explicitly with extensive and well-documented experiments, but our expectations are very high. A fuller justification of the extent to which this software engineering approach is actually paying off requires a more detailed description of the architecture, which is beyond the scope of this workshop paper; however, such a description is high on our priority list for the future.

- Scope of applicability. We believe that our attention to software engineering simplifies the broadening of EMERALD's domains of applicability – for example, detecting, analyzing, and responding to potential threats to survivability, reliability, fault tolerance, and network management stability. There is nothing intrinsic in the EMERALD architecture and implementation that would limit its applicability. The application to requirements other than security is basically a matter of writing or modifying the relevant resource objects and configuring the system appropriately, and is not expected to require major changes to the existing analysis infrastructure.

- Relative merits of various paradigms. It should be no surprise to those in the intrusion-detection community that signature-based analysis is good at detecting and identifying well-defined known scenarios, but very limited in detecting hitherto unknown attacks (except for those that happen to trigger existing rules serendipitously). On the other hand, statistical profile-based analysis can be effective in detecting unknown attacks and providing early warnings on strangely deviant behaviors; however, the statistical approach does not naturally contribute to an automated identification and diagnosis of the nature of an attack or other type of deviation that it has never identified before. Although inferences can be drawn about the nature of an anomaly, based on the statistical measures that were triggered, further reasoning is typically necessary to identify the nature of the anomaly – for example, is it an attack in progress, or a serious threat to system survivability.

Precisely because it is aimed at detecting potentially unforeseen threats rather than very specific scenarios that can be easily detected by signature-based analyses, the statistical component can be expected to turn up false positives. In the EMERALD framework, this is not necessarily a problem. We believe it is much more effective for the resolver to discard statistical anomalies that it deems nonserious rather than try to reduce the false positives in the statistical component itself (which requires greater knowledge of the potential threats – which is what can otherwise be avoided). Furthermore, once new attacks and threats are identified, it is desirable to add new rules to the expert-system rule base.

Overall, we believe that each type of analysis (such as the expert system, the statistical component, the resolver, or any additional analysis engines) will have its own areas of greatest effectiveness, but that no one paradigm can cover all types of threats. Therefore we endorse a pluralistic approach. Inference and reasoning engines, Bayesian analysis, and other paradigms may also be applicable to detection, identification, and resolution of the nature of anomalies and attacks.

- Local, hierarchical, and distributed correlation. One of the most far-reaching observations relates to the importance of being able to correlate local results from different target platforms at the same or different layers of abstraction, and also to correlate results relating to different aspects of system behavior. The inherent layered iterative nature of the EMERALD architecture is significant in this respect, because the same analytic component can be used at different layers of abstraction. We are just now beginning to conduct some experiments to demonstrate the power of this approach. In so doing, we are extending the existing EMERALD resolver to interpret the results of different analytic engines and to recommend responses appropriate to the specific layer of abstraction. Further analytic engines may also be required at various layers of abstraction, such as some reasoning tools.

- Importance of further research, prototype development, and experimentation. EMERALD continues to explore advanced concepts, as did IDES and NIDES. Although most of the necessary analysis infrastructure is now in place, R&D advances are still required for EMERALD relating to inference necessary to enhance correlation in the analysis of and response to coordinated attacks and interdependent anomalies in distributed environments, and in generalizations of applicability beyond security. These are ongoing efforts.

- Interoperability. The Common Intrusion Detection Format (CIDF) and the ongoing IETF standardization effort are important. Both are expected to increase the interoperability within and among different analysis and response systems. EMERALD is very much in line with these efforts, and compatibility is not expected to be a problem. CIDF interface definitions are based on an architectural decomposition that is aligned closely to that of EMERALD's monitor design. In particular, EMERALD's target-specific event-generation components are equivalent in function to CIDF E-boxes; EMERALD's statistical and signature analysis engines are equivalent in function to CIDF A-boxes; EMERALD's resolver is equivalent in function to a CIDF R-box. In hierarchical composition, an EMERALD service layer monitor is capable of passing alerts to a domain monitor. The service layer monitor can operate as a CIDF E-box, and the domain monitor can operate as a CIDF A-box. CIDF working documents are available online (`seclab.csl.ucdavis.edu/cidf`).

EMERALD's Expert System

With respect specifically to the integration of P-BEST into EMERALD [6], our experience has strongly reinforced our conceptual framework.

- The software engineering quality of the EMERALD monitor architecture was put to a test when a summer visitor previously unfamiliar with the system joined us to integrate the signature analysis engine into the generic monitor framework. The statistical anomaly detection engine had been developed in concert with the EMERALD API, and the NIDES expert-system-based signature engine was the first additional component to use the API. The revision and integration procedure went very rapidly (about a man-week), and minor problems that were discovered and solved were due to constraints in the expert-system tool rather than in the EMERALD API. This supports our claim that the EMERALD API is well suited for integration of various kinds of third-party modules into the monitor architecture. Although this is not an exciting *gotcha*, it was important to the development effort.

- The data-driven nature of the EMERALD monitors makes the intermonitor and intramonitor message-passing a central function of the API. The programmer is provided with a set of abstract data types, including a set of methods to handle messages and fields within messages. An example of a powerful feature of the EMERALD message format is the possibility of defining a message field as an array of message fields. This allows the programmer to effectively encapsulate one EMERALD message inside another. In the signature-analysis engine, this capability is used to include the original event record(s) in every alert message sent to the resolver, in addition to the information provided by the triggered rules. This also allows a hierarchy of analysis units (including resolvers) to be able to pass along any or all information produced earlier.

- The generality of the API with respect to the abstract data types is also reflected by the ease with which we were able to write a code-generation utility for the interface code that connects the expert system to the monitor. This utility is used when redirecting the signature-analysis engine to a completely new event stream, using the information in the resource object to fit the engine to the analysis target. The purpose of the utility is to relieve the creator of a resource object from the inner workings of the monitor. The API design made it easy to isolate the target-dependent code and let it be machine-generated.

4. Conclusions

Overall, the progress to date in developing and using EMERALD has been very promising. However, considerable further effort is needed to demonstrate the effectiveness of the software engineering approach and the power of the analytic capabilities.

- The software engineering practice used in EMERALD's modular design and the attention devoted to well-defined interfaces and information hiding in the sense of David Parnas have proven very valuable in EMERALD's development thus far, and will be even more valuable to the ability to interoperate with components developed elsewhere, to its long-term evolvability, and to subsequent generalizations of EMERALD beyond security applications to address human safety, enterprise survivability, reliability, real-time performance, and other critical attributes.

- Hierarchical and distributed correlation is necessary in analyzing highly distributed environments, because of the inability to recognize global patterns from isolated local events. However, additional analysis techniques are likely to be required.

- The iterative nature of EMERALD instantiations will enable lightweight detection components to specialize in particular areas of concern, for different event spaces and at different layers of abstraction.

A few general conclusions are also noted in an attempt to put the EMERALD experience in perspective.

- Commercial intrusion-detection systems have concentrated mostly on string matching and other forms of signature identification to detect classes of outsider attacks. To date, primarily the easy parts of the problem have been addressed by the commercial community.

- Research advances in the community at large seem to have slowed, along with the increased emphasis on detecting known types of outsider attacks. Detecting, identifying, and responding to hitherto unknown attacks and anomalies remain as very challenging problems, including highly coordinated attacks, subtle forms of misuse by insiders, and anomalous network behavior resulting from malfunctions and outages. Providing global rather than local analysis is still a very important research area that is relatively uncharted. Generalizations beyond known security attacks are also challenging.

Further Information

See http://www.csl.sri.com/intrusion.html for background and online versions of papers and reports [2, 4, 6, 8, 9]. See also Web pages for Porras and Neumann (www.csl.sri.com/users/porras/ and www.csl.sri.com/users/neumann/).

Acknowledgments

We are indebted to Martin Fong, Ulf Lindqvist, Keith Skinner, and Al Valdes, all of whom have contributed significantly to the EMERALD development. We are also grateful to those people whose work on the development of IDES and NIDES has influenced EMERALD, including quite notably Teresa Lunt. Charles Antonelli made some very helpful suggestions on the paper, and served as our official workshop shepherd.

References

[1] D. Anderson, T. Frivold, and A. Valdes. Next-generation Intrusion-Detection Expert System (NIDES). Technical report, Computer Science Laboratory, SRI International, Menlo Park, California, SRI-CSL-95-07, May 1995.

[2] D. Anderson, T. Lunt, H. Javitz, A. Tamaru, and A. Valdes. Safeguard final report: Detecting unusual program behavior using the NIDES statistical component. Technical report, Computer Science Laboratory, SRI International, Menlo Park, California, 2 December 1993.

[3] R. Jagannathan, T.F. Lunt, D. Anderson, C. Dodd, F. Gilham, C. Jalali, H.S. Javitz, P.G. Neumann, A. Tamaru, and A. Valdes. System

Design Document: Next-generation Intrusion-Detection Expert System (NIDES). Technical report, Computer Science Laboratory, SRI International, Menlo Park, California, 9 March 1993.

[4] H.S. Javitz and A. Valdes. The NIDES statistical component description and justification. Technical report, Computer Science Laboratory, SRI International, Menlo Park, California, March 1994.

[5] H.S. Javitz, A. Valdes, D.E. Denning, and P.G. Neumann. Analytical techniques development for a statistical intrusion-detection system (SIDS) based on accounting records. Technical report, SRI International, Menlo Park, California, July 1986.

[6] U. Lindqvist and P.A. Porras. Detecting computer and network misuse through the Production-Based Expert System Toolset (P-BEST). In *Proceedings of the 1999 Symposium on Security and Privacy*, Oakland, California, May 1999. IEEE Computer Society.

[7] T.F. Lunt, A. Tamaru, F. Gilham, R. Jagannathan, C. Jalali, P.G. Neumann, H.S. Javitz, and A. Valdes. A Real-Time Intrusion-Detection Expert System (IDES). Technical report, Computer Science Laboratory, SRI International, Menlo Park, California, 28 February 1992.

[8] P.A. Porras and P.G. Neumann. EMERALD: Event Monitoring Enabling Responses to Anomalous Live Disturbances. In *Proceedings of the Nineteenth National Computer Security Conference*, pages 353–365, Baltimore, Maryland, 22-25 October 1997. NIST/NCSC.

[9] P.A. Porras and A. Valdes. Live traffic analysis of TCP/IP gateways. In *Proceedings of the Symposium on Network and Distributed System Security*. Internet Society, March 1998.

[10] M.M. Sebring, E. Shellhouse, M.E. Hanna, and R.A. Whitehurst. Expert system in intrusion detection: A case study. In *Eleventh National Computer Security Conference*, Baltimore, Maryland, October 1988.

Defending against the wily surfer – Web based attacks and de'

Daniel V. Klein
Cybertainment, Inc.
dvk@erotika.com

Abstract

Intrusions are often viewed as catastrophic events which destroy systems, wreak havoc on data through corruption or substitution, yield access to closely guarded sensitive information, or provide a springboard for hackers to attack other systems.

Yet not all intrusions on the Web are the blatant, smash-and-grab, trash-the-site kind of attacks. Many attacks are more subtle, and some involve what appears to be normal access to the site (but appearances are deceiving!) This paper presents a compendium of some of the dirty tricks on the Web. These are used to steal bandwidth and server load (as well as revenue) from web sites around the Internet. Other tricks funnel hits to sites other than the intended destination, while additional, more obvious techniques are used to bypass payment schemes and gain free access to sites. A different class of attacks targets the client, instead of the server. Some of the dirty tricks are preventable up-front, while others can only be detected after the security holes have been exploited – and always, there needs to be a balance between accessibility and vulnerability. We present a compendium of problems, attacks, and solutions. Many of the attacks and preventions seem "obvious" once known – this paper aims to forearm by forewarning the reader.

1. Explanation (and expiation)

Many of the intrusion techniques cited in this paper are prevalent in the adult web site domain, although this is not to say that they don't exist elsewhere. The reasons for the prevalence of attacks on the adult market are:

1) The adult market is one in which content is actually worth money. Although E-Commerce is roaring along strongly in other arenas, it is usually material product which is being sold (e.g., although eBay and Amazon.com have huge amounts of traffic, they sell hard commodities, whereas adult web sites generally sell streams of bits).

2) Although some non-adult sites sell data (e.g. programs or stock market tips), few of these are interchangeable, but a lot of smut is.

3) People will share passwords to adult sites, because there is rarely any personal information associated with the account. People are far less likely to share their account on a stock investment site, since electronic stock trades are legally binding to the account holder.

4) Computer enabled teenagers (and there are an awful lot of them on the net today) generally couldn't care less about stocks, bonds, news, or books. Sex, on the other hand, occupies a substantial fraction of their attention.

None of these reasons make the information in this paper less valuable to non-adult web sites. As the electronic medium becomes more and more available to the general public, attacks of the kind outlined here will become more prevalent in every marketplace. The experiences of the adult market are hard won victories that can forewarn, and thus forearm other markets.

2. Domain name spoofing

If you have a new site with a hot new domain name, what kind of traffic can you expect? Who will come to your existing site, and who will visit it based on the advertisements you take out? The more difficult the name is to spell, the more likely it will be that surfers mistype the name. The more popular the site, the greater the chance that someone will try to imitate your site, or simply steal hits by parasitizing your domain name. When AT&T introduced their 1-800-OPERATOR collect-call system, MCI diverted a noticeable fraction of the income stream by activating a similar service on 1-800-OPERATER (a number they conveniently already owned). There is a whole set of Internet domain names that capitalize on surfers' inability to spell.

Domains like `netscape.com` have their typographical-error equivalents `netscpae.com` and `netscap.com`, taken by a British and California group of entrepreneurs. Although neither currently have active web pages, there is income potential from either of these sites. Even more income potential can be realized by the clever Russians who registered `quiken.com`, since the real `quicken.com` sells advertisements, and thus is an income generating site itself. Were any of these domain name parasites to create a site that visually appeared the same as their host company's site, they could easily steal credit card information or disseminate false information with the cachet of a real-looking web site.[1]

Most newbie surfers have been indoctrinated with `www.something.com`. Regardless of the real address, a web site simply *must* be prefixed with `www` and every domain must end in `.com` (as if a "domain" is a term that is readily understood outside of hacker circles). Smart companies register their domain in all of the available top-level domains (e.g., `webtv.com` and `webtv.net`, or `usenix.org` and `usenix.com`), and both with and without hyphens, where appropriate. Uninformed groups fail to do so, and lose traffic, name recognition, and money.

In 1995 a local web-based company created `pittsburgh.net`, with the marketing slogan of "Pittsburgh on the Net". I asked myself how many people would type `.com` instead of `.net`, and promptly registered `pittsburgh.com`. I also aliased it to my fledgling Pittsburgh-based web-hosting company. Without ever advertising the domain name, I started getting hits, and within 3 months (thanks to my competitor's aggressive advertising campaign), fully 40% of my hits were coming to `pittsburgh.com`.

Perhaps the most renowned of these domain name "thefts" are the hits redirected from `whitehouse.gov` to the similarly named `whitehouse.com`. Far from being the governmental information site that most surfers probably expect, it is an adult-oriented site instead.

The proliferation of top-level domains only makes this problem worse. The Pacific island nations of Niue and Tonga have gotten into the domain name business, so you can register domains like `who.nu` and `incogni.to` for $35/year. The island nation of Tuvalu auctions domain names[2], ostensibly for television-related companies, so you can also register

`color.tv`. The Cocos Islands sells domains like `mail.cc` (with premium prices being charged for 2-letter domain names), the British Indian Ocean Territory does the same with domains like `scenar.io`, and until recently, Turkmenistan was also selling domain names. However, the TMNIC realized that some of the names it registered may be legally obscene in Turkmenistan, and as a result the TMNIC registry is reviewing its naming policy for future registrations (and has suspended registrations until a new policy can be implemented). But domains such as `trademark.tm` were up for grabs until the suspension took effect.

I shudder to think the confusion that will be sown when it will be possible to have not only a `foo.com`, `foo.org`, and `foo.net`, but also `foo.web`, `foo.shop`, `foo.firm`, `foo.info`, `foo.arts`, `foo.rec`, and `foo.nom`.[3] The potential for content misdirection and identity theft is stunning.

Regrettably, there is only one defense against domain name spoofing. First, have a domain name which is difficult to misspell (and that can cost a lot of money if you want a common, readily recognizable name that someone else already owns). Second, you need to spend more money and register the domain in each one of the of the possible top-level domains (although realistically, you can probably skip Turkmenistan and the various islands).

3. Domain name stealing

The NIC provides a number of mechanisms for protecting your domain registration. Unfortunately, few novice web registrants are aware of them.

Once a domain is registered, its attributes can only be changed by the administrative, technical, or billing contact. By default, the identity of the person submitting a change request is validated via email address, and notification of changes to the domain is made after the fact (a PGP signature verification option is also available, but newbies often don't understand it).

Unscrupulous individuals can readily forge an email message that appears to originate from one of the contacts. If the change request is to modify the primary

---

[1] Prior to the transfer of the `altavista.com` domain name to Digital/Compaq, Altavista would pass queries through to the "real" `altavista.digital.com`, while selling their own ad space and rewriting the search engine's page content.

[2] According to their web site, the minimum bid is $1000. Tuvalu is also a "discriminating" registry in that it does not allow registration of pornography, hatred, or gambling content sites.

[3] As proposed by the Department of Commerce, National Telecommunications and Information Administration, Statement of Policy, "Management of Internet Names and Addresses", Docket Number: 980212036-8146-02 (see `http://www.gtld-mou.org/` for more details).

and secondary domain name servers, the original registrant is still financially responsible for the domain without benefiting from its use. The best way for a thief to do this is adjust their reverse IP lookups, such that the name of the counterfeit DNS server is the same as the real thing. When the domain change confirmation is mailed to the legitimate contacts, they are likely to miss the change in IP numbers, and see only that the DNS names are the same. Since contact email addresses are often obsolete and non-functional, when confirmation email is sent, the confirmation may go completely unnoticed. If the email addresses are valid, a clever domain thief can even maintain MX records while changing A records, redirecting the web hits while preserving email identity.[4]

4. Password hacking and sharing

The reason aphorisms are so often repeated is not because we have all heard them so often – it is because they are *correct*. An aphorism for web site maintenance is "Member site passwords are a weak point". Passwords on a web site are as vulnerable to hacking as they are anywhere, and password sharing is the same problem as it is on any computer. And as with any computer system, a good site administrator needs to check for hackers and password sharing. The advantage to the web is that log files (which are often examined daily as a matter of course) contain information that can be used to readily identify both problems.

There are numerous sites on the web dedicated to publishing accounts and passwords, and there are at least half a dozen newsgroups dedicated to nothing else.[5] The newsgroups and web sites are a mix of three things, and as with most newsgroups, the signal-to-noise ratio is fairly low. The first group consists of people actually publishing passwords. A second group is people seeking passwords (or offering to trade them, but generally only if you give away *your* secrets first). Finally, there are numerous shameless marketing ploys

---

[4] Although it sounds implausible, a number of very large adult web sites have been stolen in this way, and the theft was only noticed *months* later when someone finally decided to check server logs. As we will see over and over again, log files are your friend.

[5] A search for "pass" in newsgroup names yielded the following 6 newsgroups: alt.etc.passwd, alt.ipl.passwords, alt.japanese.neojapan.shareware.password-exchange, alt.sex.commercial-sites.password-exchange, alt.sex.password, and alt.sex.passwords. Searching for "crack" resulted in 15 more newsgroups related to cracking commercial and shareware programs. So much for honesty and integrity on the Net.

disguised as password postings. This latter group entices you to visit a web site with promises of free passwords, when in fact the supplicant is greeted with either a membership site and/or a plethora of banner ads and pop-up windows (either of which having the potential to make money for the web site maintainer).

But because valid passwords are often posted by unscrupulous individuals, the threat of password sharing is indeed real. The following chart shows 6.5 months of HTTP transfers from one member-based web site (from site-launch until just before this paper went to press). The load on the system varies throughout the week, with troughs generally occurring on the weekends, and with an average network load of 500Mb of data per day (with a recent surge up to 1Gb per day, due to a successful advertising campaign). As adult sites go, this one is a relatively small one – large sites can easily push 100 times this much data (or more) out the pipe every day.

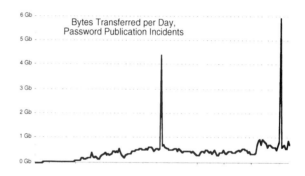

At the middle (14 Nov 1998) and just at the end of the graph (8 Feb 1999), an account/password pair was published on a password web site (by persons unknown), and the load on the server surged to nearly ten times it's normal value, almost completely filling my T1 link. While an intrusion can rarely be considered fortuitous, the timing of the second event was such that this paper benefited from an significant additional data point.

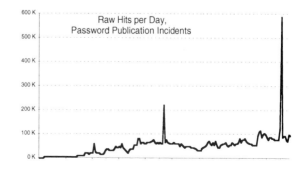

Cutting off the password in question roughly 20 hours after it was posted alleviated the server load, and restored operating parameters back to normal within a day or so. The hit rate stayed high for a slightly longer time period than the byte transfer rate, since surfers were still attempting to access the site via the now-disabled account.

A couple of statistics are worth noting on these incidents. For the previous two years (on this, and all other member sites I maintain), an average account was visited from no more than 3 domain addresses (as defined in the script in the following section), and generally one of those domains accounted for over 85% of the total hits for an account. In the second event, over 2,675 domains in 85 countries were evident (comprising an unknown number of individuals). The chart below shows the number of hits for the top-10 domains visiting the site:

47207	bellatlantic.net	8359	com.au
35687	aol.com	7874	home.com
31429	tele.dk	7668	net.au
11769	edu.tw	6373	ripe.net
8762	uu.net	5673	dfn.de

It is not at all surprising that the big ISPs account for the vast majority of the hits. What is perhaps a little more surprising is that the University system in Taiwan accounts for such a large fraction of this hits. When the top-20 TLDs are listed, we see the following distribution of accesses:

171906	.net	6922	.fr
95117	.com	6688	.it
35109	.dk	6350	.uk
24998	.de	4572	.kr
23889	.edu	3795	.fi
16952	.au	3698	.ch
14169	.ca	3611	.my
13019	.tw	3075	.no
9649	.se	3028	.at
9076	.nl	2865	.mx

Considered collectively, the greatest number of hits originated in the United States, with Denmark and Germany (long viewed as a *source* of adult materials) occupying a substantial fraction of the free-password surfers' hits.

What affect do these intrusions have on member signups? Prior to these two incidents, I posted a password myself to alt.sex.passwords on 22 Dec 1997. This was both as a test of my then-new intrusion detection software, and as my own shameless marketing ploy. I had predicted that after access to my site was cut off, people would pay to sign up, having been hooked by the content. The software worked as planned, but the marketing attempt failed miserably – most people who frequent the password sites and newsgroups are looking for a free ride. The same was true following the two real intrusions, namely that no perceptible increase in member signups occurred.

It is interesting to note that for the test incident, the greatest number of surfers originated in Russia. At the time, it made sense that smut-hungry surfers in countries that were short on hard currency would find themselves compelled to purloin access to member sites. Of course another interpretation could be that in countries where religion had not been suppressed, people were more interested in spending the winter holidays with family than surfing for smut. The latter seems perhaps more reasonable, since Russia ranked 41 in the TLDs of the real attacks, and accounted for less than 2.5% of the number of hits of Denmark, while the reverse was true of the test incident.

It is difficult to do more than speculate on the nature of the surfers, although the statistics do pose an interesting set of sociological questions. The bottom line, though, is that if your site's passwords are posted (and you don't have software to detect it), you're in serious trouble.

4.1. Detecting password sharing

The following is a simple-minded Perl script which tests for password sharing. It examines a standard HTTP log file, and tallies the number of domains from which a password has been used. The script makes the following simplifying assumptions:

1) All hits from within a domain are considered to be the same. So if a surfer shares a password with their coworkers (or legitimately views the site from two different machines in the same domain), this script will not detect it.

2) All hits from within the same Class-C subnet are also considered to be the same. For those sites for which reverse DNS is inaccurate or unavailable (or for web servers which choose not to do DNS lookup), this simplification will remove a large

number of false positive reports of password sharing (although it will remove some true positive reports, too).

Although these assumptions reduce the effectiveness of the script, experience has shown that casual sharing is not the main concern of a site, it is blatant password publication that matters most. It is also not unusual for a surfer to view a site from different ISPs at work and at home, so it is up to the site monitor to make the distinction between password sharing and office/home viewing.

```perl
#!/usr/bin/perl

#
# Parse the log files.  We only really care
# about the first three fields (and not
# really about the middle one of those).
#
while (<>) {
    ($addr, $rfc931, $acct) = split;
    next if $acct eq "-";
    $total{$acct}++;
    if ($addr =~ /^(\d+\.\d+\.\d+)\.\d+$/) {
        $addr = $1;
        }
    else {
        $addr =~ s/^.*\.([^.]+\.[^.]+)$/$1/;
        }
    $acct{$acct}->{$addr}++;
    }
#
# Extract the various cheaters in magnitude
# order
#
for $acct (sort
        { $total{$b} <=> $total{$a} }
            keys %count) {
    if (keys %{ $count{$acct} } > 2) {
        push @multi, $acct;
        }
    }
exit unless @multi;
#
# Print the cheaters out - account and
# domain/IP addresses
#
for $acct (sort
    { $total{$b} <=> $total{$a} }
        @multi) {
    print "$acct - $total{$acct}:\n";
    while (($ip, $num) =
            each %{ $count{$acct} }) {
        printf "%5d %s\n", $num, $addr;
        }
    }
}
```

Because my sites are only very infrequently attacked (and because income loss is consequently minimal), I run this script once a day. Were I more paranoid, I would run it a few times a day, and enhance it to automatically disable accounts when an obvious intrusion had occurred.

4.2. Password cracking

Dictionary-based attacks on a web site are as time-consuming as they are on any networked system, but from the standpoint of the cracker, there are two profound advantages to a web-based attack.

1) The stateless nature of the web almost guarantees that a web server does not retain a count of failed attempts (*login*, on the other hand, maintains state information and logs incidents when a surfeit of failed attempts occur, in addition to breaking the TCP connection after a small number of failures).

2) Because web servers are designed to handle multiple simultaneous connections, a cracker can easily launch multiple simultaneous attacks.

It is almost trivially simple to write a script which hammers away at a server, attempting to crack a password. Here is one such script that forks off 10 copies of itself to do the work. The script will only attempt about 10-20 connections per second, but that's fast enough if you know someone's account name...

```perl
#!/usr/bin/perl

die "Usage: $0 URL acct\n" unless @ARGV == 2;
($url, $acct) = @ARGV;

require HTTP::Request;
require HTTP::Response;
require LWP::UserAgent;
use URI;

$ua = new LWP::UserAgent;
$url = new URI $url;
$req = new HTTP::Request 'GET', $url;
#
# Read the dictionary into memory, and
# figure the size of each piece
#
open (DICT, "/usr/share/dict/words");
@words = <DICT>;
$each = @words / 10;
#
# Spawn 10 children, and give each of them
# a piece of the dictionary.
#
FORK: for $kid (0..9) {
    #
    # Parent forks off kids and continues,
    # child does the real work
    #
    next FORK if ($status = fork);
```

```
    for $w (@words[($kid * $each) ..
        ($each-1 + $kid * $each)]) {
        $req->authorization_basic($acct, $w);
        $response = $ua->request($req);
        #
        # 401 is "authorization denied".  If
        # you get anything else, you're in!
        #
        $response->code == 401 && next;
        die "Kid $kid cracked it! $w\n";
        }
    exit;
    }

0 until ($status = wait) == -1;
printf "Total elapsed time %d seconds\n",
    time - $^T;
```

4.3. Detecting password cracking

If I am going to tell you how to crack passwords on the web, then I also must show how to detect a cracker at work. Here is trivial Perl script which looks for HTTP password cracking. It simply examines a standard HTTP error log file, and tallies the number of failed attempts to access an account. It then reports those accounts for which greater than 30 attempts have been made (with the rationale that any fewer number of attempts are either a surfer who has forgotten their password, or a cracking attempt of no strength).

```
#!/usr/bin/perl

$reasons = "not found|password mismatch";
while (<>) {
    if (/reason: user (.*) ($reasons)/o) {
        next if length($1) == 0;
        $botch{$1,$2}++;
        }
    }

for $bad (keys %botch) {
    ($user, $why) = split /$;/, $bad;
    if ($botch{$_} >= 30) {
        print "user $user $why $botch{$_}\n";
        }
    }
```

I have not detected any intrusion attempts using this script (credit-card fraud is more often the means used to gain a password), but I still run this script daily, just in case someone tries to break in.

5. DNS cache poisoning

When your web browser goes to www.foo.com, how does it know how to get there? DNS provides the name-to-number mapping, so that your browser connects to the appropriate IP address. If the DNS server can be convinced that the IP address of www.foo.com is something other than what it should be, then web hits can be redirected to another site.

It turns out that it is relatively simple to do so (and in the good-old-days of the pre-cracker Internet, it used to be almost trivially so). Essentially, a cache poisoning attack works like this (the details have been simplified somewhat):

1) DNS works via UDP, to increase speed by eliminating the startup costs of TCP connections. When a DNS client wants to know a name-to-IP address mapping, it sends a UDP message to a DNS server, and awaits a UDP reply. If the server does not have the answer it its local cache, it recursively queries other servers for the answer (down a very short chain from a root server to the authoritative server for the domain).

2) Since UDP packets are connectionless and therefore stateless (all state information must be maintained by the programs which use them), it is possible to send a message to a DNS server that claims "here's the (fraudulent) answer to the (nonexistent) query you just sent me". The "answer" contains your bogus information, and most DNS servers simply accept the answer![6]

Now, why would someone want to poison a DNS cache? Here are a couple of reasons:

1) Profit – point a popular site's name at your IP address, and reap the benefits. These can be in the form of advertising income, membership income (typically from a third site, since the poisoning will eventually be corrected), or bragging rights for the crackers.

2) Sabotage – point a very popular site's name at your *competitor's* IP address, and cause a meltdown. Imagine poisoning AOL's DNS cache during the Olympics to point cnnsi.com at someone with mere T-1 connectivity. Most sites simply cannot handle 10 million hits/day.

Unfortunately, the only defenses against DNS attacks lie within BIND itself (and other DNS agents like

---

[6]   The latest versions of BIND keep track of the requests they have sent out, and will not accept an answer from a server unless they have actually asked a question. This is harder to subvert, but still possible, by sending streams of forged answers with a question-inducing query inserted in the middle of the stream.

Microsoft's DHCP) – there is little that the average web site can do to prevent them (and in any event, the most effective attacks are made against major upstream providers and ISPs).

6. Bandwidth thieves

A large number sites offer free content. Some of these sites have a huge traffic load (e.g., search engines, stock market sites, adult sites), so the costs of maintaining the sites is non-trivial. Altruism is probably not the main motivation for these sites' existence. Since the more likely culprit is monetary gain, where is the income generated if content is given away for free? The answer is advertising – the more surfers who come through a site, the more ad impressions are made, and the more money can be made. Regardless of the payment mechanism, the larger the volume of traffic, the more money to the web site.

The problem (from the standpoint of a web site) is that bandwidth costs money, but you need to have a lot of bandwidth before you can entice high-paying advertisers to your site. But advertisers who pay via profit sharing don't necessarily care if a site has high volume, as long as they make sales.

One technique used by low-volume web sites to increase their advertisement income is bandwidth theft. With this technique, the HTML on the site consists of the look-and-feel of the site, the advertisement, and the content. The first two items originate at the site itself, and generally do not produce a large bandwidth load. The last item – the content – is (typically) an image whose URL is on a different site, being parasitized. This site is the one that pays for the majority of the bandwidth, but it derives no benefit (that is, the ads being displayed do not credit the host site, but instead credit the parasite site). Bandwidth theft is most common when the URL of the image does not change.[7]

Automated defenses are possible at the cost of CPU utilization, but they also require the assumption that browsers will deliver accurate referrer information. In order to prevent bandwidth theft on an automated basis, the service for each request for an image must check for

---

[7] While the notion of an unchanging URL seems correct from a site-maintenance standpoint, it is in fact the wrong model to use when giving away free content. If a "picture of the day" page references `today.jpg`, then any other page (on any *other* site) can trivially reference the same image URL, and steal bandwidth from your site. A URL which changes daily requires the parasite to change daily, too – something which is beyond most bandwidth thieves.

the referrer URL. If the browser tells the truth (one expects that it might), then a referrer whose domain is different from the one on which the image resides is probably a bandwidth thief, and the request can be denied (or a replacement image can be supplied which suggests that a theft might be occurring).

This proactive approach is CPU intensive, since each request requires the execution of a CGI script (the author is unaware of any modules in the common web servers that do this function directly). A different, reactive approach is to maintain a referrer log file, and simply scan (programmatically, of course) for image files being requested by off-site HTML pages. When theft is detected, you can either put the thief on notice (usually a futile effort), or change the image URL.

Another reactive method is to use the advanced search features of the various search engines, to look for pages which reference your sites' images. This approach is certainly sub-optimal, as it can take a long time for search engines to index the thieves sites (if they even *permit* indexing via the `robots.txt` file).

The most effective deterrent against bandwidth theft (and regrettably, the most expensive from a bandwidth standpoint) is to simply not use static file names. Two easy ways of accomplishing this are:

1) If the free content is relatively static (that is, if it changes fairly infrequently), the directory name in which it resides can be changed. This presents a number of challenges, the first of which is that search engines need to be continually re-notified (or better, discouraged from indexing the low-level directory which contains the content). The second problem is that the bandwidth load on the server increases because various web caches will not contain the newly updated file names.

2) If the content changes frequently, then reloading (and the concomitant bandwidth load) is an issue that already has been addressed. In this case, it is far better to choose non-trivially-predictable file names for the content. This means that it is necessary to edit the HTML that references the images (and expire the HTML pages to reference the changed images).

Unfortunately, in addition to being time consuming and expensive, legal recourse is of questionable merit. When someone references your image on their HTML page, the law is unclear on whether a copyright violation has occurred[8] – after all, the thief is not republishing the image, *you* are!

7. Data theft

Another form of intrusion on the web is out-and-out theft of content. This typically presents itself as your images appearing on a different site (often with your identifying marks trimmed off, and sometimes with different marks tacked on), but can also extend itself to complete mirroring of a site. Clearly, this is a violation of copyright law, but how can you detect it? Surfing the web for your imagery requires you to look at the assorted images, and some companies have people whose job is nothing more than to surf for stolen images.

Of course it would be nice to automate the process, and some proponents of the process have proposed the "watermarking" of images. The method here is to invisibly encode identifying information in the images. The simplest mechanism is to use the comment field in the GIF or JPG image. Another method is to encode repeating serial numbers in the low-order bits of the image pixels (single bit differences are indiscernible to the human eye, but could easily be read by a program). Other, more sophisticated techniques are also proposed, and are beyond the scope of this paper.

The problem with all of these methods is that images are just data in a standardized format, and data can be manipulated. Copyrights can be trimmed off or blotted out, comments can be altered, and marks created by the watermarking system that this author experimented with were erased by simply re-saving the image with a different image viewer (without even *trying* to remove the watermark).

An alternative approach is to place visible markers on images. Many sites put a "banner bar" at the top or bottom of the picture, but these can be readily trimmed off. Other sites emboss the images with their site name, but this noticeably degrades image quality (and it is images that your paying customers are looking for). A third approach puts a visible marker (words, a logo, a copyright notice, or some combination) in a "non-

intrusive" location on the picture. In this case, a delicate balance needs to be maintained so that the marker is not so big that it pollutes the image and not so small that it can be airbrushed out. The marker also needs to be placed in such a way that trimming it out of the image would degrade the image content to an unacceptable degree.

The best solution is probably to use a combination of GIF/JPG comment fields, combined with a marker directly in the picture. But even with this solution, a human generally needs to be employed to simply look for images that have been purloined. A low tech solution, but an effective one.

8. Click-bots

A lot of money can be made on the web by creating free-content sites that sell advertising. This model has worked well for search engines, stock-market sites, Internet malls, and of course, adult sites. Advertisers typically pay sites by one of three mechanisms:

1) Per impression – that is, the number of times an ad is presented to surfers. Most of the search engines use this mechanism, since it is the most favorable to the site carrying the ads (payment is directly related to both the surfer traffic through the site and the bandwidth used by the site), and it is also the most easily tracked by the site carrying the ads.

2) Per click – that is, every time a surfer clicks on an ad, revenue is generated. This mechanism is used by some stock-market sites and also by adult sites. The payment rate is related to both the traffic through the site and the effectiveness of the ad, so in some ways, this payment mechanism is fairest to both parties. Tracking can be done by both parties, although the site displaying the ads can expect to see slightly higher click-through percentages than the advertiser (due to aborted connections, time-outs, etc.)

3) Per sale – that is, for each click-through that results in a sale a percentage of the income is paid. This mechanism is fairest to the advertiser (since ads placed in an unfavorable location do not make sales, but also do not cost the advertiser), but sales tracking can only be done on the seller site.

To some degree, a lot of advertising on the web needs to be based on mutual trust. In the adult marketplace, there is little trust (and often little technical savvy on the part of web site maintainers), so per-impression

---

[8]   In fact, the law is having very serious trouble keeping up with the the Internet and other electronic transmissions as regards all aspects of information dissemination (see Robert Reilly, "Mapping Legal Metaphors in Cyberspace: Evolving the Underlying Paradigm", and Keith Kupferschmid, "Lost in Cyberspace: The Digital Demise of the First-Sale Doctrine", *J. Computer & Information Law*, vol XVI 1998)

advertising is rarely seen. Although per-sale advertising is rapidly becoming the payment of choice, per-click advertising is still prevalent (often the payouts are scaled to the conversion rate[9]).

The problem with click-through advertising is that it can be trivially spoofed. The following simple Perl script fakes a click on a counting web page on the pigeon site[10] every 8 seconds, on average:

```
#!/usr/bin/perl

use HTTP::Request;
use LWP::UserAgent;

$ua = new LWP::UserAgent;
$ua->agent("Mozilla/3.01");
$req = new HTTP::Request(GET =>
    "http://pigeon.com/count/143");

while (1) {
    $response = $ua->request($req);
    sleep int rand 16;
    }
```

There are a number of defenses against this blatant form of spamming. The most prevalent one is the counting of so-called "uniques". Most web sites use proprietary algorithms to distinguish unique hits, and do not publish their techniques. This is ostensibly so that spammers cannot circumvent whatever checks are in place, but most likely it is to hide the crudity of the algorithms.

In general, most sites simply count one hit per IP address in a set time period (3-6 hours is a reasonable guess). While this certainly eliminates spammers, it also fails to count almost all legitimate hits from proxy servers in place at AOL, Compuserve, etc.

To circumvent unique-checking, sophisticated spammers can use the FTP indirection attack. This attack takes advantage of the fact that "classic" FTP connections use the control connection to specify a destination IP address and port for the data connection. In practice, the data IP address should be the same as the originating control connection, but the protocol can be spoofed and a third-party address can be given (newer FTP servers prevent this type of attack, but they are by no means prevalent). With this attack, an FTP server can be used as a proxy for HTTP (or other) requests, and an attacker with a specialized FTP client can use a large collection of FTP servers to generate what appears to be numerous non-unique HTTP click-throughs.

If this type of attack is used, an automated defense is difficult to implement.[11] In general, human vigilance is the only way guard against them. Periodic checks need to be made of the purported source of the click-throughs, and spammers can often betray themselves with their own cleverness. Many web sites feature hit counters. These counters are often provided by third-party web sites, which also rank sites by the number of hits they generate per day, and thus provide a popularity rating of the site (the web counter sites are free, and also make their money through advertising).

Since most ads generate a known click-through rate (depending on the ad itself and the other information on the page), the web counters can be correlated with the click-through rate to detect obvious spamming. If the frequency of click-throughs is too high, the most likely culprit is fraud.

9. Banner hijacking

Depending on site content and the advertisement itself, ads typically generate between a 1-2% click-through rate on search engines to a 5-15% click-through rate on adult sites. This disparity is due to the fact that surfers on a search engine are looking for information content (that is, the pages the search-engine has located, and not the possibly unrelated ads), while adult-site surfers have learned that numerous free images can be seen by simply clicking through ad after ad. The more successful ads are, of course, worthy of imitating. Or plagiarizing. Or out-and-out copying.

Some sites actually use their competitors' banners to advertise their own sites. Alas, there is very little that can be done to detect this so-called banner hijacking, because not only do you have to look for your banners on other's pages (which is where they *belong*, in order to advertise your site), you have to ascertain whether or not the banner's click-through URL points to your site (this is not always obvious, especially if banner rotation software[12] is in use).

---

[9] The fraction of sales over the number of clicks.

[10] A "pigeon" is a mark, a stooge, a patsy, or more simply put, the target of a scam.

[11] I am not providing an example of a script which performs this type of attack, precisely because guarding against it is so difficult.

[12] Some sites have static ads (ads which are only changed by editing the enclosing HTML), while others use ad rotation software (working in conjunction with SSI, Javascript, or Active Server Pages) for ads which can change based on advertiser-defined constraints, including having a different ad load each time a page request is made).

One way of detecting your banners is through the aforementioned watermarking, since not many sites are likely to edit the banner, unless it contains an image of a URL. Another strategy involves looking for banners with dimensions and byte counts similar to your own, then parsing the HTML of such candidates to determine whether or not your banner is being used to advertise some other site.

Fortunately, banner hijacking is relatively rare (people usually choose to steal content, instead). In cases where it exists, though, manual searching is usually the only way to find it.

10. Meta-tag Hijacking

If you have a site that you want to publicize, what is the fastest way to do it for a minimal cost? Banner ads have a limited click-through rate (and can be expensive), ads in print, TV, and radio have a long lead time and a prohibitive cost (both in production and display), and link trades and link circles are only minimally useful. Getting listed in the search engines is really the best way to get noticed. But with between 40 and 100 *million* pages catalogued in most of the major search engines, how do you get listed near the top?

There are a number of sites which will automatically examine your pages and suggest the most appropriate keywords, but the best way to get good placement is to copy the META tags[13] of the top-listed site! If it was good enough to put them at the top of the list, it will do the same for your site.

Depending on the keywords and phrases used, there may be nothing at all illegal with meta-tag hijacking, and there is nothing you can do to prevent someone from using your well-thought-out keywords. Only where copyrighted names are used is there any recourse, and your pursuit of hijackers must be aggressive, or you can lose your copyright protection.[14] But if your choice of

---

[13] In the <HEAD> section of pages indexed by many search engines, the tags <META NAME="description"...> and <META NAME="keywords"...> give the engines the information on how to index the page. This places indexing control in the hands of the web author, instead of a heuristic in the indexing engine.

[14] In a 1997 ruling, Playboy Enterprises successfully sued a number of sites which were fraudulently using the word "Playboy" in their meta tags to draw in surfers. But in 1998, another suit ruled that since Playboy had awarded the title "Playboy Playmate of the Year" to one of its models, that model was *allowed* to use the term in her site's meta tags.

keywords is merely clever, there is not much you can do to prevent your meta tags from being hijacked (although if you copyright the description, that can be protected in court). But unless you're near the top of the list, there also is not much *point* in searching out hijackers.

But if you're at the top of the list, how can you determine when your meta tags have been hijacked? By using essentially the same technique used by the hijackers – surf the search engines, and look for sites that appear near yours. Examine their meta tags, and see if they resemble (or are copies of) yours. This process can be automated, but the script is of sufficient complexity that it is beyond the scope of this paper.

11. Search Engine Misdirection

If you don't want to blatantly purloin someone else's meta tags, how do you get a lot of surfers to visit your site? The answer is simple: lie to the search engines.

My favorite example of this occurred when the first wave of public interest in Viagra™ was in full swell. Some industrious web sites simply placed a few informative paragraphs about the drug on their pages (sometimes in a tiny point size), and resubmitted them to the search engines. Many was the hapless surfer who was lured into an adult-oriented site while researching information on the drug.

Another technique is for a site to make a comparison between their product and their competitor's, and list that page on the search engines. In this way, no matter which product the surfer is looking for, they will find the misdirecting site's pages (and more hits mean the potential for more sales).

Unfortunately, there is nothing at all that can be done to prevent this type of attack (other than a ban by the search engines). The only defense is the ever-useful advice of *caveat emptor*. It is up to the surfers not to fall for the misleading ads.

12. Frame spoofing

An interesting vulnerability in frames enables the author of a nefarious web site or email message to "spoof" information presented by another web site.[15] This vulnerability exists in all the popular web browsers that support frames, and is exploitable both with and without Javascript being enabled.

---

[15] See http://www.securexpert.com/framespoof/ for complete details and a working example.

Almost every site using frames is vulnerable to this form of attack, which enables an attacker to have their information represent itself as having originated at your web site. In this way, an attacker can steal credit card information, disseminate misleading or damaging information, steal passwords, etc.

The vulnerability occurs simply because Netscape and MSIE fail to protect the `frames[]` array from cross-domain write access. This enables one web site (or an HTML email message) to replace a frame displayed by another site with content that is under the attacker's control.

All that is required for a web site to exploit the vulnerability is either one of the following:

1) The attacker has opened the victim site's window – either by sending HTML email, or from a scripted web page (required for the Javascript-based variant of the attack).

2) The attacker knows the name of a frame in the victim site (for the HTML-based variant).

Detecting this type of intrusion from a web site is well-nigh impossible, since the attack is done on the *browser*, and not on the web site. Using the search engines to hunt for links to your frames is one defense, but a weak one (especially since attacks can be HTML email based). Checking referring URLs is another reactive test, but it is time consuming and extremely labor intensive.

Protecting against this form of attack is done in a twofold manner, since both surfers and sites can guard against it. For surfers, not having more than one window open at a time is the surest defense (since exploiting the bug requires a window to attack and a window to attack from).

For web sites, SecureXpert offers solutions only to their paying clients, so I am unable to comment on them. However, eliminating frames from your HTML is certainly one defense, albeit a draconian one.

13. Revenge of the Nerds

It is worth noting that surfers are not the only ones guilty of hacking and spamming. Web sites are often just as guilty of the same offenses. Many of the site-induced intrusions involve Javascript, so preventing the attacks is as simple as disabling Javascript (a technique

which regrettably also compromises some sites'' functionality). Some examples of these attacks are shown below:

13.1. The surfer-motel

Surfer's check in, but they can't check out. This is an annoying technique that many web sites use to spam surfers and entice them to spend money by inundating them with new windows. Javascript is used to open a new window whenever the surfer attempts to leave the site.

Typically, one company will have dozens (or hundreds) of web sites, so when the surfer attempts to leave one web site, a new window pops up for one of the other sites. This is done using the `onUnload` method in Javascript, which is invoked whenever a window or frame is replaced with another window (or when the window is closed). So one site would have code that looks like this, which references another site:

```
<html>
<head><title>One Site</title></head>
<body onUnload="
    window.open('http://other.com', 'S2')">
```

This simple example can be extended to create "the window that would not die" (in this case, the Javascript should be placed in a file named `rude.html`, so that the URL points to itself).[16]

```
<html>
<head><title>Rudeness!</title></head>
<body onUnload="
window.open('http://www.rude.com/rude.html',
    '_blank')">
<h1>Try and get rid of me!</h1>
</html>
```

As long as Javascript is enabled, any time the offending window is unloaded or closed, it reappears. On the OS/2 version of Netscape 3.5, if the surfer tried the radical approach of killing the browser (with no less powerful an incantation than CTRL-ALT-DEL), it would immediately restart itself and re-open this window!

13.2. URL masking

This is a fairly benign attack using Javascript, wherein the surfer is persuaded to go to a site other than what they intend. Ordinarily, the URL of a hyperlink is displayed in the bottom left of the browser window

---

[16] An absolute URL (including the site name) is required, otherwise Netscape outsmarts the malicious code.

when the mouse is moved over the link. Some sites obscure this, or even intentionally mislead the surfer by using Javascript. Here is a simple example where a link advertises one site, but takes the surfer to a competitor.

```
<A HREF="http://www.pepsi.com/uncola.html"
    onMouseOver=
        "window.status='http://www.coke.com';
        return true"
    onMouseOut=
        "window.status='';
        return true">It's The Real Thing</A>
```

In this example, when the surfer moves the mouse over the hyperlink, the browser indicates that it will go to one company, when in fact it is the competitor that is visited when the link is traversed. Combining this attack with frame spoofing can create a fraud that is very difficult to detect by the average surfer.

13.3. Credit-card Churning

Unscrupulous web sites can steal from unsuspecting surfers in a number of ways. One of the most prevalent forms of attack is with recurring billing. A credit card is required (as a means of proving the surfer is the age of majority) for a "free" one-week membership, but the fine print states that the card will be re-billed at monthly intervals if the membership is not canceled. Many surfers fail to read the fine-print, and so are re-billed each month for membership in a site they have long forgotten about. Another technique is to place the "cancel my membership" page in a hard-to-locate place.

Of course, some sites ask for credit cards with no intention of giving a membership, but only to steal credit-card information. Fortunately, this virulent attack is rare, but it is all too easy to make. Surfer awareness is the only defense – only deal with companies you know, or who use credit-card verification systems that you know. And as obvious as it sounds, you should *always* examine your credit card bills for mysterious charges.

14. Conclusions

Although the Internet started out as a nice, safe place to travel, we must realize that with all the gold to be won, the day of the Information Superhighwayman is upon us. Unless we are careful and ever-watchful, he (or she) will come riding – riding, riding – up to our electronic front door.[17]

---

[17] With apologies to Alfred Noyes (1880-1958) author of *The Highwayman*

Some attacks, such as those upon surfers using Javascript, are indirectly the result of well-intentioned but security-unaware browser developers, and the exploitation of their security holes by webmasters. With no oversight of proprietary browser develpment, there is little that the average surfer can do to protect themselves. Other attacks, such as those involving data theft, password cracking and password posting, are the actions of malicious surfers or competitors. These attacks can be defended against with proactive or reactive detection systems.

Whatever the origins of the attacks, awareness and constant (potentially automated) vigilance are the only means to defeating them. And since the law appears to be not a idiot, but merely a long way from catching up from the recent rapid advances in technology, it is up to the netizens themselves (and most especially, the potential targets of attacks), to provide their own security perimeters.

Hopefully this brief examination of some of the common attacks used on the Web will raise the reader's awareness enough to effect a secure perimeter.

Preprocessor Algorithm for Network Management Codebook

Minaxi Gupta

College of Computing
Georgia Institute of Technology
801 Atlantic Drive, Atlanta, GA 30332-0280
minaxi@cc.gatech.edu

Mani Subramanian

Georgia Institute of Technology
manis@cc.gatech.edu

Abstract

As the size of networks increases, real-time fault management becomes difficult due to the volume of traffic. A single problem can generate numerous symptoms, which are received as events by a network management system. These events could be correlated to deduce the source of the problem. One of the correlation techniques used is *codebook approach*, developed by Yemini et. al. Codebook is a matrix relating problems with symptoms. We present a way to transform the original algorithm used in deriving the codebook. Our algorithm improves the efficiency by reducing the matrix as well as by ensuring the selection of minimum number of symptoms required to uniquely identify each problem in the codebook. This avoids an exponential growth in the number of symptoms as number of problems increase, which in turn shows up as saving in real-time processing.

1 Introduction

As the size of networks increases, real-time fault management becomes difficult due to the volume of traffic. A single problem can generate numberous symptoms, which are received as events by a network management system. These events could be correlated to deduce the source of the problem.

There are various fault correlation techniques available. Prominent ones out of these are: *Rule-based reasoning* (a rule base contains expert knowledge in the form of if-then or condition-action rules), *Case-based reasoning* (these systems store knowledge as a repository of successful cases of solved problems and when the system is presented with a problems, it searches for similar cases in its database), *Reasoning with generic models* (generic models rely on generic algorithms to correlate events based on an abstraction of system architecture and its components), *Probability networks* (these networks works on the probability of correctness of hypothesis about the state of the system), *Model-based reasoning* (this involves creating a model which represents the underlying system being monitored, an example of this would be a finite state machine), and *codebook approach* (this approach treats detection and identification of exception events in a system as a coding problem). Out of the above mentioned available event correlation and management approaches, we have selected *Codebook Approach* because of its superiority over the other techniques. The basic idea of this approach is to form a matrix relating potential problems with the symptoms that manifest them. Such a matrix is usually very large and for fast run-time detection, one needs to apply efficient algorithms to reduce its size (the resultant matrix is referred to as codebook, and is the main focus of this paper), still maintaining enough information to be able to detect and uniquely identify the root cause of the problem. Run-time decoding of problems uses the codebook and employs best-fit approaches to conclude the occurrence of problems.

The basis of our present work is the original work by Yemini et. al. ([1, 2]) on codebook approach. In this paper, we present a method of pre-processing the matrix made up of problems and symptoms which produces optimal (minimal), mathematically provable codebook if the matrix lends itself to an optimal solution. The work presented in this paper improves upon the original codebook approach. The meaning of the terms used will be explained in more detail in subsequent sections.

2 Codebook Approach

In codebook approach ([1, 2]), event correlation (correlating observed symptoms to specific problems) is split into two separate activities: (1) generating efficient codes for problem identification, and (2) decoding the event stream. Using this technique, detection and identification of problems in the system can be done efficiently due to following reasons. First, the redundant and inefficient data is eliminated during code generation, leaving a greatly reduced amount of data to be analyzed during the decoding phase, and second, comparing codes against observed symptoms significantly reduces computational complexity.

There is a four-step process that accomplishes the above. It includes

- Specifying an event model (possible problems that can occur in the system under consideration) and a propagation model (how these events propagate to generate observable symptoms) for components in the system. This specification includes the exceptional events associated with each type of component, their corresponding local symptoms, and the potential relationships with other components along which events can propagate.

- Creating a representation of possible problems and their symptoms for the system to be monitored. The preferred way for this type of representation is a matrix. This matrix contains a mapping of symptoms to likely problems in the system. Typically, such a matrix will contain 1s and 0s in each cell. Since some problems can occur with higher probability than other, probabilities can be included in this matrix to ensure more focus on problems that are more likely. By eliminating loops and repetitions of rows and columns, the matrix is made *well-formed*.

- Finding a minimal codebook by reducing the amount of information in the above matrix to the minimum required to identify uniquely problems. Codebook should be able to tolerate loss of events or generation of spurious symptoms, this can be done by introducing redundancy in the selected symptoms.

- Continuously monitoring and decoding the symptoms by locating the *best-fit* problem in the optimal codebook which matches a particular set of symptoms.

3 Optimal Codebook Generation

Our work assumes that first two stages of the codebook have been accomplished as described by Yemini et. al. [2]. We start with a well-formed matrix. The goal is to reduce it to generate the optimal (minimal) codebook. Initially, we assume no error tolerance by our codebook. This means that loss of symptoms, or generation of spurious symptoms will result in incorrect decoding of problem occurrence at run-time.

To motivate the need for such a codebook, an example follows.

A well-formed matrix for a system with three problems represented by symptoms

---

along rows and problems along columns is shown in Figure 1.

	p1	p2	p3
s1	1	0	1
s2	0	0	1
s3	1	1	1
s4	0	1	0
s5	0	1	1
s6	1	0	0
s7	1	1	0

Figure 1: A *well-formed* matrix for three problem case

An optimal codebook, however, for above well-formed matrix would end up as in Figure 2.

	p1	p2	p3
s1	1	0	1
s5	0	1	1

Figure 2: Optimal codebook for matrix in Figure 1

As this simple example shows, only two symptoms are needed to distinguish among three problems, hence keeping seven symptoms (as the original well-formed matrix did) to be decoded at run-time is an overkill. In the subsequent discussion, we will explain the mathematical limits of the optimal number of symptoms that a codebook should have depending on the number of problems and how to achieve that limit.

3.1 Well-Formed Matrix

Ideally, a well-formed matrix for n problems should contain only $2^n - 1$ symptoms at maximum. This is because, mathematically, there can be only 2^n combinations of 1s and 0s possible if there are no common rows. Out of these, the row containing all 0s does not help us distinguish any problems from each other(mathematically speaking, the row containing all 1s also does not help us distinguish any problem from any other, but in real world, that can be useful, hence we keep that), so those can be eliminated. We will

assume that the well-formed matrix provided to us as input is an ideal one (that it has all possible combinations of 1s and 0s). This is what we mean by *a matrix lending itself to optimal solution*. A non-ideal matrix may be have far fewer rows to lend itself to optimal solution.

3.2 Mathematical Limits

Let's start with some motivation for what the algorithm should accomplish and what the mathematical limits are on the optimal codebook.

Given n problems, to be able to distinguish each problem from all others, we need following number of distinct cases

$$(n - 1) + (n - 2) + ... + 1 = n(n - 1)/2 \quad (1)$$

This is because the first problem needs to be distinguished from (n-1) other problems (hence, there are (n-1) cases), the second problem needs to be distinguished from (n-2) other problems (because the second problem has already been distinguished from the first) and so on. The (n-1)th problem just needs to be distinguished from 1 other problem, the last one. For a four problem case, the cases can be pictorially explained in Figure 3.

Total number of cases for four problem case: $3 + 2 + 1 = 6$ If we substitute $n = 4$ in Equation 1, we get the same result.

Each symptom eliminates several cases. If k symptoms are required to distinguish n problems, we want following to hold true:

$$2^k - 1 \geq n \quad (2)$$

The reason for this is as follows. If k symptoms are selected, we have 2^k combinations of 1s and 0s available at our disposal. Out of this, the combination consisting of all 0s needs to be ruled out, since that won't

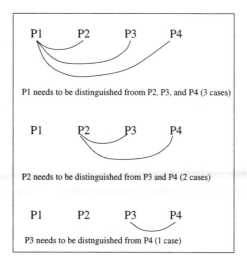

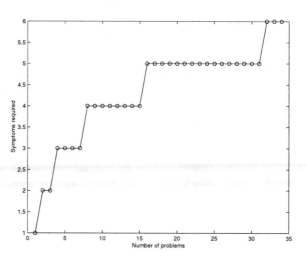

Figure 3: Enumeration of *cases* for four problem case

Figure 4: Windows of symptoms for various problem ranges

help distinguish any of the problems from any other.

There is a window of problems, that a certain number of symptoms can distinguish. This window (denoted by w) is given by

$$2^{k-1} \leq w \leq 2^k - 1 \qquad (3)$$

Figure 4 gives a feel for that window of problems. As is clear from the graph, the window keeps getting wider with n. The fact that these k symptoms are sufficient can be proven by checking that they have at least $n(n-1)/2$ cases embedded in them.

3.3 Pre-processing the Well-Formed Matrix

The pre-processing that we propose on the well-formed matrix is guided by the following observation. Intuitively, to select the minimum set of symptoms for the codebook, the best approach is to eliminate as many cases as possible with each symptom that we select. Let us now see how we can do that.

To distinguish n problems, if we select the first symptom of the type

1 0 0.... 0 (only one 1, rest (n-1) are 0s),

This would help us distinguish the first problem from all the other problems, but no other problems can be distinguished from any other problems. Hence it eliminates (n-1) cases out of the $n(n-1)/2$ that we need to eliminate. However, it is not the optimal one to select. Let us consider the case where we select a symptom that has approximately equal number of 1s and 0s (approximate, because for odd number of problems, number of 1s and 0s are not equal), i.e., the symptom was of the type

1 0 1 0 .... 1 0 (approximately n/2 0s and n/2 1s)

The 1s and 0s need not be in any specific order – we call such symptoms as *balanced* symptoms). This could eliminate 50% of the cases we need to eliminate right after the first symptoms is chosen (because of complementary nature of the symptom). Eliminating 50% would mean eliminating $n(n-1)/4$, which is larger than (n-1) for n>4 (implying larger the problems, better it is to start with balanced symptoms). The exact number of cases eliminated for each problem will depend on the particular combination of 1s and 0s in the balanced symptom.

For subsequent symptoms also, if we could eliminate as many rows as possible (upto 50%) of the remaining cases at each stage following similar procedure, we are guaranteed

---

to select the minimum number of symptoms, because this would imply that we select approximately $\log_2(n + 1)$ symptoms (this expression can be derived from Equation 2). We are now ready to detail pre-processing steps.

- Step 1: Sort the well-formed matrix, bring the *balanced* symptoms on top.

- Step 2: Eliminate *compliments* to prepare the matrix for our algorithm that selects codebook.

We would illustrate the effect of each step on sets of three and four problems.

4   Pre-Processing Algorithm

4.1   Step 1

We first sort the well formed matrix in our hand. We call this new matrix as *sorted-well-formed matrix*. The idea behind sorting is to keep the balanced symptoms on the top of the matrix (as explained in the previous section, balanced symptoms are the best ones to select). Figuring out whether a symptom is balanced or not takes O(n). This can be done in one pass and the time taken for this would be O(mn), where n is the number of problems and m is the number of symptoms. The next pass can naively go through this list of numbers and puts the balanced symptoms before the unbalanced ones (it will be a little more involved for matrices with odd number of problems, because for odd number of problems, rows with (n-1)/2 and (n+1)/2 1s in them will be balanced, as against the n/2 for even number of problems). The sort also takes time O(m^2), where m is the number of symptoms. There are many better algorithms that can be employed for this purpose, but since it does not affect the complexity of our solution, we would keep this simple one for the time being.

We now illustrate examples of sorting three (odd number of problems) and four (even number of problems) problem matrices.

A three problem well-formed matrix can have only seven combinations (of course many permutations of the rows are possible and the real world matrix may not even have all of them). Figure 5 shows a three problem well-formed matrix.

	p1	p2	p3
s1	0	0	1
s2	0	1	0
s3	0	1	1
s4	1	0	0
s5	1	0	1
s6	1	1	0
s7	1	1	1

Figure 5:   Another *well-formed* matrix for three problem case

After sorting, it would not change for this particular case because all but the last combination of all 1's are balanced (except the last one).

For four problems, maximum well-formed matrix would look like (fifteen combinations possible) Figure 6.

	p1	p2	p3	p4
s1	0	0	0	1
s2	0	0	1	0
s3	0	0	1	1
s4	0	1	0	0
s5	0	1	0	1
s6	0	1	1	0
s7	0	1	1	1
s8	1	0	0	0
s9	1	0	0	1
s10	1	0	1	0
s11	1	0	1	1
s12	1	1	0	0
s13	1	1	0	1
s14	1	1	1	0
s15	1	1	1	1

Figure 6:   *Well-formed* matrix for four problem case

After sorting, the balanced symptoms get pushed to the top and the well formed matrix for four problems changes to give us Figure 7.

	p1	p2	p3	p4
s3	0	0	1	1
s5	0	1	0	1
s6	0	1	1	0
s9	1	0	0	1
s10	1	0	1	0
s12	1	1	0	0
s1	0	0	0	1
s2	0	0	1	0
s4	0	1	0	0
s7	0	1	1	1
s8	1	0	0	0
s11	1	0	1	1
s13	1	1	0	1
s14	1	1	1	0
s15	1	1	1	1

Figure 7: *Sorted-well-formed* matrix for four problem case

4.2 Step 2

Eliminate all the compliment rows from the well-formed matrix. If the matrix had all possible combinations in it, it would cut down the matrix size in half. The reason we eliminate the compliments is because although the compliments mean different symbols physically, they do not contain any different information from each other mathematically. To see that, consider symptoms in Figure 8.

	p1	p2	p3	p4
s1	1	1	0	1
s2	0	0	1	0

Figure 8: Figure showing *compliment* symptoms

The first symptom distinguishes p1, p2 and p4 from p3. The same is the case with the second symptom.

While deciding to eliminate one of the compliments, we give preference to the symptom with more 1s in it. The reason for this choice is completely physical. The symptom with more 1s is likely to be more useful (because it shows up for more problems) than the one with more 0s. If there are equal number of 1s and 0s, we simply choose the one that

has more 1s in the beginning. From the face of it, it seems more like a convention. But in reality, this helps select better symptoms. There can be other choices as well for choosing symptoms, logically, this seems to work the best.

This operation takes $O(m^2 n)$ time, where m is the number of symptoms because for every row, one may have to go all the way down to find the compliment and at each stage, $O(n)$ comparisons are required for n problems.

After eliminating the compliments, while giving priority to the symptoms with more 1s than 0s, we get Figures 9, and 10 matrices for three and four problems respectively.

	p1	p2	p3
s3	0	1	1
s5	1	0	1
s6	1	1	0
s7	1	1	1

Figure 9: *Minimized-sorted-well-formed* matrix for three problems

	p1	p2	p3	p4
s9	1	0	0	1
s10	1	0	1	0
s12	1	1	0	0
s7	0	1	1	1
s11	1	0	1	1
s13	1	1	0	1
s14	1	1	1	0
s15	1	1	1	1

Figure 10: *Minimized-sorted-well-formed* matrix for four problems

In the matrix for four problem case, s9 was given a priority over s6 while eliminating compliments because, although they have the same number of 1s and 0s in them, s9 has more 0s in the beginning than s6. Also, the matrix might look a little different depending on the exact algorithm that is used while re-shuffling the symptoms. We just mark the symptoms that we would eliminate and later just copy the un-marked ones in order.

These matrices are called *minimized-*

sorted-well-formed matrices.

The number of balanced symptoms in the matrix for even and odd number of problems can be expressed by the formulae in Equations 4 and 5 respectively.

$$\frac{{}^nC_{n/2}}{2} \quad \text{even case} \qquad (4)$$

$$\frac{{}^nC_{(n-1)/2} + {}^nC_{(n+1)/2}}{2} \quad \text{odd case} \qquad (5)$$

This is because for even number of problems, we just need to choose $n/2$ positions for 0s and 1s can go in the rest of the positions (and vice versa). For odd number of problems, there are two ways to choose balances symptoms. Hence correspondingly, for odd number of problems, there are two terms. Since we have eliminated compliments, the number of combinations that we get need to be halved, hence the above formulae. These formulae can be verified with the following results.

5   Codebook Algorithm

Having pre-processed the well-formed matrix, we will analyze the behavior of codebook algorithm using pre-processed matrix. Because of the pre-processing steps, the algorithm will always generate minimal codebook if the well-formed matrix contains adequate symptoms to uniquely distinguish between problems, i.e., it is always optimal.

The idea behind the algorithm is very simple. We start with the first problem and see how many symptoms will uniquely distinguish it from all other problems. For all other problems, we first check to see if the symptoms that have been already selected will suffice to distinguish it from all other problem. If the answer is yes, then we move on to the next problem, if not, then we determine which symptoms are to be added. We work our way through the input matrix sequentially.

We will illustrate the working of this algorithm on the *minimized-sorted- well-formed matrix* for three problems first.

- It chooses s5. s5 distinguishes p1 from p2 (s3 distinguishes p1 from p2, but does not show up for p1, while s5 shows up whenever p1 happens).

- To distinguish p1 from p3, the algorithm selects s6. Now p1 has been distinguished from all other problems.

- Now it will move on to other problems. In this case, it is just p2. The algorithm will first check to see if already selected symptoms are enough. It turns out that both s5 and s6 can be used to distinguish p2 from p3 as well. It should be noted that even s5 can be used to distinguish p2 from p3, though it does not show up for p2 (as explained later, a sanity check will eliminate the worst case scenario of running into a case where mathematically a problem can be diagnosed, but practically it can not be). Only when we pick a new symptom do we make sure that the symptom actually shows up for that particular problem.

The algorithm selects two symptoms for three problems, which is the minimum required mathematically. The resulting codebook is shown in Figure 11.

	p1	p2	p3
s5	1	0	1
s6	1	1	0

Figure 11: Codebook for matrix of Figure 5

Running this algorithm on Figure 5 without pre-processing it, produces Figure 12.

	p1	p2	p3
s4	1	0	0
s6	1	1	0
s1	0	0	1

Figure 12: Codebook for matrix of Figure 5, without pre-processing

This is not the optimal codebook because it has one more symptom than the minimum codebook. This shows that without pre-processing, optimal algorithm could fail to produce optimal codebook.

The algorithm will work on *minimized-sorted well-formed matrix* for four problems as follows.

- It chooses s9 because that is the first symptom that shows up for p1. s9 distinguishes p1 from p2 and p3.

- To distinguish p1 from p4, the algorithm will select s10 (the algorithm always starts from the first symptom). At this point, p1 has been distinguished from all other problems.

- For p2, s9 (which has already been selected), distinguishes it from p4 but not from p3 and s10 distinguishes it from p4. So, p2 is also taken care of.

- p3 can be distinguished from p4 using s9. So, all problems can be distinguished from each other.

- The algorithm does a sanity check at this stage (because it claims to have distinguished all problems in less symptoms than mathematically required). It turns out that if only s9 and s10 are used, even if p2 occurs, it would not show up. To avoid this, the algorithm selects s12 and is done generating the codebook at this time.

The resulting minimal codebook for four problem case would be as shown in Figure 13.

	p1	p2	p3	p4
s9	1	0	0	1
s10	1	0	1	0
s12	1	1	0	0

Figure 13: Codebook for matrix of Figure 6

It is clear that the algorithm selects three symptoms for four problems. It is easy to show that if the initial rows of the matrix are not made the right kind by pre-processing, because of the nature of the algorithm, it would selected many more symptoms (maximum number equal to the number of problems) than the optimal (hence the argument that the pre-processing work that we have done will eliminate the possibility of bigger codebooks). For small problem sets, this difference is not very prominent, but for larger problem sets, it could effect the run-time problem identification adversely. However, it should be noted that there could be some real-world matrices that will not have enough balanced symptoms (in particular, they may have lesser than the optimal codebook requirements). In that case, the algorithm will be forced to generate a sub-optimal codebook. In practice, the redundancy in the matrices is so much that such a case would be rare, else we will not really need codebooks at all!

6 Discussion

Figure 14 shows that the number of problems that can be detected at run-time by same number of symptoms increase exponentially. We have used the lower limit of the window of problems that can be detected using the same number of symptoms to be on the conservative side. We have used the relation $n = 2^{k-1}$ (lower end of the window from Equation 3) as our y-axis parameter.

We now compute net savings due to pre-processing input matrices.

At the higher end of a window (for exam-

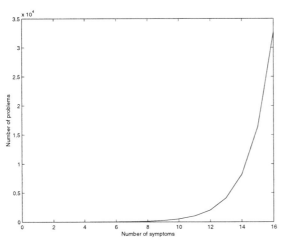

Figure 14: Number of problems that can be detected at run-time using same number of symptoms increase exponentially

ple, $n = 15$, $k = 4$), savings are given by

$$n \quad - \quad \lceil \log_2(n+1) \rceil \qquad (6)$$

At the lower end of the same window ($n = 8$, $k = 4$), savings are given by

$$n \quad - \quad (\lceil \log_2(n) \rceil + 1) \qquad (7)$$

Equations 6 and 7 give the reduction in the number of symptoms our preprocessor algorithm guarantees over worst case codebook (if the pre-processing of well-formed matrix was not done and codebook algorithm was run on it). The way we compute savings is as follows. Without pre-processing, in the worst case, for n problems, n symptoms will be selected by codebook algorithm to uniquely identify the problem. However, if the well-formed matrix is pre-processed, only $\lceil \log_2(n+1) \rceil$ or $\lceil \log_2(n) \rceil + 1$ symptoms are needed for optimal codebook, depending on which end of the window one is in (these formulae are derived using Equation 3). Average number of symptoms required for a given number of problems are given by

$$(\lceil \log_2(n+1) \rceil \quad + \quad \lceil \log_2(n) \rceil + 1)/2 \qquad (8)$$

Hence the average savings are given as

$$n - (\lceil \log_2(n+1) \rceil \quad + \quad \lceil \log_2(n) \rceil + 1)/2 \qquad (9)$$

Figure 15 brings about some of these points more explicitly. It compares the number of symptoms in the final codebook generated using the codebook algorithm with and without the pre-processing of input matrix. As is very clear from the figure, pre-processing reduces the number of symptoms substantially. Also, as the number of problems increases, the savings increase, making the difference more prominent (and in turn, ensuring more real-time savings).

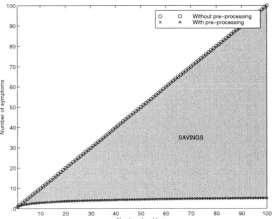

Figure 15: Comparison of number of symptoms in output codebook with and without pre-processing of input matrix

7 Summary

We have developed a two step pre-processing algorithm that ensures that the codebook algorithm would generate mathematically provable optimal codebook. Using the pre-processing algorithm for a given number of symptoms, number of problems that can be identified increases exponentially. For a practical situation, number of problem being finite, number of symptoms needed reaches a plateau, if the pre-processing algorithm is used.

The Packet Vault: Secure Storage of Network Data

C.J. Antonelli
M. Undy
P. Honeyman

Center for Information Technology Integration
The University of Michigan
Ann Arbor
`{cja,mundy,honey}@citi.umich.edu`

Abstract

This paper describes the packet vault, a cryptographically secured archiver of network packet data. The vault captures network packets, encrypts them, and writes them to long-term CD-ROM storage for later analysis and for evidentiary purposes. The cryptographic organization of the vault permits selected traffic to be made available without exposing other traffic.

1. Introduction

The goal of the packet vault project at the Center for Information Technology Integration is to provide cryptographically secured long-term storage of network packets for later use as input data for intrusion detection algorithms or for possible evidentiary purposes.

Creating a complete, permanent record of all activity on a subnet addresses security threats in several ways. First, intrusion detection algorithms can be executed using the record as the input packet source. Detectors can be run over the same record with different parameter settings, outputs of different detectors can be compared, and new detectors can be created and evaluated against the record. Conducting such experiments requires a complete record of packets.

Second, in response to an intrusion in progress, the packet vault can be attached to a subnet under attack; the packets it stores may be used to determine quickly the source and nature of the intrusion, and thus help shape the response. In addition, the vault can be permanently connected to a suspect subnet, allowing the record to be examined periodically.

Finally, a properly constructed corpus of packet data may serve as evidence in legal proceedings.

In the remainder of this paper, we describe the goals of the packet vault, then discuss the hardware, software, and cryptographic organization of the vault. We then describe our experiences, discuss some issues — including legal issues and the strength of DES — in operating the vault, and conclude with a discussion of future work.

2. Goals

The architecture of the packet vault reflects the following goals:

- **Commodity.** We want to build a packet vault from commodity hardware and software, notwithstanding the attraction of expensive machines with fast buses and I/O devices. With a vault built from cheap parts in hand, we feel we can trade money for speed by buying faster parts (in a year).

- **Completeness.** To create a complete record, it is vital to capture and store every packet. We suspect that an adversary can exploit any form of packet triage; the only way to defend against all such attacks is to build a vault that stores packets at the maximum rate the network delivers them.

- **Permanency.** We decided from the outset that our storage medium would be CD-ROM, because of consistently bad long-term experiences with data storage on magnetic tapes, and because we wanted to learn a bit about CD-ROM writers. We are not concerned with the relatively low data rates of the writers, as we can depend on them to improve, and in any case we can use multiple writers.

- **Security.** Should the CD-ROMs containing network traffic become available for unsupervised inspection, either intentionally or by larceny, it is critical that the data stored on them be protected with strong cryptography. Accordingly, our design goals acknowledge the possibility of loss of physical control by assuming the worst, anticipating potential publication of the encrypted data. It is also vital that the data be organized in such a way that some subsets of the traffic can be revealed without exposing others. Ideally, we would like to publish keys that unlock certain data on a given CD-ROM, without the possession of those keys exposing other data on it.

We observe that our goals of commodity and completeness are in tension, particularly at network speeds above 10 Mbps. Our goal is to construct a vault that can store all packets on a typically loaded 10 Mbps Ethernet network, and to depend on faster hardware to improve the rate at which packets can be acquired.

3. Architecture

A critical question is whether a single commodity machine can accept packets from the network, encrypt them, and write them to CD-ROM without becoming overloaded. Early experiences with bursty Ethernets coupled with the real-time requirements of CD-ROM recorders[†] convinced us that two machines would be necessary.

The packet vault hardware is composed of two 133 MHz PCI-bus Pentium machines interconnected via a private 100 Mbps Ethernet. One machine (the "listener") is connected to the network being monitored and is used to capture and encrypt packets, which are then sent over the private Ethernet. The listener never stores packets on magnetic disk.

The other machine (the "writer") receives encrypted packets and assembles them on magnetic disk for subsequent writing to CD-ROM. The two magnetic disks on the writer are attached to a common SCSI bus. A second SCSI bus dedicated to the CD-ROM recorder (CD-R) prevents bus contention. Figure 1 shows the hardware architecture of the packet vault.

We chose UNIX for both listener and writer for its familiarity and flexibility. OpenBSD was chosen for the listener for its kernel packet filtering support; early availability of CD-R drivers dictated the choice of Linux for the writer.

We use BPF [1] on the listener to capture all packets seen on the 10 Mbps network being monitored and write them to an *accumulator* file in a memory file system (MFS [2]). We modified the BPF code to pass

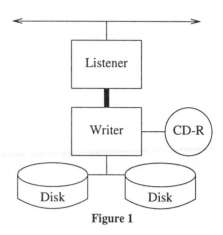

Figure 1

packets directly from the kernel network buffers to MFS, obviating two copies between user and kernel space. A listener process monitors the size of the accumulator file and renames it when it reaches 4 MB in size or after 1 minute has elapsed, which keeps the size of the MFS packet files manageable. The names of the packet files reflect the time of day they were created.

Another process on the listener polls the MFS for new packet files, encrypts their contents, and uses rcp to copy the files over the private 100 Mbps link to the writer. Unencrypted data are stored only in the MFS, so in the event of a system failure no unencrypted data remain.[‡]

When enough packet files have accumulated on the writer to fill a CD-ROM, a background process is spawned on the writer. The writer process generates an ISO-9660-compliant image on magnetic disk containing the packet files and the cryptographic material necessary to permit later recovery of the packet data. The image is written, then purged from magnetic disk. A double-buffering scheme avoids disk contention between image generation writes and subsequent packet file writes on the same physical disk. The packet data path is shown in Figure 2.

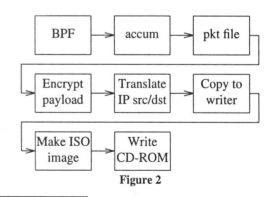

Figure 2

[†] Our CD-ROM recorder, like all early commodity recorders, possesses a small (512 KB) data buffer and thus requires the attached host to maintain a constant data rate during the entire time the CD-ROM is being written; failure to maintain the required rate ruins the CD-ROM.

[‡] We run the listener with swapping disabled, but acknowledge potential attacks on RAM hardware [3].

---

4. Cryptographic Organization

The cryptographic organization of the vault follows from our requirement that vault data be publishable — in this way we anticipate the possibility of unrestricted access to a mass storage device filled with vault data. We also endeavor to provide access to individual packet contents with fairly fine granularity.

Our basic strategy is to encrypt all packet payloads; the challenge is to devise a means of associating different keys with different packets at some level of granularity. The ends of the spectrum are unattractive: one key per CD-ROM risks a serious breach if lost, while managing a different key for each packet becomes unmanageable.

Our unit of granularity for associating packets with keys is the *conversation*, defined as a set of packets with the same pair of source and destination IP addresses. Including port numbers would offer finer control, but would also require special treatment for non-TCP streams and create problems with port-agile applications.

Each CD-ROM *volume* holds sufficient information to reconstruct the packet traffic it stores, thus no ancillary information need be managed. We use a multi-level encryption scheme. Symmetric key encryption is used to seal packet payloads and any additional information necessary to reconstruct the packets (explained below). Asymmetric key encryption is used to encrypt the symmetric keys. A trusted third party such as the Regents of the University of Michigan holds the private key. Figure 3 shows the cryptographic organization on CD-ROM.

Our implementation uses 1024 bit PGP [4] for asymmetric key and DESX [5] for symmetric key encryption. Starting with Karn's DES implementation [6] we added both pre- and post-whitening steps for each block:

$$DESX_{k.k_1.k_2}(x) = k_2 \oplus DES_k(k_1 \oplus x)$$

DES encrypts 64-bit blocks, so this requires $64 + 56 + 64 = 184$ bits of key material, and conservatively extends the effective key length of DES in our environment to at least 95 bits with respect to key search (in the sense of Kilian and Rogaway [5]), while adding a trivial amount of computation to each block encryption.[†]

[†] If an attacker could obtain all the plaintexts for all encrypted packets on a volume, and if the average packet length is 100 bytes, this would yield 6 million plaintext/ciphertext pairs. Rogaway's effective key length expression becomes $55+64-1-\log_2(6\times10^6) = 95$ bits [7].

Translation table symmetric key
Regent's public key

Volume master symmetric key
Regent's public key

Translation tables
Translation table key

Trans. header	Packet payload

Payload key

Figure 3

To hinder traffic analysis, we obscure source and destination addresses by substitution. A translation table mapping real to substituted addresses is encrypted with DESX using a *translation table key* K_T unique to each volume. To speed up searches for specific conversations, a second table holds all pairs of translated addresses for which at least one conversation exists on the CD-ROM. The absence of a given pair of addresses in the second table means the CD-ROM contains no packets of that conversation, obviating an exhaustive search to establish this fact. Both translation tables are written to CD-ROM.

A key is constructed for a given conversation by combining the concatenated, untranslated source and destination IP addresses with a 192-bit *volume master key* K_V using exclusive-or, and then using DESX in CBC mode to encrypt a 192-bit constant with the combined value:

$$K_{C_i} = DESX_{K_V \oplus (SA_i | | DA_i)}(CONST)$$

The resulting 192-bit *conversation key* K_{C_i} is used to encrypt packet payloads of the conversation:

$$C_i = DESX_{K_{C_i}}(P_i)$$

A new volume master key and translation table key are generated for each volume. Currently, they are computed from previous keys:

$$K_{V_{i+1}} = DESX_{K_{V_i}}(K_{V_i})$$

$$K_{T_{i+1}} = DESX_{K_{T_i}}(K_{T_i})$$

where K_{V_0} and K_{T_0} were randomly generated. This scheme does not exhibit good long-term randomness; we plan to replace this with a practically strong random data generator [8].

A new pair of PGP keys are generated per vault instance. The public key is used to seal the volume master and translation table keys before they are written to CD-ROM.

Finally, we have built a rudimentary decryption engine that reconstructs all packet traffic stored on a

---

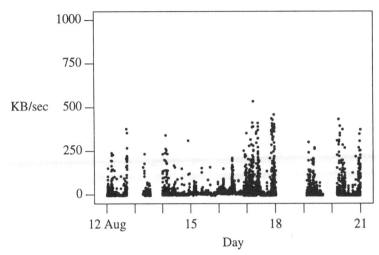

Figure 4 This graph shows vault throughput measured in kilobytes per second during the period 12–21 August 1998. Because values are averaged in 30-second intervals there is some peak clipping; the maximum observed value is 1.2 MB/sec.

CD-ROM given the private PGP key of the vault that created it. We have used the engine to verify the implementation of our cryptographic organization.

5. Experiences

The packet vault has been operational for the last year, irregularly collecting packets from a 10 Mbps Ethernet. The network is usually lightly loaded but there are periods when experimental video work causes traffic to exceed 70%. During the period 12-21 August 1998 we operated the vault continuously, collecting about 7.7 GB on 15 CDs. There were four interruptions of significant duration caused by vault failures during this period. Figure 4 shows a trace of the vault throughput.

The major challenge in the construction and operation of the vault has been systems engineering and integration. Bottlenecks discovered along the way were removed until the vault could handle the incoming network traffic. For example, it was discovered that passing packets in and out of the kernel from BPF to MFS was too slow, so we modified the listener's kernel to skip the kernel/user space copies.

Disk usage on the writer must be monitored closely because of the large data volumes. Currently, the vault does not clean up when interrupted. To achieve reliable operation on restarting, six locations spread across both machines must be checked for abandoned temporary files.

The data path consists of several stages, some of which process data in parallel, others sequentially. Payload encryption and network copying are the most costly operations in this pipeline, yet both of these operations occur sequentially. Generating the image

and writing the image to a CD are also costly, but as larger buffers are available for these steps only the average throughput is of importance.

If the sustained input rate exceeds the throughput of any stage in the data path, eventually some buffer becomes exhausted and the vault fails. The first failure is almost always caused by the MFS filling up, which crashes the listening process. Experimentally, with a 70% utilization of the source Ethernet, the vault crashes after about two minutes. Increasing buffer sizes is of limited practical value; doubling the memory allocated to MFS extends this time to four minutes.

At 70% network utilization, while the writer is busy generating a CD image, its disk and processor utilizations increases dramatically, and the `rcp` time increases by a factor of two to three. It takes about 7 minutes to generate an image under these conditions. A bug validated our assumption that double-buffering was needed: a failure to toggle the drive on which the image was being created resulted in packet files for every other volume being written to the same disk on which an image was being built; the resulting overload backed up the data path and crashed the vault.

The other obvious target for performance optimization is the encryption code. We use a machine-specific implementation of the DES code compiled with full optimization and aggressively cache the DES key schedules. These changes speed up the encryption task by over 80%, but opens the door to a denial of service attack by an adversary who manufactures packets that defeat the caching.

6. Discussion

The focus of this work is the creation of a cryptographically secured record of packet activity on a given subnet. The usefulness of such a record is in many ways dictated by the evidentiary requirements of the legal system. Our ability to construct an accurate record must also take into account the creativity and persistence of the adversary, which we consider to be nearly omnipotent. However, we do not address the threats outlined in Schneier and Kelsey [9], in which logging takes place on physically insecure systems; we assume the vault to be under strict physical and administrative control.

6.1. Legal issues

A study conducted by the Office of Policy Development and Education at the University of Michigan identifies a number of thorny legal issues connected with operation of the packet vault [10].

University of Michigan Policy forbids the interception of electronic mail without consent or a court order. Even in the absence of this policy, it is conceivable that a court would find that the vault is intercepting electronic mail under Title I of the Federal Electronic Communications Privacy Act (ECPA). Interception for research purposes might not fall under the so-called "system administrator exemption," which permits interception in the normal course of business or as necessary to protect the rights or property of the service provider, and could therefore be unlawful. In a similar vein, the Family Educational Rights and Privacy Act (FERPA) prohibits disclosing student records to anyone who does not have a specific need to see them.

More generally, the courts have have read the First Amendment of the United States Constitution to prohibit government action that would tend to discourage citizens from speaking their minds. This "chilling effect" applies here, as awareness of the vault's presence would tend to limit free speech by those whose subnets are being monitored.

The vault is a research instrument, so its use is under the purview of the University's regulations on research involving human subjects. While most such research requires informed consent, and the signing of a consent form, it is possible to get an exemption from a University Institutional Review Board. Exemptions can be granted to projects that involve little risk to subjects or where informing the subjects of the nature of the experiment could bias results. Since anyone who sends email to a user on a monitored subnet would arguably be a research subject, obtaining consent from all of them would be problematic.

Other issues potentially raised by use of the vault include increasing the likelihood of copyright violations, bypassing an institution's policies with respect to creating permanent records subject to Freedom of Information Act (FOIA) requests, increasing the likelihood of civil discovery "fishing expeditions" against the material contained in the vault, weakening users' Fourth Amendment protections against search and seizure, and increased exposure of the vault's operators to civil liability.

The question of whether encrypted text is legally the same as clear text has no definitive answer. In some cases, the purported protection offered by encryption is irrelevant; for example, it is likely that copyright infringement takes place when a work is copied, not when it is read.

The study recommends that, at a minimum, all users be notified of the vault's existence. This resolves some of the above legal issues. However, notification would not cure First Amendment "chilling," nor would it address the FOIA or FERPA issues. In addition, it is not clear how to obtain consent from remote correspondents of local users.

A recommended stronger form of consent would allow users to volunteer to be monitored, but requires us to separate on different sets of subnets those users who consent to monitoring and those who do not or to modify the vault to discard certain packets. Both approaches are problematic.

Other recommendations include physically securing all archival materials, maintaining an access audit trail, capturing fewer types of packets, and using the vault only for investigation of specific, ongoing security incidents.

For these reasons, we have chosen not to attach the vault to any production subnets at Michigan, nor to gather many packets. The data we do have were collected on a semi-private CITI subnet for a limited period after all users of the subnet were notified in advance.

In corporate environments, by contrast, the repeated refusal by the Congress to pass laws restricting workplace monitoring suggests that a business is free to monitor workers' communications on its computer systems without consent or knowledge. In fact, in securities trading environments, Wall Street regulations require such monitoring. Use of our vault is less controversial in these environments (at least for now).

6.2. Limits of DES

Recently, the Electronic Frontier Foundation's DES cracker and a worldwide network of personal computers jointly won RSA Data Security's DES Challenge III, obtaining the encryption key to a DES-encrypted message in 22 hours via a brute-force search of the key space [11]. Two previous challenges were successfully cracked by similar methods. Since the vault uses DES at the core of its encryption strategy, these events call the security of the data stored on vault CD-ROMs into question, especially in the long term.

First, we believe our use of DESX inhibits the use of brute-force DES crackers because it is difficult for an attacker to derive a plaintext/DES-ciphertext pair from a set of plaintext/DESX-ciphertext pairs obtained by a chosen-plaintext attack [7]. However, we have not quantified the effect of DES's rapidly declining strength on our cryptographic organization.

Second, we can replace DES with more secure triple-DES; this increases the key length of all symmetric keys as recommended by Blaze *et al* [12] and is a straightforward modification. However, triple-DES is roughly three times as slow as DES; even though processors today are more than three times faster than they were when we started our project, the additional encryption cost may be prohibitive.

Finally, we can look to other recent proposed encryption algorithms and the results of the Advanced Encryption Standard effort to deliver a more secure encryption algorithm for our vault, although this is necessarily a long-term prospect.

In any event, recent developments have shown that ciphers once considered secure are rapidly being broken as technologies and analysis techniques mature. It is not reasonable to assume that any cipher will be strong enough to withstand decades of determined attacks, which implies that loss of physical control of the vault media will lead to exposure of the data they carry.

6.3. Limits of Passive Protocol Analysis

Ptacek and Newsham point out a shortcoming in passive protocol analysis due to the inability of an intrusion detection system to determine accurately what is happening on networked machines [13]. They identify three classes of attacks: insertion, in which the detector is made to see traffic that the victim does not; evasion, in which the victim sees traffic the detector does not; and denial of service, in which the detector is fed traffic designed to cause it to fail.

The packet vault is largely immune from these attacks — because the vault obtains packets directly from the link level device driver, it does nothing beyond reading and storing each packet that arrives on the interface. Fragment reassembly, management of TCP connection state, *etc.* are left to the analysis phase after the CD-ROMs are written. This causes attacks on the vault by, say, deliberately overlapping fragments to fail, as the vault does not reassemble them; further, the complete evidence is stored for later analysis. There is some potential for denial-of-service attacks, including the one mentioned earlier that defeats the caching of key schedules.

As long as the recording rate exceeds the arrival rate, then the packet vault defeats evasion and denial of service attacks. Insertion attacks are possible, but permanent storage of all packets permits later replay on appropriately instrumented test gear.

6.4. Evidence handling

Sommer outlines general principles for the production of reliable, computer-derived evidence [14]:

- the scene of the crime must be "frozen"
- there must be continuity of evidence
- all procedures used in examination should be auditable

The packet vault records onto CD-ROM — an immutable material that effectively "freezes" the evidence — all data that traverse a snoopable subnet. While it is possible that some packets traversing the network during periods of peak load are not seen by the vault, its architecture precludes the generation of spurious packets, *i.e.,* the vault does not manufacture evidence. The vault thus provides evidence that can be used to support other materials, such as audit logs.

Continuity of evidence is indicated by the data handling architecture of the vault. The monotonically increasing time-stamped sequence of stored packets lends further support for continuity of evidence. Including a digital signature with the CD-ROM contents would help prove the authenticity of any CD-ROM that purports to have been generated by the vault.

The vault source code and, potentially, the contents of the CD-ROMs are available for public inspection, which allows the procedures to be audited.

6.5. Future work

The next major step involves focusing on intrusion detection methods, replaying vault data in a virtual network testbed. Better administrative and fault-handling scripts are also needed for graceful shutdown and restart of the vault. An occasional inability of the writer to allocate buffer space for the private Ethernet link remains to be resolved. The high disk loads caused by creating an ISO-9660 image *en masse* could be ameliorated by constructing the image incrementally. We plan to replace our hastily constructed key generator with a practically strong random data accumulator and generator [8]. We will investigate the issues in replacing DES by triple-DES or another cipher to provide a more secure cryptographic organization for our vault. Determining and recording the number of packets dropped during the generation of and digitally signing each CD-ROM would improve the evidence handling capabilities of the vault. Finally, these and other steps are necessary to convert the vault from a research instrument to a highly-available packet capture and storage mechanism.

7. Acknowledgements

We thank Mike Stolarchuk for his contributions to the architecture of the packet vault. He also wrote the BPF layer modifications, and provided invaluable systems engineering assistance. Dan Boneh suggested the conversation key mechanism. Joe Saul thoroughly investigated the legal issues in operating the vault. We thank Dan Geer for his helpful review and commentary. This work was partially supported by Bellcore.

8. References

1. Steven McCanne and Van Jacobson, "The BSD Packet Filter: A New Architecture for User-level Packet Capture," pp. 259–269 in *Proc. of Winter USENIX Conf.*, San Diego (January, 1993).

2. Marshall Kirk McKusick, Michael J. Karels, and Keith Bostic, "A Pageable Memory Based Filesystem," pp. 137–143 in *Proc. Summer USENIX Conf.*, Anaheim (June, 1990).

3. Peter Gutmann, "Secure Deletion of Data from Magnetic and Solid-State Memory," pp. 77–89 in *Proc. of Sixth USENIX Security Symp.*, San Jose (July, 1996).

4. William Stallings, "Protect Your Privacy: The PGP User's Guide," *Prentice-Hall*, New Jersey (1995).

5. Joe Kilian and Phillip Rogaway, "How to Protect DES Against Exhaustive Key Search," pp. 252–267 in *Advances in Cryptology - Crypto '96, Lecture Notes in Computer Science*, ed. N. Koblitz, Springer-Verlag (1996).

6. Phil Karn, `karn@unix.ka9q.ampr.org` (December, 1995).

7. Phillip Rogaway, *RSA Laboratories' CryptoBytes* **2**(2) (Summer, 1996).

8. Peter Gutmann, "Software Generation of Cryptographically Strong Random Numbers," pp. 243–257 in *Proc. of Seventh USENIX Security Symp.*, San Antonio (January, 1998).

9. B. Schneier and J. Kelsey, "Cryptographic Support for Secure Logs on Untrusted Machines," pp. 53–62 in *Proc. of Seventh USENIX Security Symp.*, San Antonio (January, 1998).

10. Joseph M. Saul, Peter Honeyman, and Virginia Rezmierski, "Policy Issues Related to Network Monitoring: The Secure Packet Vault," Unpublished, Ann Arbor (July, 1997).

11. Electronic Frontier Foundation, in `www.eff.org/DesCracker/`.

12. Matt Blaze, Whitfield Diffie, Ronald L. Rivest, Bruce Schneier, Tsutomu Shimomura, Eric Thompson, and Michael Wiener, "Minimal Key Lengths for Symmetric Ciphers to Provide Adequate Commercial Security ," in `www.counterpane.com/keylength.html` (January, 1996).

13. Thomas H. Ptacek and Timothy N. Newsham, *Insertion, Deletion, and Denial of Service: Eluding Network Intrusion Detection,* Secure Networks, Inc. (January, 1998).

14. Peter Sommer, "Computer Forensics: an introduction," in `www.virtualcity.co.uk/vcaforens.htm` (1997).

Real-Time Intrusion Detection and Suppression in ATM Networks

R. Bettati   W. Zhao   D. Teodor

Department of Computer Science
Texas A&M University
College Station, TX 77843-3112

Abstract

Distributed mission critical systems require support for ultra-secure communication, in which intrusions must be detected and suppressed in real time, possibly before the affected messages reach the receiver. When the distributed application has real-time requirements, the effects of intrusion are particularly severe. In addition to covered channels and potentially tampered data at the receiver, such systems may experience violations of timing requirements and timing instabilities in components not directly related to the intrusion. Systems with real-time requirements have admission and access control mechanisms in place to ensure that timing requirements can be met during normal operation. Such admission control mechanisms require load profiles of traffic (for example in form of leaky bucket descriptors) so that resources can be appropriately allocated to meet application requirements during system operation. In this paper, we report on our project aiming at real-time detection of intrusions in ATM networks. We take advantage of the specification of the traffic profile during connection setup, and use a traffic modeling technique to determine the profile of the traffic on the connection in an arbitrary point in the network, thus providing a base line for detection of load deviations. We designed and analyzed a security device that uses the profile information, detects violations. The traffic is modeled in an accurate but efficient manner. As a result, our device is able to detect an intrusion within 25 μs, yet is simple enough to be economically realized in existing VLSI technology.

1   Introduction

High-performance networks with support for Quality of Service (QoS), such as Asynchronous Transfer Mode (ATM), are increasingly being deployed to support distributed mission-critical computing, at shipboard level or at wider scale [1]. For example, ATM technology provides the backbone for various core technology subsystems of the SmartShip program for AEGIS class cruisers [11], such as integrated condition awareness system, damage control system, machinery control system, and integrated bridge system. The networks used in many of these systems must meet stringent timing and security requirements. In this paper, we report on our project aiming at providing real-time intrusion detection for these types of networks. By real-time detection, we mean that a solution should detect and suppress network intrusions within very short time periods, say, 100 μs.

In addition to its high speed, ATM's ability to provide QoS support to users makes it increasingly popular for many such systems. While QoS for a connection can be characterized by many parameters, for real-time applications it is bandwidth guarantees and delay bounds that are perhaps the most important parts of the QoS specification. Unfortunately, relying on bandwidth or delay guarantees makes this type of systems very vulnerable to denial-of-service attacks, in addition to traditional intrusions. Indeed, as with other types of networks, potential attacks in an ATM network include the modification of connection and path data in a switch in ways that are beneficial to the attacker. In this way, the attacker would be able to insert, divert, or delete traffic in an unauthorized manner. Although such attacks can be local in nature, they can have a global impact by affecting not only the attacked connections, but other connections as well. For example, localized or intermittent flooding by an intruder can cause the network to violate the QoS requirements of many unrelated connections. This may in turn cause applications to time out, and the effect may range from invocation of timing recovery actions to total loss of system control. Thus, the damage can be widespread and very serious for a mission critical system and, hence, must be confined in real-time.

Deleting and suppressing flooding by intruders is difficult to achieve effectively at switch or network level, as it may easily masquerade as "friendly" traffic. Detection approaches therefore often have to rely on end-to-end mechanisms with very long latencies.

During normal operation, connections in networks with support for QoS guarantees need to go through a connection *establishment* phase. The new connection specifies its QoS requirements along with a characterization of the amount of traffic that it will carry. The admission control component of the system will then determine whether enough resources are available to satisfy the requirements of the new connection without violating guarantees of previously established connections. Once the connection is established, a policing mechanism typically enforces that the sender adheres to the traffic specification defined at establishment time. If an appropriate traffic model is used, and a sufficiently detailed traffic specification is provided at connection setup time, both can be used to accurately profile traffic during the lifetime of the connection. The traffic model should be capable of describing the traffic generated at the source as well as the traffic at an arbitrary point within the network. In an ATM network, traffic belonging to different connections gets repeatedly multiplexed and demultiplexed at the entrance to the network and in the switches. Consequently, the traffic pattern of a connection undergoes several changes as it traverses the network. The traffic pattern of a connection inside the network may be substantially different from its pattern at the source. In particular, it differs substantially from the traffic specification provided during connection setup time.

An important contribution of our work is a traffic model that very accurately characterizes traffic flows in a network, and so allows for the definition of accurate *traffic descriptors*. We will describe in Section 2.2 how we use *maximum* and *minimum traffic functions* to define an envelope on the amount of traffic generated by a sender or a set of senders in a distributed application. As we will demonstrate, these functions are powerful enough to describe all types of traffic encountered in time-critical applications, both at the sources and inside of the network. At the same time, these mathematical functions are concise and easy to manipulate.

Based on the traffic modeling techniques developed, we design and analyze a security device that uses traffic information to detect intrusions. The device meets the ATM forum UNI data specification. An evaluation shows that it is able to perform covert network traffic detection, suppression, and alert in a timely fashion (within 25 μs) even under peak traffic conditions. Its implementation is both cost effective and stable.

The rest of this paper is organized as follows: In Section 2, we introduce our traffic modeling techniques. The design and analysis of the security device is presented in Section 3 while Section 4 concludes the paper with final remarks.

2 Traffic Modeling

In order to provide a valid characterization of the traffic of a connection anywhere along the path of the connection, the traffic model must be flexible enough to capture perturbances as the traffic travels along its path. Also, the network must be modeled as to capture the elements that add perturbance to the traffic as it flows through the network. To model the traffic we use pairs of deterministic traffic bounding functions. To capture the active elements within the network we model it as a network of servers and distinguish between constant and variable servers.

2.1 The Network

For our purposes, an ATM network consists of ATM switches connected by communication links. An ATM switch itself consists of input ports, the switching fabric, and output ports. A cell that arrives at an input port of a switch is transported by the switching fabric to an output port, where it is transmitted along the physical link associated with the output port. Messages are segmented into fixed-size cells. This simplifies the traffic analysis because the cell transmission time is constant, and time can be normalized appropriately.

For the purpose of traffic analysis, the network is traditionally decomposed into a collection of *servers* [4]. Each server provides an abstraction for a network component in the system. For example, the input ports, the switching fabric, the output ports, and the physical links can each be modeled as a server.

We distinguish two types of servers: constant servers and variable servers [4, 9]. *Constant servers*, such as physical links, input ports, and most common switching fabrics, impose a constant delay to each cell and do not modify the traffic flow characteristics of a connection. *Variable servers*, on the other hand, add a non-constant delay to each cell, and so modify the traffic characteristics of connections. An output port, for example, acts as a multiplexor and may simultaneously receive cells belonging to different connections competing for transmission on the link associated with the port. Thus, cell blocking may occur, and cells may be forwarded in an order that is determined by the scheduling policy adopted by the switch. An output port, which is a multiplexor, must therefore be considered as a variable server.

Constant servers do not affect the traffic flows. Therefore, they need not be further considered to derive the characterization of traffic flows inside a network. Variable servers, however, modify the traffic that flows through them, and their effect on traffic has to be understood, so that the accuracy of a traffic descriptor does not excessively suffer as the traffic traverses one or more variable servers. In the following section, the network will therefore be modeled as a network of variable servers only.

2.2 Maximum and Minimum Traffic Functions

We define the *output traffic function* $R_{i,X}(t)$ of connection M_i at the (variable) server X to be the amount of data of Connection M_i departing from Server X during the time interval $[0, t)$. Obviously, $R_{i,X}(t)$ precisely describes the traffic of Connection M_i at the output of Server X. The fact that this function is time-dependent makes it an unlikely can-

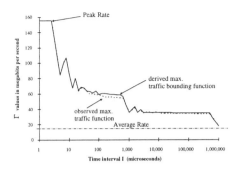

Figure 1: Maximum Rate Function

didate for a traffic descriptor. We consider two more concise functions, which deterministically bound the expected traffic of a connection, and therefore can be used as envelope to characterize the traffic.

We call Function $F_{i,X}(I)$ the *maximum traffic function* for Connection M_i at Server X if for any $I > 0$,

$$F_{i,X}(I) = max_{s \geq 0} (R_{i,X}(s + I) - R_{i,X}(s))$$

That is, the maximum amount of traffic output from Server X for Connection M_i during any time interval of length I is at most $F_{i,X}(I)$.

Similarly, we define $f_{i,X}(I)$ to be the *minimum traffic function*. That is, for any $I > 0$,

$$f_{i,X}(I) = min_{s \geq 0} (R_{i,X}(s + I) - R_{i,X}(s))$$

Again, during any interval of length I, the amount of traffic output from server X for Connection M_i is at least $f_{i,X}(I)$. Figure 1 shows a related measure, the *maximum rate function* $\Gamma(I) = \frac{F_{i,X}(I)}{I}$ of a traffic flow. In this example, a traffic stream is measured by a network analyzer as it enters an ATM network, and the maximum average rate $\Gamma()$ is plotted as a function of the averaging interval I.

We use the functions $F()$ and $f()$ as traffic descriptors for the traffic of connections in the networks. $F()$ and $f()$ form the tightest deterministic time-invariant characterization of the traffic at the output of a server. As $F()$ and $f()$ may be defined by a large number of points, they are cumbersome to manipulate and *bounds* on the maximum and minimum traffic functions are used to characterize the traffic.

We define the *maximum traffic bounding function* $B(I)$ to be an upper bound on $F(I)$, that is, $B(I) \geq F(I)$ for all I. Similarly, we define the *minimum traffic bounding function* $b(I)$ to be a lower bound on $f(I)$, that is, $b(I) \leq f(I)$ for all I. Since we base our detection mechanism on $B()$ and $b()$, the more tightly they bound the actual traffic, the more accurate is the resulting classification into compliant and non-compliant traffic.

In the context of real-time communication protocols, maximum traffic bounding functions are used to allocate resources, and tight bounding functions are sought to prevent excessive over-allocation of network resources. In practice, a trade-off must be made between tightness of the bounding function on one side, and the overhead incurred to manipulate it on the other, together with the inherent *a-priori* uncertainty about the traffic characteristics at the sources.

Traffic functions can be easily approximated with piecewise linear bounding functions at any level of resolution. Consider a maximum traffic function $F()$. Assume that we know one point of the function $F()$, that is, we know $B' = F(I')$ for some value of I'. We then have a first-order approximation of $F(I)$, which is given by

$$B'(I) >= [I/I'] \cdot B + min(I', I - [I/I'] \cdot I')$$

This can be recursively used to bound the function if more points are known. In this form, coarse bounds (three to five linear segments) on maximum traffic functions can be used for resource allocation purposes, where a broad categorization of traffic streams into classes – for example teleconference, or advertising, or sports – is sufficient. More accurate bounds (say, ten linear segments) can then be used to closely characterize individual traffic streams.

Once the traffic bounding functions are known at the entrance to the network, they can be derived for any point along the path of a connection. This derivation requires to obtain the traffic at the output of a server from the traffic at its input.

Let X and Y be two adjunct servers, and let Connection M_i first traverse Server X and then Server Y. Then,

$$F_{i,Y}(t) = F_{i,X}(t + d)$$

and

$$f_{i,Y}(t) = f_{i,X}(t - d)$$

where d is the worst-case delay experienced by Connection M_i at Server Y. The value for d depends on the scheduling methodology used in the server

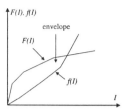

Figure 2: Maximum and Minimum Traffic Function Define an Envelope

and on the traffic functions of other connections using that server. For a FCFS service discipline, for example, the worst-case delay on Server X can be bounded as follows, assuming that Server X serves N connections, and the traffic of a connection M_j is bounded at the output of the previous server by the maximum traffic bounding function $B_{j,PREV}()$:

$$d = max_{I \geq 0} \left(\sum_{i=0}^{N} B_{j,PREV}(I) - I \right)$$

Various analytical techniques to derive worst-case delays based on traffic bounding functions for other scheduling policies, such as Static Priority, Generalized Processor Sharing, and various forms of Earliest-Due-Date have been proposed ([4, 5, 7, 8, 12] among many others). The above formula imply that, for Server Y, the upper and lower traffic at its output, modeled by $B_{i,Y}(t)$ and $b_{i,Y}(t)$, can be derived from the traffic at its input (i.e., the output of the previous Server X).

Figure 2 illustrates how the maximum and minimum traffic functions define an envelope for the amount of traffic on the connection at the output of a server. The network will, during run time, dynamically examine the traffic and verify if the traffic lies within this envelope. In the case of a violation is found, then a (potential) intrusion is detected. Actions can be taken to immediately suppresses the violation. These functionalities are implemented in a security device, which we discuss next.

3 Design and Analysis of a Security Device

The device must perform the functions of detection, suppression and alert when non-compliant traffic is found to be passing through the network, in a timely manner. *Detection* refers to determining if a

---

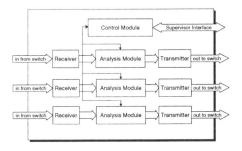

Figure 3: Block Diagram of ATM Switch Security Device

cell being transmitted out of a particular port on a switch is in accordance with the maximum and minimum traffic functions defined for the connection, that is, its VPI/VCI pair. *Suppression* involves the discarding of the offending cell and *Alert* refers to a method by which the security device reports the VPI/VCI pair of the offending cell and the switch output which produced it. Optionally, *Alert* also refers to the reporting of the reason for which the cell is found to be in violation, whether it be due to an illegal VPI/VCI pair or due to a violation of the traffic envelope.

The determining factor in the design was the need to implement the device with components that are widely available, inexpensive, and of proven stability. Because of the high data rates involved in the transmission of cells in ATM networks, it was necessary to use as much parallelism of functions as possible in hardware in order to implement the design with standard components and realizable clock speeds.

As illustrated in Figure 3, the device relies on three units functioning in tandem to handle the traffic produced by each ATM network switch output. These three units, labeled *Receiver*, *Analysis Module*, and *Transmitter*, function in sequence to capture, analyze, and retransmit the network traffic from one ATM network switch output Port: The Receivers queue the incoming data from the ATM network switch and present the data to the Analysis Modules in manageable pieces. The Analysis Modules capture the data from the Receivers and perform the necessary functions of detection, suppression and alert and pass this data to the Transmitters if it is found to be valid. The Transmitters capture the outgoing data from the Analysis Modules and transmit it to the subsequent switch in the ATM network.

Overseeing the operation of the Receivers, Analysis Modules and Transmitters is the Control Module. It is the responsibility of this module to accept data from the Supervisory Interface regarding new connections that need to be admitted in the ATM network and pass this data to the appropriate Analysis Module. Additionally, the Control Module must detect a traffic alert from any one of the Analysis Modules and, when it occurs, must capture the data regarding the cell which caused the alert from the appropriate Analysis Module. Then, the Control Module must transmit this data to the supervisory interface.

The end result is a device that can capture, analyze and retransmit the ATM network traffic on the multiple output ports of an ATM switch, update path information , and report traffic infractions under conditions of peak data rate transmission. The analysis portion of the device's function may be of two types. Under the first variant, arriving network traffic will be checked for validity in terms of whether or not the connection with which that traffic is associated does indeed pass through the network switch and port from which the data originated. The second variant will perform exactly the same verification as the first variant and, in addition, will also verify that traffic that has been found to be traveling across a valid connection has not exceeded the traffic limits placed on that connection.

3.1 Transmitter and Receiver

The receivers and transmitter capture and send the cell data from and to the physical outputs and inputs of the ATM switches between which the device lies and process it according to the particular physical interface characteristics of those switches. This includes any functions of decryption, decompression, and bit-level synchronization. The exact design of these units will be highly dependent on the physical media and beyond the scope of this description. The physical blocks comprising these modules is not a matter of choice since it is already described in the ATM forum literature ([2, 3]) and components for use in these modules are available.

The only design issue that needs to be noted with regard to the function of the receivers and transmitters is that they present data to the Analysis Module in parallel 16-bit words and synchronize the their presentation to the Analysis Module clock. The stipulation that data be presented to and read from the Analysis Modules in 16-bit words arises out of the need to have this device operate at clock speeds that are reasonable for implementation in integrated circuit designs that utilize the major logic families currently available. At the highest speed scenarios of data rates of 622.08 Mbps, it implies that 38.9 million 16-bit words need to be processed by every Analysis Module, which implies a maximum clock rate of 38.9 MHz for the Analysis Modules.

3.2   Analysis Module

The Analysis Module admits a new cell into a 16-bit shift register, word by word from the receiver. In parallel, as components of the VPI/VCI pair belonging to the cell in transit are received from the Receiver (contained in the cell header, consisting of the first five bytes of data) they will also be copied into six four-bit latches.

Once all 24 bits of the VPI/VCI pair associated with the cell in transit have been captured in these four-bit latches, the 24 bits of output from them will be presented to the *memory lookup module* in two 12-bit words, with one word being presented at a time. The control to present these two 12-bit words will be performed by a 12-bit by 4-input multiplexor.

The two words that are presented to the memory lookup module will be interpreted by this module as an address that is uses to perform the actual analysis of the cell's validity. Depending on the version of the Analysis Module to be implemented, this function will change. Primarily, the memory lookup module will verify if the cell belongs to a connection that does indeed pass through the switch and port from which it originated. Optionally, the module will also verify if the network connection along which the cell in question is traveling has is within the envelope defined by the maximum and minimum traffic bounding function for that connection at that output port.

This result will be used by the sequence/detect module to determine if the cell is valid or not. If the cell is valid, it will enable the output from the last set of latches in the 16-bit shift register to be sent out to the transmitter. If the cell is not valid, the sequence/detect module will suppress output of the cell from the shift register to the transmitter by simply presenting null data (all zero bits) to the

input state of the Receiver. In this case, the sequence/detect module will also trigger the interrupt logic in the Control Module. The Control Module will then know that an invalid cell has been detected and will perform the necessary operations to read the VPI/VCI pair of the offending cell from the outputs of the six 4-bit latches, which have been storing this information throughout the entire process.

All the devices used in this circuit are currently feasible in TTL and HC logic families. In addition, a number of tri-state buffers are implicitly used in this design to allow the Control Module to select between the data inputs and outputs of the different Analysis Modules to which it is attached. The interconnection of the functional blocks of the Analysis Module is shown in Figure 4.

The sequence/detect module is a simple sequential state machine with external decode logic. It controls all the inputs and outputs required to perform the functions just described. This state machine is designed using the same type of edge triggered D-type latches and combinatorial logic used to construct the other component blocks of the Analysis Module.

The reasoning behind the design of the Analysis Module was to be able to take advantage of the large number of operations that can be performed in parallel in order to reduce the number of clock cycles necessary for the device to perform its function.

The effect on the performance of the physical communication link passing through this device will be that any cell in transit will be delayed by the amount of time necessary to read in the cell's header and perform the lookup of the VPI/VCI pair contained in these five bytes in the memory lookup module. This means that the controlling factor of the transmission delay a cell will experience in every security device through which it passes will be the sum of these two periods of time, in addition to delays incurred due to link-level synchronization at receivers and transmitters.

The Control Module's logic will be triggered within less than one cell transmit time if the transiting cell is found to be invalid (nine clock cycles, to be precise). This means that the Control Module will know about the violation in less than one cell time and can begin sending data bout the violation to its supervisory control interface within less than one cell time.

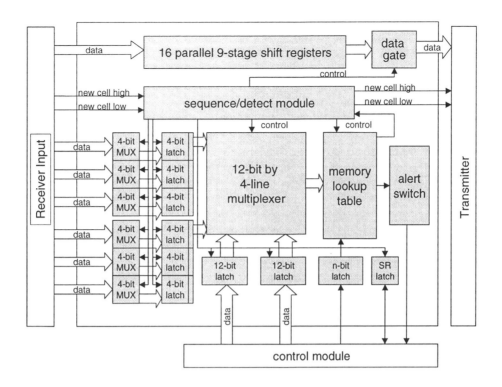

Figure 4: Analysis Module Block Diagram

3.3 Control Module

The Control Module performs its job asynchronously from the Analysis Module. It handles communication with the supervisory interface and with the hardware in the Analysis Module to which it is attached. To the supervisor interface, the Control Module must report traffic violations detected and read from the Analysis Modules and get information about new valid data paths that have been created in the network. When the Control Module receives data about a new valid path, it must be able to distinguish through which Analysis Module the path passes and must update the valid path information within this module.

A Motorola 68PM302 Integrated Multiprotocol Processor is an ideal candidate because of its current availability at reasonable cost and its capability to provide a broad range of built-in features that closely match the needs of this application. It provides sufficient I/O to be able to perform all the necessary read and write operations to and from the Analysis Module hardware. It offers the interrupt circuitry necessary for the Analysis Module to alert the Control Module of a traffic violation. Finally, it provides a high-speed serial interface, which could be used in conjunction with a DS1 compliant

transceiver in order to communicate with the Control Module's supervisory interface.

4 Final Remarks

In this work we propose an intrusion detection mechanism for high-speed networks based on the characterization of the traffic arrival patterns on connections. This approach well complements other traffic characterization schemes. Its strength lies in the fact that the management of characterization parameters is greatly simplified. Indeed, we take full advantage of the fact that applications must declare the traffic specification during connection setup if they want their QoS requirements to be met. This traffic specification provides the upper bound of the traffic envelope. An additional minimum traffic specification would provide the lower bound. No sophisticated anomaly detector is needed ([6, 10]) to determine whether an intrusion occurred, since the envelope parameters have been provided during connection setup. For example, if a maximum traffic function is exceeded for a connection, an alert must be triggered to indicate that an intrusion may have happened and that the system is operating at a higher load than what is safe for the given QoS guarantees.

Our traffic model in terms of maximum and minimum traffic functions then gives us a flexible method to formulate the envelope for each connection at an arbitrary point in the network. This allows for a targeted deployment of our proposed ATM security devices across the network, and for an accurate methodology to determine the parameters for the traffic envelopes for connections.

We presented a module level description of a detection device and have shown it to be implementable with currently available off-the-shelf components and custom ASICs available at current levels of integration technology. The performance of the device has been evaluated under worst-case conditions for network traffic. It has been shown that the delay experienced by network traffic in existing virtual connections in the network is trivial when compared to its expected transit time within the network and that the management functions of creating and destroying virtual connections are not a function of the creation/destruction rate of these connections. Through the description of its operation, it is evident that, while utilizing such a framework of traffic security enforcement, the full bandwidth of the network is available to all users for authorized utilization and that traffic delays network cells will experience are constant even under sustained peak traffic conditions.

The details for the components of the device presented here have concentrated primarily on the mechanisms by which actual enforcement should occur and how to limit the impact which it has on overall network performance. Many portions of the larger issues of this method of security enforcement have been glossed over. Foremost among these issues is the topology and physical architecture that should be used to implement the network by which supervisory control data is transferred between the modules that actually provide the enforcement and the workstations that keep the operators of the security body appraised of the state of the network. An integral component of this decision will be an assessment of exactly what criteria to use in order to derive the level of enforcement that the modules designed in this document will be required to perform. Based on this, assessments may be made with regard to what the overall bandwidth and worst-case delays of the overlaying network must be in order to provide an interface to the individual enforcement modules that is deemed to be acceptable from the network management perspective.

References

[1] ABIS Task Force, DoD Advanced Battlespace Information Systems Task Force Report, 1996.

[2] ATM Forum, "DS3 Physical Layer Specification," ATM Forum, January 1996.

[3] ATM Forum, "622.08 Mbps Physical Layer Specification," ATM Forum, January 1996.

[4] R. L. Cruz. "A calculus for network delay," *IEEE Transactions on Information Theory*, 37(1):114–131, Jan. 1991.

[5] R. L. Cruz, "Quality of Service Guarantees in Virtual Circuit Switched Networks," *IEEE Journal of Selected Areas in Communication*, Aug. 1995.

[6] J.S. Javitz, A. Valdes, "The SRI IDES Statistical Anomaly Detector," *Proceedings of the IEEE Computer Society Symposium on Research in Security and Privacy*, Oakland, CA, May 1991.

[7] C. Li, R. Bettati, W. Zhao, "Static Priority Scheduling for ATM Networks." *Proceedings of the Real-Time Systems Symposium*, San Francisco, CA, Dec. 1997.

[8] J. Liebeherr, D.E. Wrege, and D. Ferrari. *"Exact admission control in networks with bounded delay services."*, *IEEE/ACM Transactions on Networking*.

[9] A. Raha, S. Kamat, and W. Zhao. "Admission control for hard real-time connections in ATM LAN's," In *Proceedings of the IEEE Infocom'96*, Mar. 1996.

[10] K. Tan, "The Application of Neural Networks to UNIX Computer Security," *Proceedings of the International Conference on Neural Networks '95*, Perth, Australia, 1995.

[11] Xylan Corporation. *Xylan announces participation in SmartShip program*. Xylan Press Release. URL: http://www.xylan.com/news/pr-053097.html.

[12] H. Zhang and D. Ferrari, "Rate-Controlled Service Disciplines." *Journal of High-Speed Networks*, 3(4):389-412, 1994.

A Statistical Method for Profiling Network Traffic

David Marchette
Naval Surface Warfare Center B10
Dahlgren, VA 22448
dmarche@nswc.navy.mil

Abstract

Two clustering methods are described and applied to network data. These allow the clustering of machines into "activity groups", which consist of machines which tend to have similar activity profiles. In addition, these methods allow the user to determine whether current activity matches these profiles, and hence to determine when there is "abnormal" activity on the network. A method for visualizing the clusters is described, and the approaches are applied to a data set consisting of a months worth of data from 993 machines.

1. Introduction

The task of monitoring the traffic on a large network is a daunting one. At a minimum, one needs to filter out all the "normal" or "uninteresting" traffic in order to focus attention on those connections that are unusual or indicative of potential problems. The problem addressed in this work is the one of characterizing "normal" traffic, and recognizing and flagging "abnormal" traffic.

At one level, "abnormal" can refer simply to those connection attempts that are considered undesirable and hence are disallowed by the firewall. Once a suspicious connection attempt has been detected, the traffic from that source can be pulled and perused to determine if allowed connections may have been used successfully to compromise the network.

The problem with this approach is that it can only catch those things one already knows about. Every network administrator has a bad ports list and a bad IPs list, and any connection matching one of these lists is scrutinized. However, some connections are only bad if they are to certain machines, but are perfectly normal to others. For example, one may allow individuals to set up ftp servers, provided they follow certain guidelines to ensure relative security. So one may see a fair amount of ftp traffic in and out of the network to a (periodically changing) subset of machines. Suppose a machine that has never had ftp traffic suddenly starts to get ftp connections. An alert network manager might

want to check to make sure that the system administrator for that machine has intended to set up an externally available ftp site, rather than someone taking advantage of a misconfiguration or vulnerability. This can be particularly important if the machine in question is an infrastructure machine, contains sensitive information, or is otherwise an important target for attackers. In fact, any traffic that is "unusual" for a give machine or class of machines should be flagged for further analysis.

The problem then is to determine what is "normal" and hence what is "unusual" for the network. This paper will describe two techniques based on some statistical approaches to clustering and discrimination. The techniques will be described and an example for a large (nearly 1000 machine) network will be provided.

The data considered in this work consists of six fields: date/time, source IP address, source port, destination IP address, destination port, and protocol (TCP or UDP). These data can be obtained through programs such as netlogger or tcpdump. Other information, such as SYN/ACK flags, packet size etc. can easily be incorporated within the basic framework described herein. The data consist of a subset of the external connections to our network for the months of March and April 1998. The subset of the data chosen comprised those machines that had at least 10 connection attempts to at least two distinct ports in the month of April. Only those connection attempts in which the source was external to our network and the destination was internal were considered. The month of April was used to define "normal" activity, and the data from March was used to obtain performance statistics. The availability of reported attacks during the month of March, and the fact that we had done considerable analysis of the April data set dictated this choice.

2. Measuring Network Traffic

The first and most obvious way to measure network activity is to keep count of the number of accesses to each port within a given time period (hourly, daily, etc.). When the count for a port on a given machine or set of machines is unusually high, this is an indication of a potential problem. The determination of what constitutes "unusually high" can be made through studying the normal fluctuations of these quantities in historical data.

Table 1 shows one way of utilizing counts to monitor a network. The incoming telnet sessions are tabulated for the current day and compared with the activity for the previous two months. These are real data collected on our network. Obviously the IP addresses have been changed. The analyst can scan a list such as this for daily counts that exceed the normal for the previous months, pull the traffic to that machine to determine who is making these connections, and, if warranted, pull additional traffic for the appropriate machines. Obviously this kind of analysis can only be done for a relatively small number of ports and machines, but for some of the most obvious services this can provide the analyst with considerable information about the traffic on the network.

The above idea can be extended to allow the consideration of all the ports in a natural way, by normalizing the counts by the overall traffic, thus obtaining a probability estimate, instead of a "connections per day" measure. So now one has an estimate of the probability of having an access to any given port for any given machine. This can then be used as above to determine whether the traffic for a given time period is abnormal, or it can provide feedback for individual accesses. Port access attempts which have a low probability can be flagged as unusual and worthy of further investigation.

These ideas can be extended to consideration of "sessions", or sequential accesses from a single source IP. There are at least two approaches here. One can count sessions in much the same manner as above,

and flag low probability sessions as unusual. This is essentially the approach taken by Forrest et al [3]. Or one can model the sessions (for example as a Markov chain) and flag a session that deviates from the model. Work in this area is ongoing and we will not consider these ideas further in this paper.

Once again it is important to remember that these methods are not designed to catch intruders by themselves, but rather to filter the traffic to eliminate from consideration that which is obviously "normal". Experience has shown that on a network of hundreds to thousands of machines, with millions of connections a day, events with very low probabilities happen quite frequently, far too frequently to be dealt with on an individual basis (assuming the usual number of security personnel reviewing the log files).

2. Clustering Machines by Network Activity

The above method works well when dealing with a small number of machines. Once the number of machines on the network rises into the hundreds, one would like to aggregate machines into "activity types". Intuitively, one would imagine that machines with similar functions should have similar normal activity. This is the case, although ones intuition as to which machines should be similar may not be entirely accurate. The idea is to do this aggregation in an automated manner. In the statistics literature this type of aggregation is called "clustering".

One of the most widely used clustering methods is the k-means method. This requires knowledge of the number of clusters in the data. Once one has

Table 1: Telnet access counts

Destination IP	Daily Count	March Count	March Counts/Day	Feb Count	Feb Counts/Day
331.409.17.39	2	14	0.5	8	0.26
331.409.25.95	3	3	0.1	15	0.48
331.409.28.98	20	323	11.5	834	26.9
331.409.48.49	1	5	0.18	0	0
331.409.6.81	1	2	0.07	17	0.55
331.409.66.35	1	8	0.29	11	0.35
331.409.66.59	2	12	0.43	20	0.65
331.409.50.73	1	1	0.04	0	0
331.409.88.26	10	78	2.8	32	1.03
331.409.90.10	1	64	2.29	43	1.39
331.409.90.4	8	28	1	31	1

decided how many clusters are represented within the data, the algorithm proceeds as follows:

Algorithm: k-means

0. Initialize the k cluster centers (for example at k randomly chosen data points)
1. While the clusters change do 1.1 - 1.2
1.1 Determine (via a nearest distance calculation) which data belong to which cluster.
1.2 Recompute (via the mean) the cluster centers.
2. Return the clusters.

The algorithm is simple to implement and works quite well in most situations. Note that there are a couple of issues that need to be addressed. First, one must decide on the number of clusters in the data. There is no easy answer as to how to do this. Typically it is done by visualizing the data, and through guess work. Once one has decided on the value of k one must pick starting centers for the clusters. This can be done via visualization of the data if the dimension is low enough for this to be practical, or through trial-and-error.

To illustrate the k-means method, the data has been reduced as follows: counts were kept for the first 1024 ports in both TCP and UDP, and a separate count is kept for all ports above 1024, again both for TCP and UDP. These counts are then normalized by the overall amount of traffic to produce a probability vector of size 2050 (1024+1+1024+1). These vectors will be referred to as "activity vectors". 993 machines were considered in the example. Obviously 993 2050-dimensional vectors would task most visualization techniques to the breaking point. The method we use is to plot the data as an image, with the pixel values corresponding to the port-probabilities. Even this is difficult to display on a typical computer screen. The data has been further reduced by eliminating from the display those ports with a probability of less than 0.2. This results in vectors of length 61 for these data.

Figure 1 shows the results of a k-means clustering with the number of clusters set at 10 (arbitrarily). The cluster centers were initialized at random. The different images correspond to the different clusters (a cluster containing a single machine is not shown). Each row corresponds to a machine, while each column corresponds to the probability vector, color coded for different probability values. It is clear from this figure that the clusters are distinct, and most of them are fairly homogeneous.

One uses these clusters as follows: all the machines within a cluster are aggregated in the sense that all their data are used to produce an activity vector for that group. These vectors are then used to classify individual connections to one of the machines within a given cluster according to their probabilities.

One problem with this approach is that there are some clusters which are not homogeneous, for example the fourth cluster in the figure. Clusters like this tend to be catch-alls where machines that don't fit any other cluster criterion are put. Rather than place a hard classification for each machine, it could be noted that some machines appear to fit well with several clusters, and use partial assignments. These could then be used to produce, for example, a weighted average of the activity vectors, which would better indicate the connection probabilities. While this can be done within the k-means clustering scheme, it is more natural in the scheme which we now describe.

The k-means clustering method could be thought of in terms of estimating the structure (or probability density) of the data via a mixture of "clumps". These clumps, in the k-means framework are spherical, and could be taken to be normal distributions. One could then use the wide literature on fitting mixture models (see, for example, McLachlan and Basford [4]). Unfortunately, fitting normal mixtures to 2050-dimensional data is simply not possible, without very serious constraints, which essentially reduce the model down to the k-means model. Typically what one does in these situations is reduce the dimension of the data through a projection, and then construct the model within the projected space. This is the approach taken here.

We utilize a method of Cowen and Priebe (see [1] and [2]), called approximate distance clustering (ADC). The idea is to select out a subset of the data, referred to as the witness set. For each data point, determine the distance to each element of the witness set and retain the smallest distance. This is the value to which that point gets projected. Thus we are projecting from 2050 dimensional space to 1 dimension. The method can be extended to utilize several witness sets, in which case the projecting dimension is the number of witness sets.

Algorithm: ADC

0. Initialize the witness set (for example select k randomly chosen data points)
1. For each point determine the distances to each point in the witness set
2. Return the smallest of the distances.

Once one has projected the data, one constructs a normal mixture model estimate of the density of the data. The clusters then become determined by the components of the mixture: each cluster consists of those points whose posterior probability is highest for the cluster's component. This allows a natural method for giving partial cluster assignments: use the posterior probabilities.

A mixture model is a weighted sum of normal densities. The weights (called mixing coefficients or proportions) are constrained to be positive and sum to one. The formula for an m-component mixture model is:

$$f(x) = \sum_{i=1} \pi_i \varphi(x, \mu_i, v_i),$$

where the π_i correspond to the mixing coefficients, μ_i the means, and v_i the variances.

As in the k-means method, most mixture model algorithms require the user to decide on the number of components in advance. We use a method that simultaneously estimates the number of components and the component parameters, which is described in Priebe et al [5]. The clusters chosen by this method are shown in Figure 2.

Algorithm: AKMDE

0. Start with a single component with mean and variance chosen from the data.
1. While a stopping criterion is not met (for example AIC) do 1.1-1.3
1.1 Construct a nonparametric estimate (kernel estimator) using the current mixture
1.2 Add a new term where the two models differ most.
1.3 Estimate the new model parameters
2. Return the mixture.

The basic idea of the AKMDE algorithm is as follows: one uses a nonparametric (kernel) estimator of the density to test whether the parametric model is adequate, and if not, a term is added. So, one uses the mixture to construct the "best" nonparametric estimator that one can, assuming the mixture to be correct. The two estimators are then compared. If the kernel estimator is significantly different than the mixture, then a new term is placed where the difference is greatest, and the new mixture model is constructed. This continues until the mixture matches the kernel estimator sufficiently closely.

The details of the AKMDE are beyond the scope of this paper. The interested reader is urged to check out the paper for more details.

Figure 3 shows the mixture model constructed on the ADC projected data. The top curve shows the overall density, while the bottom curve shows the mixture model. The x-axis represents the means of the components while the y-axis represents the mixing coefficient. The bar at each point represents one standard deviation on either side of the mean. The figure indicates that there are basically four to five obvious clusters. Figure 2 treats each component as a single cluster, rather than trying to combine components into clusters in this manner. The clusters displayed in Figure 2 are ordered by their means in the same manner as the components displayed on the bottom of Figure 3. The small component with a mean near 0.7 contains no machines and thus does not appear in the cluster picture.

3. Results

The data for the month of March 1998 was run through the k-means and ADC/AKMDE clusters, assigning to each record a probability. There were 1,757,206 records. There were a total of 27 source IPs which were determined to be attackers against one or more of the 993 machines in the data set. These consist of only those attacks that could have been detected via these methods. For example, while accesses from certain foreign countries to our facility may have been considered attacks, these were not included in the data unless the attack was detected without consideration of the source. These kinds of attacks can easily be detected by resolving the source IP.

We define attacks very broadly to include any information gathering that might indicate future attacks. An example of this kind of information gathering is using traceroute to determine the routes to our network, and hence the potential bottlenecks which could be attacked to deny service. While traceroutes are a legitimate and useful tool, we want to know about them to determine whether they show a pattern over time, which might indicate potential future attacks.

Table 2: Attacks

Attack Type	#
Bad Ports (111, 161, etc)	5
Suspicious Telnets	6
Suspicious FTPs	1
Netbios Probes	6
Zone Transfers (53 TCP)	2
Port Scans	1
Traceroute	1
Finger Probe	1
NNTP	1
NFS	1
Misc Ports	2

The attacks considered here are grouped into 11 basic categories as shown in Table 2. Since the techniques described here work on individual access attempts, the attacks are denoted by the service or access which best describes the attack. Note that two of the attacks, the traceroute and the port scan, are not single port accesses, and yet they are still easily detected using this approach, as will be seen below.

The port scan was an unusual one which appeared to be looking for services above the usual 1024 range, and so might have been hard to detect using the approach implemented here. Recall that we only consider the first 1024 ports individually, grouping all other ports into a "big port" range. Obviously one could extend this approach to include more ports if desirable. Note also that a port scan is defined in terms of a sequence of access attempts rather than any individual one, and so this method is not the method of choice for detecting these scans.

With that said, it is of interest to note that the scan was easily detected, since the machine scanned had seen very little activity beyond the first 1024 ports.

Port scans that focus only on commonly accessed ports will not be picked up via this method. Clearly, techniques that take into account the number of different ports accessed are more appropriate for detecting general port scans.

The data are reduced by setting a threshold on the probability and filtering out (ignoring as "normal") all records with probability exceeding the threshold. The results for several thresholds are given in Tables 3-5. Each table indicates the threshold probability, the number of records that are flagged at or below that probability, the number of attacker IPs which remain in the data to be detected via further processing, and the type of attacks that were missed at that threshold. Table 3 presents the results for the individual machines. This effectively treats each machine as a cluster and uses the activity vector for that machine to determine the probability for the access attempt. Tables 4 and 5 present the results for the two clustering techniques described above. All thresholds in the tables are the same to allow comparisons at a given threshold. Figure 4 shows a plot of these results for various thresholds, plotting number of records against the number of attacks detected.

Table 3: Results on March Test Data: Unclustered Results

Threshold	Number of Records	Number of Attackers	Type of Attacks Missed
0	50,217	21	1 Telnet, 2 netbios, ftp, nfs, 1 misc
0.0001	50,288	22	1 Telnet, 2 netbios, nfs, 1 misc
0.001	54,069	23	2 netbios, nfs, 1 misc
0.005	58,962	23	2 netbios, nfs, 1 misc
0.01	63,410	23	2 netbios, nfs, 1 misc

Table 4: Results on March Test Data: ADC Results

Threshold	Number of Records	Number of Attackers	Type of Attacks Missed
0	17,069	9	Telnets, netbios, news, ftp, finger, tracerout, misc
0.0001	60,975	13	Telnets, netbios, news, ftp
0.001	108,529	14	Telnets, netbios, ftp
0.005	140,435	23	3 netbios, ftp
0.01	160,875	27	none

Table 5: Results on March Test Data: k means Results

Threshold	Number of Records	Number of Attackers	Type of Attacks Missed
0	61,023	12	Telnets, netbios, ftp, misc
0.0001	78,642	20	netbios, ftp
0.001	112,961	21	netbios
0.005	131,393	23	4 netbios
0.01	146,742	23	4 netbios

This is a fairly significant reduction in the amount of data to be processed. When eliminating 90% of the data the ADC method still detects all of the attacks. It is important to stress again that these techniques should be thought of as data filters. Other intrusion detection algorithms must be applied to the filtered data to detect the actual attacks. Also, these techniques can only detect abnormal traffic. If a machine or group of machines normally have a certain amount of traffic to a given port, this technique is not designed to detect an unauthorized connection to that port. Other techniques, and often other data sources, must be utilized to detect these kinds of attacks.

One strength of this approach is that it does not require a network security expert to implement it, nor does it require perfectly clean (attack free) data. Assuming the undetected attacks in the training data are rare, they will not have too great an effect on the system. With that said, the performance does degrade if the training data does include attacks.

An interesting point to note is that the individual machine results were not uniformly better than the cluster results. Consider in Figure 4 the point at which each method first detects all the attacks. The ADC method is superior under this metric. Intuitively, one would think that this should not be the case. The reason for this counterintuitive result is as follows. Imagine that a machine was attacked in April but the attack went undetected. This machine then would have a number of access attempts to a port which should have been flagged as abnormal but were left in the training set, thus increasing the probability associated with that port. This can cause new accesses to that port on that machine to be considered "normal" for thresholds below this probability. Now imagine that the machine is clustered with others. Presumably these machines did not all have access to this forbidden port, which forces the probability of access to be reduced. One now considers these accesses to be "abnormal".

This does not come without penalty. If the clusters are not perfectly homogeneous, "normal" ports may be given lower probabilities than they should have, due to the fact that different machines have (slightly) different access patterns. This results in the superior performance of the individual machine method in the low thresholds. It gets far more attacks than the others do while passing fewer "abnormal" packets.

One issue in these approaches is the time required to implement them. There are two issues here. The first is the time required to generate the statistics. This is highly dependent on the size of ones network and the number of connections that are typically seen to the network. The calculation of these statistics on our class B network takes less than a minute for two months worth of data, in part because of the design of the database. Since this is done once a month, or at most once a week, this is not an unreasonable computational burden.

The second issue is the time required assigning a probability to a new connection and deciding if it is "abnormal" or not. First the statistics for the destination host must be retrieved from the database in which these are stored, then a table lookup provides the probability associated with the destination port. Finally, the probability is compared with the threshold to determine if the connection is to be classed as "abnormal". All of this can be done in real time or near real time on most networks, particularly if care is taken to optimize the retrieval and look-ups.

If one uses one of the clustering methods the time is essentially the same, the savings comes in the storage requirements. First one determines which cluster the host is associated with, then the statistics for the cluster are retrieved and the processing is the same from there on.

4. Future Issues

It is not obvious that the distance measure used in both the k-means and ADC algorithms, Euclidean distance, is the appropriate one for these data. It would be of interest to consider other distances with an eye toward encoding domain specific information into the process. This would allow a more natural method for encoding unregistered ports, for example handling the ranges of ports used in ftp traffic and traceroutes.

The ADC method relies on projecting the data to a lower dimensional space. It would be interesting to consider projections to 2-, 3-, and higher dimensions. Also, the ADC can be coupled with the k-means rather than using the AKMDE. All these are areas of current research.

Time can be taken into account through the consideration of pairs, triples, etc., of connections. These can be clustered in the same manner as above, by constructing probability vectors associated with their frequency. The clustering methods could then be applied to these vectors. More thought will be required when one takes into account both incoming and outgoing connections to produce a description of an entire session.

Another issue that must be addressed is the updating of the clusters. As new machines are acquired, old machines are retired or change their function, the clusters must be updated to reflect the new environment. One way to do this is to utilize a sliding window. Every week (or appropriate time unit) the statistics are updated by considering only those records within a recent window of time which were not flagged as attacks or as otherwise suspicious activity. This must be done with care to avoid a gradual shift caused by incorporating missed attacks in the statistics.

As mentioned above, the approach should be fairly robust to incorporation of missed attacks in the training data. One possible approach to eliminating these from the data is to incorporate outlier detection algorithms into the process. One problem with this is the high dimensional nature of the data. It remains to be seen whether missed attacks remain outliers when the data is projected via the ADC or other projection methods.

Much more extensive tests are needed to determine the best way to utilize these ideas. The optimal choice of the number of clusters is a difficult problem. Ultimately one must decide if it is necessary to cluster the machines into a small number of clusters instead of treating each machine as an individual. The latter should provide better accuracy while the former can require substantially fewer computations on a large network. The work described here is the first step to answering these questions.

References

[1] Cowen, L.J. and Priebe, C.E., "Randomized Nonlinear Projections Uncover High Dimensional Structure", Advances in Applied Mathematics, Vol. 9, pp. 319-331, 1997.

[2] Cowen, L.J. and Priebe, C.E., "Approximate Distance Clustering", Computing Science and Statistics", Vol. 29, pp. 337-346, 1997.

[3] Forrest, S., Hofmeyr, S., and Somayaji, A., "Computer immunology", Communications of the ACM, Vol. 40, No. 10, pp. 88-96, 1997.

[4] McLachlan, G.J., and Basford, K.E., *Mixture Models: Inference and Applications to Clustering*, Marcel Dekker, 1988.

[5] Priebe, C.E., Marchette, D.J., and Rogers, G.W., "Alternating Kernel and Mixture Models", The Johns Hopkins University Department of Mathematical Sciences Technical Report #574, 1997.

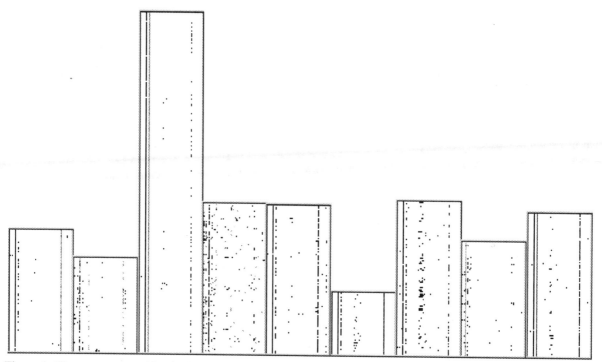

Figure 1: Clusters generated by the k-means algorithm. Each rectangle corresponds to a cluster. The x-axis corresponds to port number, while the y-axis corresponds to individual machines. Only those ports that have a probabilitity obove 0.2 for some machine are shown. The probabilities are indicated by gray scale value, with black corresponding to a probability close to 1.

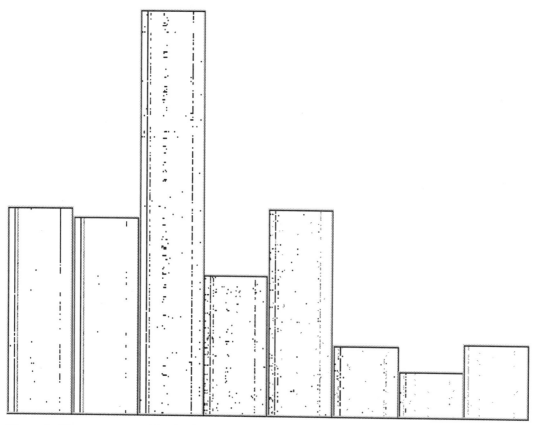

Figure 2: Clusters generated by the ADC method. The coding scheme is the same as in Figure 1.

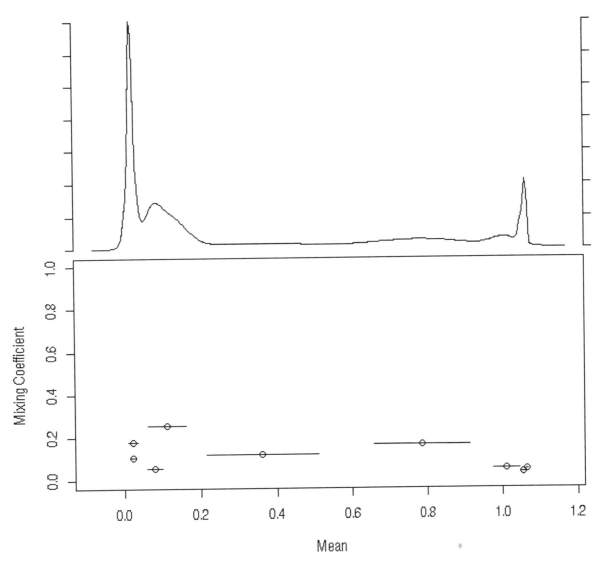

Figure 3: The mixture model generated on the ADC projected data using the AKMDE. The top plot shows the mixture density, while the bottom plot indicates the mixture components. Components are plotted as a point at the mean and mixing coefficient, with a bar indicating one standard deviation on either side of the point.

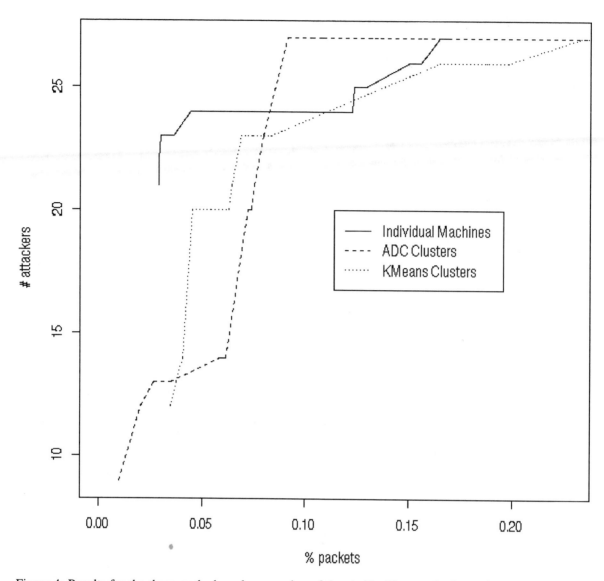

Figure 4: Results for the three methods under a number of thresholds. The x-axis shows the percentage of packets that are flagged as "abnormal". The y-axis indicates the number of attacks that remain in the "abnormal" data.

Transaction-based Anomaly Detection

Roland Büschkes, Mark Borning
Aachen University of Technology - Department of Computer Science
Informatik 4 (Communication Systems)
D-52056 Aachen, Germany
{roland, borning}@i4.informatik.rwth-aachen.de

Dogan Kesdogan
o.tel.o communications GmbH & Co
Dept. Enterprise Security
D-51063 Köln
Dogan.Kesdogan@o-tel-o.de

Abstract

The increasing complexity of both tele and data communication networks yields new demands concerning network security. Especially the task of detecting, repulsing and preventing abuse by in- and outsiders is becoming more and more difficult. This paper deals with a new technique that appears to be suitable for solving these issues, i.e. anomaly detection based on the specification of transactions. The traditional transaction and serialization concepts are discussed, and a new model of anomaly detection, based on the concept of transactions, is introduced. Applying this model to known attacks gives a first insight concerning the feasibility of our approach.

1 Introduction

Modern tele and data communication networks provide users with all kinds of services. In the future, the variety of available services will increase, ultimately offering any service anytime and anywhere. Yet, the growing range of available services also increases the complexity of the underlying networks. Therefore, it is becoming increasingly difficult to detect, repulse and prevent abuse by both in- and outsiders. Classical security mechanisms, i.e. authentication and encryption, and infrastructure components like firewalls cannot provide perfect security. Therefore, *intrusion detection systems* (IDS) have been introduced as a third line of defense.

The techniques classically applied within IDS can be subdivided into two main categories [20]:

- Misuse Detection, and

- Anomaly Detection.

Misuse detection (see e.g. [7, 11, 13]) tries to detect patterns of known attacks within the audit stream of a system, i.e. it identifies attacks directly. The main disadvantage of this approach is that the underlying database of attack patterns must be kept up-to-date and consistent. Because misuse detection techniques depend on the knowledge of recognized attack patterns, they cannot detect new attacks.

Explicitly describing the sequence of actions an attacker takes, misuse detection is based on the specification of the undesirable or *negative behavior* of users and processes. The opposite approach would be the specification of the desired or *positive behavior* of users and processes. Based on this normative specification of positive behavior attacks are identified by observing derivations from the norm. Therefore, this technique is called *Anomaly Detection*.

The main problem with anomaly detection techniques is to determine the positive behavior. Two general approaches exist:

1. Learning user and process behavior, and

2. Specification of user and process behavior.

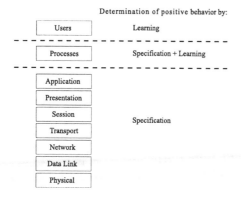

Figure 1: Anomaly Detection Approaches.

The former approach is often based on statistical methods like the calculation of means, variations and multivariate statistics [9]. Other methods use learning algorithms like e.g. neural networks or Bayesian classifiers [2]. This approach is particular popular for the profiling of users.

The latter approach, specification-based anomaly detection, was first proposed in [10]. In this paper we describe a new model alled transaction-based anomaly detection and its application in communication networks. In general the transaction-based approach is similar to the specification-based approach as it formally describes positive behavior. In contrast to the specification-based approach it specifies the desired actions and sequence of actions by the definition of transactions. This explicit definition of allowed transactions becomes an integral part of the local security policy.

Figure 1 summarizes the different approaches to anomaly detection and their possible application. On the one hand, the expected behavior of the network protocol stack is well defined. This allows the application of non-intelligent techniques to monitor it. On the other hand, users are less predictable in their behavior and therefore intelligent techniques must be applied. It would be theoretically possible to formally define process behavior, but in many cases their complexity makes this approach impossible. Nonetheless, from our point of view non-intelligent monitoring techniques should be preferred over intelligent ones whenever possible. Although intelligent techniques can improve the security of a system, they rarely give a clear picture of the level of security they can guarantee. In contrast non-intelligent techniques like e.g. specification-based approaches extend the general security policy, and clearly define their guaranteed level of security.

The paper is subdivided into six main parts. Following this introduction we first define the requirements on a formal specification of positive behavior. Subsequently we introduce our transaction-based approach, briefly reviewing the general transaction model known from the database systems domain and adapting it to the IDS scenario. In section 4 we introduce sample applications of our model. After comparing the transaction-based concept with other approaches in section 5, we finally draw some conclusions and finish with an outlook on future work.

2 Specification Requirements

Any misuse or anomaly detection component should adhere to some basic design principles. These design principles also define the common criteria for the comparison of individual techniques. In the following we will review them briefly.

Obviously, the specification of positive behavior requires some formalism. Although formalisms are often very expressive and powerful, they also involve the danger of being too complicated. Complicated mechanisms tend to introduce errors, and errors open new security holes.

An appropriate formalism should therefore provide at least for the following properties:

1. ease of specification,

2. ease of monitoring,

3. completeness (no false negatives),

4. soundness (no false positives),

5. efficiency, and

6. universal validity.

As the first five desired properties in this list are well-known, we will only briefly elaborate on the requirement of universal validity to motivate our approach. Current IDS still mainly focus on the monitoring of operating system environments like UNIX or NT. Only recently the first papers dealing with the monitoring of network infrastructures [1, 3, 14, 16, 19] have been published.

However, future communication platforms like middleware (CORBA), electronic commerce, intelligent network or mobile phone (UMTS) architectures will also be vulnerable to attacks.

Misuse detection techniques can obviously not yet be studied in this context, as these systems are not in place and therefore no attacks have been identified. Anomaly detection techniques have the advantage that they can be applied right from the start of such systems. As an additional advantage, they can provide the administrators not only with information concerning potential attacks, but also with general information concerning system activity, faults and performance. Following this approach anomaly detection components establish an essential part of general network management platforms.

From our point of view two general observations hold for present and future communication platforms:

- Communication protocols can generally be specified as state transition systems.

- The protocols can be considered as defining valid transactions.

Therefore, our approach tries to maximize its universal validity by utilizing the transaction model, which is typical for many processes and especially communication processes.

3 Transaction-based approach

Transactions are a well known concept, originating from the field of *database managing systems* (DBMS) and now widely applied in other environments like distributed systems [4]. Before we will discuss their application in the context of intrusion detection we will briefly review the general concept.

3.1 The Classical Transaction Concept

Transactions generally consist of a sequence of read and write operations. If several transactions concurrently read from and write to a database, the following problems can arise:

1. Lost Update Problem

$Process_1$	Time	$Process_2$
read(x)	1	
	2	read(x)
update(x)	3	
	4	update(x)
write(x)	5	
	6	write(x)

Table 1: Lost update problem.

2. Dirty Read

3. Phantom Updates

The Lost Update Problem is depicted in Table 1. $Process_1$ reads the variable x. Immediately after $process_1$ $process_2$ also reads x. Subsequently both processes update x and write it back to the database. Obviously the update from $process_1$ is lost.

To avoid these problems transactions describe atomic operations. The provision of an atomic operation [4] means that the effect of performing any operation on behalf of one client is free from interference with operations being performed on behalf of other concurrent clients; and either an operation must be completed successfully or it must have no effect at all. Atomic transactions are often characterized by the ACID principle [6]:

1. Atomicity: All operations of a transaction must be completed, i.e. a transaction is treated as a single, indivisible unit.

2. Consistency: A transaction takes the system from one consistent state to another.

3. Isolation: Each transaction must be performed without interference with other transactions.

4. Durability: After a transaction has successfully been completed all its results are saved in permanent storage.

Obviously, the simple serial execution of transactions preserves the ACID properties, but is not efficient. Therefore, the task of a *scheduler* is to maximize concurrency and to execute transactions interlocked. The scheduler ensures that the transactions are executed in a *serially equivalent* way. Schedulers usually belong to one of the following categories:

1. Blocking scheduler

Operation	Return value	Comment
BeginTransaction	TransId	Starts a new transaction
EndTransaction(TransId)	Commit $\vee$ Abort	Ends a transaction
Commit(TransId)		Commits a transaction
Abort(TransId)		Aborts a transaction

Table 2: Transaction commands.

Figure 2: Layered Transaction Model.

2. Non-blocking scheduler

A blocking scheduler applies read/write-locks in order to serialize transactions. A non-blocking scheduler does not use such locks. Instead, it coordinates the transactions using e.g. timestamps. A non-blocking technique of particular interest in the context of intrusion detection is the optimistic concurrency control. This technique is based on the assumption that the likelihood of conflicts (attacks) is low. Therefore, the transactions simply proceed and after termination the scheduler checks them for any conflicts.

What actually has to be considered by the scheduler as a transaction must be specified by the clients. The sequence of operations which should be executed according to the ACID principle is grouped by a BeginTransaction/EndTransaction pair. This groups several valid commands and defines a single meta command.

Depending on whether or not the scheduler is able to execute the transaction without conflicts it is committed or aborted (see Table 2).

3.2 Transaction-based Anomaly Detection

One common argument concerning the difficulty of detecting intrusive behavior is that attacks normally consist of single steps, each of which performs a legal operation. These legal steps are generally used to interfere with another process also performing legal operations. Considering the victim's and the attacker's sequence of operations as transactions, an attack will obviously not be successful if the ACID properties are guaranteed for the victim's transaction.

Although it will probably not be efficient to design transaction-based operating and network systems, the transaction concept itself can be used to detect intrusions. Like an optimistic scheduler, an IDS can check

each transaction at its end concerning its serially equivalent execution and its adherence to the ACID properties. If the check fails, the transaction is trapped. This is the general idea of transaction-based intrusion detection.

As we focus on communication systems in this paper, our model is based on the ISO/OSI reference model [5], which is made up of seven protocol layers[1]. The protocols of each of these layers can be described by *deterministic finite state machines* (DFSM) (Figure 2).

A DFSM A is a 5-tuple $A = (Q, \Sigma, q_0, \delta, F)$ with Q being the set of states which can occur during a transaction, Σ the union of all inputs, q_0 the initial state, $\delta : Q \times \Sigma \to Q$ the transition function, and F the set of final states. The syntax and semantics of a DFSM are unambiguously determined by the transition function.

The initial state of the DFSM is considered to be consistent. The DFSM passes through the operations (input events) that form the transaction. The transaction is successful if the final state is also consistent. To ensure this, atomicity, consistency and isolation properties have to be checked. The atomicity is checked on the base of the DFSM. The DFSM defines a language $\mathcal{L}(A)$. By checking whether $w \in \mathcal{L}(A)$ holds for a trace w extracted from the audit stream the transaction is tested for the atomicity property.

Subsequently the assertions (consistency property) are checked, which are expressed with the help of first order logic (FOL). Each DFSM can include assertions. Assertions can be valid only for a specific transaction (local assertions) or, on a more global level, for a certain layer (layer assertions, see Figure 2).

Finally the serially equivalent execution (isolation) of the transaction is checked (only if necessary).

---

[1]However, for concrete examples we use the TCP/IP protocol stack.

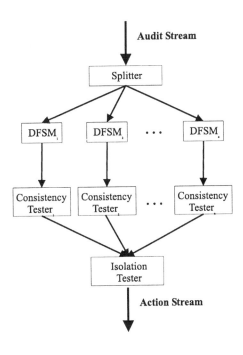

Audit Stream

Figure 3: General architecture.

The overall architecture is shown in Figure 3 and described in more detail in the following subsections.

3.2.1 The Splitter

The audit stream contains all events received from the different sources. As we focus on network protocols in this paper the audit stream consists of packets received from the network. The task of the splitter is to distribute these single events to the corresponding state machines. The assignment of events to a state machine is straightforward, as it follows the rules of the corresponding communication protocols. A TCP session, for instance, is uniquely identified by the 4-tuple *(source address, source port, destination address, address port)*, whereas a UDP packet is identified by its socket address. For a fragmented IP packet the 16-bit identification field, in combination with the `more fragments` bit of the flags field, the source address, the destination address and the protocol type allows the splitter to feed the corresponding audit data into the appropriate state machine.

The splitter is also responsible for the scheduling of the isolation tester. The scheduler monitors the event stream for any potential conflicts and feeds the isolation tester with the necessary information.

3.2.2 Template State Machine

As mentioned above, the theory of DFSMs is in general sufficient to represent the protocol state machines. Nonetheless, a major disadvantage of the DFSM theory is the nonexistence of variables. Therefore, a separate transition has to exist for each possible value of a variable during a protocol run. This blows up the state machines substantially.

To keep the state machines small we introduce the concept of a *Template State Machine* (TSM). A TSM represents a protocol in a value independent way. The actual instance of the protocol template, i.e. the concrete DFSM, is derived during run time from the audit data.

A TSM $\mathcal{A}$ is a 6-tuple $(Q, \Sigma, V, q_0, \delta, F)$ with

- Q - set of states which can occur during a transaction,

- Σ - the union of all inputs,

- V - set of variables,

- q_0 - initial state,

- δ - transition function, and

- F - set of final states.

The transition function δ is defined as follows:

$$\delta : Q \times (AExp(\Sigma, V))^+ - \rightarrow Q$$

$AExp(\Sigma, V)$ is defined by

$$
\begin{aligned}
e \quad ::= \quad & z \mid x \mid e_1 + e_2 \mid e_1 - e_2 \in AExp(\Sigma, V) \\
\text{with} \quad & z \in \Sigma, \text{and} \\
& x \in V.
\end{aligned}
$$

The semantics of the TSM, i.e. the derivation relation $\Rightarrow$, is defined by:

$$\Rightarrow \subseteq \big(Q \times \Sigma^+ \times (V \rightarrow \Sigma_\perp)\big) \times (Q \times (V \rightarrow \Sigma_\perp))$$

with

$(q, (z_1, \ldots), \sigma) \Rightarrow (q', \sigma')$, if
ex. $(e_1, \ldots) \in (AExp(\Sigma, V))^+$ with
$\delta(q, (e_1, \ldots)) = q'$ and
$\forall i : [(\sigma(e_i) = z_i \wedge \sigma' = \sigma) \vee$
$(\sigma(e_i = \perp \wedge e_i \in V \wedge \sigma' = \sigma[e_i/z_i])].$

In contrast to the DFSM, the semantics of a TSM is not determined solely by the transition function, but also by the instantiation of the variables.

The TSM mechanism serves several purposes:

- It enables the formal and compact specification of a protocol, which can dynamically be fed into a monitor.

- It prevents state explosions.

- It can be used for the graphical specification of protocols.

- It can be used for a consistency and correctness check of the protocol specification.

In this paper we concentrate on the two former points.

3.2.3 Consistency Tester

After the atomicity of a transaction has been checked with a TSM, the next step is to ensure that the transaction leaves the system in a consistent state. The consistent state itself is defined by so-called assertions. In general, we distinguish between two kinds of assertions, local assertions and layer assertions, respectively.

To express the assertions we use first order logic (FOL) with the restriction that the negation is only allowed for atomic formulas (FOL^+)[2].

Local Assertions Local assertions are related to a specific TSM, and are checked during the execution of transitions. Therefore, we have to add Boolean expressions to our TSM concept.

The transition function is adapted as follows:

$$\delta : Q \times (\text{AExp}(\Sigma, V))^+ \times \text{BExp} \longrightarrow Q$$

BExp is defined by

$$
\begin{aligned}
b \quad ::= \quad & \texttt{true} \mid \texttt{false} \mid e \\
\mid \quad & e_1 = e_2 \mid e_1 < e_2 \mid e_1 \neq e_2 \\
\mid \quad & b_1 \wedge b_2 \mid b_1 \vee b_2
\end{aligned}
$$

---

[2]Any formula can be transformed in an equivalent negation-free formula.

The semantics of a TSM changes in the following way:

$$\Rightarrow \subseteq \left(Q \times \Sigma^+ \times (V \to \Sigma_\perp)\right) \times \left(Q \times (V \to \Sigma_\perp)\right)$$

with

$(q, (z_1, \ldots), \sigma) \Rightarrow (q', \sigma')$, if
ex. $(e_1, \ldots) \in (AExp(\Sigma, V))^+$, $b \in Bexp(\Sigma, V)$ with
$\delta(q, (e_1, \ldots)) = q'$ and $\sigma(b) = \texttt{true}$ and
$\forall i : [(\sigma(e_i) = z_i \wedge \sigma' = \sigma) \vee$
$(\sigma(e_i) = \perp \wedge e_i \in V \wedge \sigma' = \sigma[e_i/z_i])]$.

Obviously, we do not need the whole expressiveness of FOL^+ for local assertions, as quantifiers do not necessarily make sense within the context of a TSM. Each transition is triggered by a single packet, which is checked for obeying the local assertions. No quantifiers are necessary in this context.

Layer Assertions Layer assertions are valid for all TSMs belonging to a single layer. In contrast to local assertions layer assertions can make use of the complete FOL^+, including universal and existential quantification. They can be checked either at the initial state or at a final state, i.e. before or after checking for atomicity. In general, a violation of an assertion should be detected as early as possible. Therefore, layer assertions will be checked at the initial state of a TSM whenever possible.

As layer assertions can be expected to be more complex than local assertions, they will not be checked during the execution of the corresponding TSM. In general, failure of a check of a layer assertion during run-time is possible, because intermediary states of the TSM must not necessarily fulfil the layer assertions. Intermediary states only describe the transformation process from one consistent state to another. This does not imply that all intermediary states have to fulfil the layer assertions, they only have to fulfil the local assertions. The layer assertions must hold for the initial state and for the final state.

3.2.4 Isolation Tester

The isolation tester is responsible for checking the isolation property, i.e. for checking whether a transaction performed without interference from other transactions. For general processes running on a single node the application of the isolation tester is obvious: it can detect attacks based on race conditions. To do so, the splitter has to monitor the audit stream for accesses to critical objects (e.g. directories and files) and start the isolation tester, which checks for a violation of the isolation property.

With regard to communication processes the use of an isolation tester is not immediately obvious. Nonetheless, certain attacks on the protocol level can be interpreted as a violation of the isolation property. This is especially true if we take the distributed nature of a communication process into account, i.e. if we do not only consider the effects of a protocol run on a single system, but broaden our transaction concept to include all nodes involved in the communication process. This results in the so-called compound transaction concept.

3.3 Compound Transactions

Signaling and communication protocols form the core of modern tele and data communication networks. They define the communication between two or more nodes. Therefore, it is not sufficient to consider only local transactions. Instead, it must also be possible to monitor *distributed transactions*.

Distributed transactions describe the parallel execution of single transactions on different nodes. This is not always sufficient in our context. Therefore, we enhance the concept of distributed transactions and also take the communication between the single transactions into account, i.e. the transactions communicate with each other, and the progress of one transaction depends on the progress of the other. The communication itself can also be considered as a transaction. Together with the local protocol actions of the sender and the receiver the communication forms a *compound transaction*.

Compound transactions cannot only be used to describe the horizontal communication between peer layers, but also the vertical communication between different layers within a protocol stack.

Whether a communication process is monitored as a distributed or a compound transaction depends on the level of granularity demanded by the IDS. We use the following syntax to distinguish between these two kinds of transactions:

1. Distributed Transactions: $A \parallel B$

2. Compound Transactions: $A \leftrightarrow B$

In order to describe the communication process between

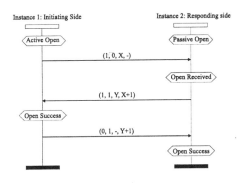

Figure 4: MSC for TCP's three-way handshake.

the involved components, we use *Message Sequence Charts* (MSCs).

MSCs [8] are a well-known technique for the visualization of communicating processes. A single MSC consists of different instances, which can communicate with each other. Each instance represents a DFSM, which is additionally allowed to communicate with another DFSM. Figure 4 shows the MSC for TCP's three-way handshake protocol in graphical notation.

An MSC is not a description of the complete behavior of a system. Rather it expresses one execution trace. To specify a system more detailed a collection of MSCs may be used [12].

The concrete textual syntax of the core language of MSCs [12] is given in Figure 5. The events in and out are used for the communication with other instances and the environment.

The correspondence between message outputs and message inputs has to be uniquely defined by message name identification. A message input must not be executed before the corresponding message output has been executed [12]. In addition, the activities along one single instance axis are completely ordered, but no notion of global time is assumed. Events of different instances are ordered only via messages, which imposes a partial ordering on the set of events being contained.

This partial ordering is checked by the IDS. The communication processes on both sides are identified by a unique transaction identifier (TransId). The transaction identifier is composed of the session characteristics already mentioned in section 3.2.1. For a TCP session, for example, the pair of socket addresses and the corresponding sequence numbers are used. To check the compound transaction for its correct execution two checks have to be performed:

```
msc        ::=   msc mscid; mscbody endmsc;
mscbody    ::=   instdef mscbody | ε
instdef    ::=   instance instid; instbody endinstance
instbody   ::=   event instbody | ε
event      ::=   in msgid from instid;
           |     in msgid from env;
           |     out msgid from instid;
           |     out msgid from env;
           |     action actid;
```

Figure 5: Basic Message Sequence Charts.

- Check the local transactions for their successful execution (aborted or committed?).

- Check the communication between the local transactions according to the MSC.

Step 1 is similar to the general approach taken for distributed database transactions. Each node involved in the transactions is polled by a coordinator for the success of its local transaction. Based on the information gathered from the nodes the coordinator decides on whether to commit or abort the transaction and informs the nodes (two-phase commit protocol).

In our case the coordinator will either be the receiver or a trusted third party (TTP). Our monitoring of distributed transactions follows the approach taken by the two-phase commit protocol. Nonetheless, for compound transactions the communication between the nodes has also to be taken into account. Communication between the nodes is checked to conform with the corresponding MSC. As we do not assume a global synchronized time, this check focuses on the partial order of the events defined by the MSC, particular the message in- and outputs. In the sense of the state operator λ_M defined in [12] we check that a message input is not executed before the corresponding message output. The coordinator therefore requests the input and output events from the participating nodes and performs this check.

Compound transactions can be mapped onto distributed transaction. The checking of the MSC simply defines an additional local transaction that leads to a local decision about committing or aborting the whole transaction based on its course of communication.

This method will only work if the source of the audit data is reliable. Otherwise, an attacker could send the requesting node a faked set of in- and output events. The IDS components therefore need to communicate in an authentic way.

4 Examples

To demonstrate the feasibility of our approach, we will examine two aspects related to our model using practical examples. On the one hand we will elaborate on the aspect of how to subdivide a communication process horizontally and vertically into transactions for monitoring. On the other hand we will have a closer look at certain attack scenarios and describe how they will lead to trap events based on violations of the ACID principle. Regarding the latter we will distinguish between attacks which are to be considered in the context of local transactions (e.g. Ping of Death) and attacks to be considered in the context of compound transaction (e.g. IP spoofing).

The typical scenario for these examples is a *Virtual Private Network* (VPN).

4.1 Scenario

Future applications will increasingly involve several distributed sites, which will typically be interconnected by a VPN.

VPNs are a well suited scenario for studying IDS and distributed IDS functionality as they involve two or more parties belonging to different security domains with different trust relationships. We consider three general scenarios for our approach:

1. Local security domain.

2. Cooperation of trusting security domains (e.g. sites interconnected via a VPN).

3. Cooperation of non-trusting security domains (e.g. VPN sites and network provider).

The two latter scenarios are of special interest to distributed and compound transactions.

4.2 Atomicity

The check for atomicity of a transaction helps to detect various attacks as abnormal behavior. This includes *SYN flooding*, a *denial of service* attack.

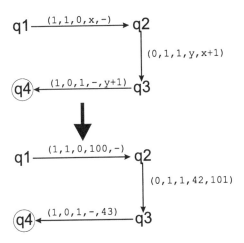

Figure 6: TSM for the 3-Way-Handshake.

With SYN flooding a server is hit by a large number of connection requests. The sender address is normally spoofed.

By defining the TCP connection establishment process as a transaction it becomes obvious that the corresponding DFSM on the victims side is not completed. The final state q_4 is not reached, and therefore the atomicity property is violated.

Figure 6 shows the corresponding TSM of the 3-way-handshake. The 5-tuple used obeys the following scheme:

$$(b_0, b_1, b_2, c_0, c_1)$$

with

- b_0 - Boolean value, indicating whether a packet was sent ($b_0 = 0$) or received ($b_0 = 1$);

- b_1 - Boolean value, indicating whether or not the SYN flag was set;

- b_2 - Boolean value, indicating whether or not the ACK flag was set;

- c_0 - sequence number of the local node;

- c_1 - sequence number of the remote node, incremented by 1 (acknowledgement number).

Obviously, a SYN flooding attack can be detected by the violation of the atomicity property. The protocol itself recognizes the incomplete 3-way-handshake through a timeout. This timeout triggers the receiver to send a reset (RST bit set). As a result the next message received by our monitor is an invalid 5-tuple, which aborts the transaction.

An example for an attack involving two sides in the detection process (second scenario) is *IP-spoofing* based on sequence numbers. In fact, the SYN flooding attack is part of this attack. If host C hijacks a connection between sender A and receiver B, the local transaction monitored at site B will end with a `Commit(TransId)`. By considering the communication as a distributed or compound transaction the whole communication is decomposed into two or three local transactions. Only if all of these local transactions commit, the distributed or compound transaction also commits. For IP-spoofing the local transaction at sender A will obviously abort and therefore the whole communication transaction will be aborted.

Other attacks that can be detected by monitoring the atomicity of a transaction include e.g. *port scanning attacks*.

4.3 Consistency

The consistency of a transaction guarantees that the communication process is error free and adheres to the protocol specification. This also helps to detect various attacks.

One example is the *Ping of death*. This attack is based on the fragmentation of IP packets. According to [17], IP packets including the header may have a size of up to 65535 octets. Without any option fields the header has a size of 20 octets. Packets which exceed the size accepted by layer 2 of the protocol stack[3], are fragmented and reassembled at the receiver side.

An ICMP ECHO request consists of an eight octet ICMP header [18], which is followed by the request data. Therefore, the maximum size of the data field is 65507 octets.

Nonetheless, it is possible to construct and send an invalid packet, in which the data part contains more than 65507 octets. This is based on the fragmentation process. The fragmentation is done by specifying an offset and the size of the fragment. For the last fragment it is therefore possible to exceed the 65535 octet limit for the whole packet.

A layer assertions therefore specifies that the total size of a packet cannot exceed 65535 octets. This layer assertion has to be put into action by the TSM, i.e. the layer assertion is transformed into a local assertion and

---

[3]Defined by the maximum transmission unit (MTU).

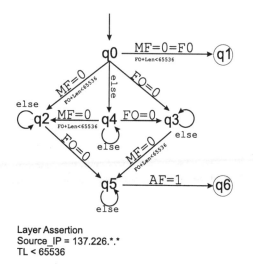

Layer Assertion
Source_IP = 137.226.*.*
TL < 65536

Figure 7: TSM for the reassembling of IP fragments.

a corresponding check. In our example the check can be done when receiving the final fragment, because for this fragment the sum of the fragment offset and fragment length has to be less than 65536.

Figure 7 shows the corresponding TSM using the following abbreviations:

- *FO* (Fragment Offset) - offset (in 8-byte units) of the fragment from the beginning of the original datagram;

- *MF* (More Fragments) - one bit in the *flags* field turned on for each fragment comprising a datagram except the final fragment;

- *AF* - Boolean expression, indicating whether or not all fragments have been received;

- *TL* (Total Length) - total length of the IP datagram;

- *Source_IP* - IP source address of the fragment sender.

The TSM uses both local and layer assertions. The local assertions are part of the inscription of the transitions, the layer assertions are explicitly specified below the TSM.

The local assertions ensure that the fragment with $MF = 0$ is checked if the sum of the fragment offset and the fragment length is actually less than 65536 octets. This puts the second layer assertion into action.

The first layer assertion defines the admissible general conditions of the communication. In this simple example the set of valid sources is limited to IP addresses of the form 137.226. *.* or written as a FOL^+ expression:

$$\exists a_3, a_4 \in \{0, \ldots, 255\} : SrcAddr = 137.226.a_3.a_4$$

This assertion is checked before the run through the TSM.

4.4 Isolation

Isolation means that each transaction must be performed without interference with other transactions, i.e. the intermediate effects of a transaction must not be visible to other transactions [4]. As already stated the violation of the isolation property is not immediately obvious in the network context discussed so far, although e.g. IP-spoofing based on sequence numbers could also be interpreted as a violation of the isolation property. We will therefore not elaborate on this topic in this paper. Nonetheless, as one major design goal of our approach is universal validity, we will briefly stress its validity in the context of processes. With processes, monitoring of the isolation property helps to prevent security failures due to improper synchronization of processes or race conditions.

An abstract example for improper synchronization is given in Table 1. A concrete example for such a lost update problem [10] describes a scenario in which a user invokes the *passwd* program to change his password while an administrator is editing the password file. The two programs modify the password file simultaneously, leaving it with an incorrect content.

Following our approach we can consider either one or both of the accesses to the password file as a transaction. By doing this, the transaction is monitored for its isolated execution and the password file cannot be left with an incorrect content. In contrast to the network scenario the allowed transactions have not already been defined by any kind of protocol specification. When entering the process and user level depicted in Figure 1, the allowed transactions must be explicitly specified in the security policy. In order to avoid restrictions for the normal user it is sufficient to define transactions on the basis of valid action sequences for administrators and security critical processes.

4.5 Durability

So far, we have not considered in detail the property of durability. As atomicity, consistency and isolation are properties which focus on the execution of the transaction, the durability property influences the period after the successful execution of a transaction. The effects of a successful transaction have to survive even hard- and software failures or, in our case, attacks.

What does that mean in the context of an IDS? For databases the durability property (in combination with the atomicity) ensures that after a failure the database state to be reconstructed is well defined. This property is also useful for systems under attack. After an attack has been detected it is often difficult to determine the latest safe state. If the administrator cannot determine the exact time of a successful intrusion, he cannot be sure that his backups are free from security leaks. Therefore, an IDS should not only support the detection of attacks, it should also support the administrator in the reconstruction of the system and the reestablishment of a safe state. Nonetheless, the details of this approach will be discussed elsewhere.

5 Related Works

The approach most similar to ours is described in Calvin Ko's paper "Execution Monitoring of Security-Critical Programs in a Distributed System: A Specification-Based Approach" [10]. It follows a specification-based approach and also describes the meaning of atomic actions in relation to intrusion detection. However, [10] does not follow the parallels to the classical transactional model and therefore, from our point of view, looses some of its generality. For instance [10] cites the examples of a super user editing the password file and an user changing his password in the same file. The given solution is a specification in the form of a so-called *Parallel Environment Grammar* (PEG). In the PEG the parallel execution of two programs[4] is specified as shown in Figure 8.

Although we focus on communication processes in this paper it is obvious that the transaction model also applies to this process centric scenario. Following the transaction model it is sufficient to specify the most high-level

---

[4]The concrete and therefore longer PEG for the password file example can be found in section 5.4 of [10]. The general structure is the same as for this simple example.

```
    Environment Variables
1.  Int E=0;

    Start Expression
2.  <progA> || <progB>

    Hyperrules
3.  <progA> -> <writeA, E>.
4.  <writeA, 0> -> <openA> <closeA>{E=E-1;}.
5.  <open> -> open_A {E=E+1;}.
6.  <close> -> close_A.

7.  <progB> -> <writeB, E>.
8.  <writeB, 0> -> <openB><closeB>{E=E-1;}.
9.  <openB> -> open_B {E=E+1;}.
10. <closeB> -> close_B.
```

Figure 8: Parallel Environment Grammar (PEG).

(su level) action as a transaction. It is not necessary to explicitly specify the parallel execution, because of the check for the serially equivalent execution performed by the scheduler.

Another system related to ours is the Bro system [15]. The specifications made by Bro can be integrated into our approach as a part of the Assertion-section of a transaction or a layer. As we do not yet have specified the exact data types to be used in our approach, we are currently considering the reuse of some of the data types already specified by Bro.

The main limitation of our model is related to the specification process. In general, the specification of communication processes can be extracted immediately from the protocol specification. Therefore, the specification can either be provided by the vendor or any other trusted third party (ease of specification). Any attack based on an implementation error can be indirectly detected by our approach because it will be recognized as an anomaly. Any closer examination and classification (error or attack) of the anomaly can be done either by a human operator or a misuse intrusion detection component.

Nonetheless, the transaction model cannot deal with specification or management errors, which form the other two sources of vulnerabilities. The transaction model only deals with implementation errors. If the specification of a communication protocol or its transformation into a specification for the anomaly detection system itself is faulty, attacks based on these errors will remain undetected because by definition they follow the specification and can therefore not be considered to be anomalies. The same holds for any management errors of the environment.

6 Conclusions and Outlook

In this paper we have proposed a new technique for anomaly based intrusion detection. The detection of anomalies is based on the definition of correct transactional behavior. This definition of correct, desired behavior defines the system's multi-level security policy, which is monitored during run-time by the IDS. In contrast to classical database and other transactional systems we do not enforce the distinct transactions to be executed according to the ACID properties. Instead, in the sense of an optimistic scheduler, we monitor the system only for any potential conflicts.

Obviously, it is neither desirable nor feasible to monitor all host activities and connections. The monitoring will therefore be performed dynamically, i.e. the different sensors will be activated and configured on demand by a control instance being part of the general network management environment. This is one of the main design criteria for our *Aachener Network Intrusion Detection Architecture* (ANIDA), which forms the broader context to which the described anomaly detection approach belongs.

Our approach is currently under development and first results of the prototype will be available soon.

Acknowledgements

We would like to thank Dr. Thomas Noll for his helpful comments and suggestions.

References

[1] K. Bradley, S. Cheung, N. Puketza, B. Mukherjee, and Ronald A. Olson. Detecting disruptive routers: A distributed network monitoring approach. In *Proceedings of the IEEE Symposium on Security and Privacy*. IEEE, May 1998.

[2] R. Büschkes, D. Kesdogan, and P. Reichl. How to increase security in mobile networks by anomaly detection. In *Proceedings of the 14th Annual Computer Security Applications Conference (ACSAC'98)*. ACM, December 1998.

[3] S. Cheung and K. Levitt. Protecting routing infrastructures from denial of service using cooperative intrusion detection. In *Proceedings New Security Paradigms Workshop 1997*, Cumbria, UK, September 1997.

[4] G. Coulouris, J. Dollimore, and T. Kindberg. *Distributed Systems - Concepts and Design*. Addison-Wesley, 2nd edition, 1994.

[5] Fred Halsall. *Data communications, comuter networks, and open systems*. Addison-Wesley, 3rd edition, 1992.

[6] T. Härder and A. Reuter. Principles of transaction-oriented database recovery. *Computing Surveys*, 15(4), 1983.

[7] K. Ilgun, Richard A. Kemmerer, and Phillip A. Porras. State transition analysis: A rule-based intrusion detection approach. *IEEE Transactions on Software Engineering*, 21(3):181–199, March 1995.

[8] ITU-T. *ITU-T Recommendation Z.120: Message Sequence Chart (MSC)*. ITU-T, Geneva, 1993.

[9] H. Javitz and A. Valdes. The SRI IDES statistical anomaly detector. In *Proceedings of the IEEE Symposium on Research in Security and Privacy*, pages 316–326, May 1991.

[10] C. Ko. *Execution Monitoring of Security-Critical Programs in a Distributed System: A Specification-Based Approach*. PhD thesis, University of California, Davis, 1996.

[11] S. Kumar. *Classification and Detection of Computer Intrusions*. PhD thesis, Department of Computer Science, Purdue University, August 1995.

[12] S. Mauw and M. A. Reniers. An algebraic semantics of basic message sequence charts. *The Computer Journal*, 37(4), 1994.

[13] A. Mounji. *Languages and Tools for Rule-Based Distributed Intrusion Detection*. PhD thesis, Facultés Universitaires Notre-Dame de la Paix Namur, Belgium, September 1997.

[14] B. Mukherjee, L. Heberlein, and K. Levitt. Network intrusion detection. *IEEE Network*, pages 26–41, May/June 1994.

[15] V. Paxson. Bro: A system for detecting network intruders in real-time. In *Proceedings of the 7th USENIX Security Symposium*, January 1998.

[16] Phillip A. Porras and Peter G. Neumann. Emerald: Event monitoring enabling responses to anomalous live disturbances. In *Proceedings of the 20th National Information Systems Security Conference*, October 1997.

[17] J. Postel. *RFC 791: Internet Protocol*, September 1981.

[18] J. Postel. *RFC 792: Internet Control Message Protocol*, September 1981.

[19] S. Staniford-Chen, S. Cheung, R. Crawford, M. Dilger, J. Frank, J. Hoagland, K. Levitt, C. Wee, R. Yip, and D. Zerkle. Grids: A graph-based intrusion detection system for large networks. In *Proceedings of the 19th National Information Systems Security Conference*, Baltimore, 1996.

[20] A. Tucker Jr., editor. *CRC Computer Science and Engineering Handbook*. CRC Press, December 1996.

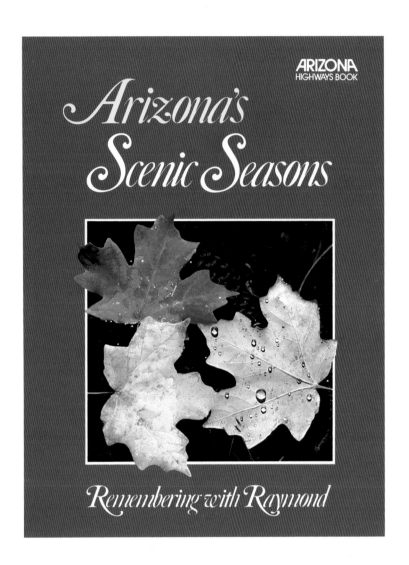

Arizona's Scenic Seasons

ARIZONA
HIGHWAYS BOOK

Remembering with Raymond

ARIZONA
HIGHWAYS BOOK

Selected writings of
Raymond Carlson
Editor
Arizona Highways Magazine
1938-1971

Photography by
Arizona Highways
Contributors

Arizona's Scenic Seasons
Remembering with Raymond

Prepared by the Related Products Section
of *Arizona Highways Magazine*
Hugh Harelson, Publisher

WESLEY HOLDEN— Editor
DON DEDERA—Text Editor
J. PETER MORTIMER—Picture Editor
W. RANDALL IRVINE—Design and Production

Library of Congress Catalog Number 83-073646
ISBN 0-916179-00-1
ISBN 0-916179-01-X (soft cover)

This book is set in H. B. Poppl-Pontifex and headlines in Caslon 471
Italic with Swash by Arizona Typographers, Phoenix, Arizona, and
printed and bound by Toppan Printing Company, Ltd., Tokyo, Japan.

Arizona Highways Magazine, a monthly publication of the
Arizona Department of Transportation: Hugh Harelson,
Publisher; Don Dedera, Editor; Richard G. Stahl, Managing Editor;
Gary Bennett, Art Editor; J. Peter Mortimer, Picture Editor;
Lorna Holmes, Assistant Art Editor; Robert J. Farrell, Assistant Copy Editor;
Wesley Holden, Managing Editor, Related Products Section.

(Front cover) Peter Kresan (Back cover) Dick Dietrich
(Following panel) Oak Creek Canyon. Ron Swartley

Remembering Raymond...

Summer Wears a Green Gown...

If ever I would leave you,
It wouldn't be in summer...

Black River reflections in the White Mountains.
David Muench

Summer...She wears that old, old look. Paris shears have not altered the hem of her skirt nor changed the line of her bodice. Bespectacled little chemists, stirring the brew in their odorous dye pots, have concocted no outlandish colors for her to go swishing about in. Slick and glossy fashion editors of slick and glossy fashion magazines seldom call on her for an interview. She carries no appointments for sittings before high-powered cameras operated by high-powered young men. She's just as plain as can be. Her plainness is the essence of poise and dignity.

She wears a green gown, and it is mighty becoming. It isn't a monotonous green, mind you. It is the gray green of the saguaro, the silvery green of ripening grain, the dark green of the pine, the bright green of the sycamore, the light green of weeds on a canal bank, the green of olives with a faintly bluish cast, the just-right green of new mown grass.

She's composed, serene and smiling, and carries herself as if she were somebody, which, in truth, she is. She's so cool and calm in her lovely green gown, and she has the loveliest name. Her name is Summer.

(Left) Butterfly in the Coconino National Forest. George McCullough

(Right) Summer in the White Mountains. Jerry Jacka

(Left, below) Rocky Mountain mule deer in the Kaibab National Forest. James Tallon

(Below) Nature's garden in the Apache-Sitgreaves National Forest. Jerry Jacka

Tranquillity

There are many definitions of tranquillity. It might be described in one way as one being at peace in Nature's world around and about. It comes to the sailor on the placid seas; it comes to the mountain man, surrounded by the green and serene forests. It comes to the dweller in the desert land.

Here is distance and stillness and peace... here only the marks of the Sun, of the fitful wind, of the changing seasons which represent the errant notations of time's dreamy passing.

When you live in a big land, but not over-populated, just a few minutes drive and there you are; in the tranquil world of Nature. If you make your peace with that world you have attained man's most desirable state of being: tranquillity...

The lonely acres may be the answer to the yearning that is deep within all of us that sometime, someplace we may be where Nature's handiwork is unaltered and our companions are the Sun, the wind, and the eternal skies with their depths of blue at day and their star-filled radiance at night.

The desert is a place for contemplation and reverie. One might ponder the inscrutable ways of the Creator that provide a brave living for the flora and fauna of the desert that live and survive and even flourish under conditions that could be described, even generously, as harsh...

Here the boundary of one's world is the shimmering horizon even beyond where the mountains are nothing more than hazy, purple curtains. Our world has no boundaries. Our thoughts and dreams and hopes soar beyond the boundaries of our world and, perhaps, that is the very essence of tranquillity.

Dawn on Hawley Lake near Pinetop. David Muench

Rain

It just happened to be one of those years—the year it rained. Rainy years have been few and far between in this arid land of ours, but the welcome rains came last winter and spring...

People who live in wetter areas of our blessed land, who might receive seven or eight inches of rain in a single day, might not be impressed by our boastful figures, but when your average rainfall is six inches a year (a figure that hasn't been reached in years), an over-average is something to be very happy about.

Rain and the miracle of spring brought life to the desert land and millions, maybe billions, of wild flowers raised their colorful heads in grateful salute...Rain sure can pretty up the land...

Folks can get mighty philosophical about rain. Like the old-timer said, squinting up at the blue, clear sky, "It'll rain! It always has!"

(Left) Tonto Creek below the Mogollon Rim.
(Right) Rustler Park in the Chiricahua Mountains.
(Below) Approaching thunderstorm at Sunset Crater.
Jerry Sieve photos

A soft Sleepiness

You can't always tell by the cool calculations
of the calendar or the bobbing babble of the
thermometer. The testimony of the way-
ward Sun is not always reliable. You awaken
one fine morning and for some indefinable
reason you know summer is just around the
corner. There is a languor in the shadows
and a soft sleepiness in the air that bespeak
summer's approach. There is a drowsiness
in the gossip of the green, green leaves
caressed by the soft, warm breeze. You
know that spring has had her fling and
another season is getting ready to cavort
over the landscape.

Cooley Lake in the White Mountains. Jerry Jacka

Canyons Calling

Wherever you go in this land of ours you'll come across canyons. You'll even find them on mountaintops as you will when you visit Chiricahua National Monument in the Chiricahua Mountains in Cochise County. The canyons themselves in this area are bounded by rock formations in every conceivable size and shape, mounded deftly by all the tools of the weather.

Where the hills and the mountains break off into the desert you come upon marvelous canyon formations. Sabino Canyon joins the desert and the mountains in Pima County retaining both the design of desert and mountain, losing nothing but gaining from the two, and remaining a canyon in every detail, truly a scenic spot and delightful to see.

And so it goes in this, the canyon country. You will find big canyons and little ones, each with a personality of its own. Tombstone, Aravaipa, Bloody Tanks, White Horse, Six Shooter, Echo, Cave Creek, White and Red and Black and Green—all canyons as picturesque as their names, to mention a few in the endless list. When the time comes to travel again the exciting trails through our West, and it will come soon, you can seek out canyons for yourself. The canyons and the country will be here. The canyons are part of the country, and like the country they never change, for they are governed only by the moods of time, wind, and the weather....

(Left) Morning mist in the rocky canyons near Sedona. Steve Bruno
(Right) Ribbon Falls in the Grand Canyon. Jody Forster
(Following panel) Hiking through time in the Grand Canyon. George McCullough

Navajoland

Navajoland is a wonderful island of geology, geography, anthropology, and meteorology, a parcel of landscape unique in these United States. It is a big land, and within its borders resides the largest Indian tribe in the country.

It is mostly high plateau land, in places cruelly carved with deep canyons, in places supporting harsh mesas, and in places there are a few mountain ranges (Navajo Mountain, the Chuskas, the Lukachukais, for instance) whose pine-covered summits extend regally and eternally into the deep blue canopy of sky.

It is not a "pretty" land, but a harshly beautiful land. The gentle greens of gentler lands are not to be found here. The predominant colors are red and orange and burnt yellow, searing splashes of cruel color under the relentless tyranny of the Sun.

Here the capricious wind finds room for its gambolings, turning red cliffs into rolling sand dunes, carving those very cliffs into strange and contorted formations—all evidence of the mighty power of the singing wind.

Navajoland is an arid land, so arid it puzzles the beholder that the patient Navajos can find enough fodder to support their grazing herds of sheep. And when the storms come they do so with such fury one marvels the red earth itself can endure such onslaughts.

In this land of distance and elusive horizons live the Navajos, whose love of their land is a religion. They are inured to the vagaries of the elements. They accept the wind, the Sun, the lack of rain, all the tempestuous quirks of time and weather—with stoic resignation, for all such things are their gods' will.

They find their land good. It was good when they moved into it hundreds of years ago. It is good today....

Navajo shepherds in Monument Valley.
Herb and Dorothy McLaughlin

(Left) Sunset over Willcox Playa.
Josef Muench
(Below) Sulphur Spring Valley
in southeastern Arizona.
David Muench
(Right, below) Sunrise over
the Pinaleño Mountains near
Safford. Jerry Sieve

Skies and Grass

The words of the old refrain have been with us since childhood, and too often, like the words of a familiar prayer, a great hymn, or an intimate ballad, they lose their meaning by being sung and resung, told and retold.

America...O beautiful for spacious skies... Old words, old tune, yet brave new words, brave new tune.

These are our skies, the skies of Arizona, one of the precious things about this big land of mountains and desert. These are the skies that cloak distant horizons, a fitting backdrop for such regal settings. There is strength in our skies and bigness and promise and might. There is poetry, too, and music, and they have something sacred about them, like religion. There are the kind of skies that lift men's eyes, the kind of skies you should look at with your soul...

The skies of our land are ever-changing, yet changeless. Each day brings a new, bright sky, with new patterns in sunlight and clouds, enhanced by varying shades of blue. These are skies that make a proper canopy over a new land, where only yesterday, it seems, new trails were cut, new lands were found by the adventuresome people searching the new horizons.

Grass, not gold, is the basis of empire. Civilizations have perished because of the lack of it and the neglect of it. Nations have become great because of an abundance of it. It is one of God's greatest gifts to man, least appreciated, most abused. It is the supreme triumph of the chemistry of soil, rain, Sun.

Grass is Earth's natural cover. When this panoply disappears, the Good Earth is exposed to the ravages of wind and rain. The soil becomes lifeless, and all life supported by the soil perishes. Grass for our people has meant sorrow, despair, exultation. Grass is triumph and tragedy.

A sea of grass is beauty and utility. A million delicate roots clutching the soil, holding it in place, nurturing it! A million blades of grass bespeaking a bountiful land, the well-being of the people who are of the land....

Desert Storm

There is anger in the storm. There is anger in the howling wind, and anger, too, in sonorous and sinister rolls of thunder as if some mad gods were kicking tin cans across the sky. The cruel lightning flashes are like strokes of great swords held by madder gods flailing each other to settle their lordly quarrels. Ever since the beginning of time humankind has been afraid of the storm. Our distant uncles and their kinfolks sat huddled and shivering in their caves when outside the elements were cutting capers and clawing at the Earth. They attributed the storm to the fury of supernatural beings and shivered all the more. They defied the forces of the sky and weather, and today simpler peoples do the same thing, with the sun the beneficial god and inclement weather signs of disapprobation of lesser and more perverse gods holding court with the Sun. We understand the storm now, but we cannot control it....

There is drama in the storm. Sky and Earth meet and are one, and the beholder, if he has a comfortable seat, is afforded

divine entertainment. This is especially true in our western country where the sky is endless and the land stretches on and on. The faraway mountain ranges, seen as bright purple through the rarified atmosphere, turn darker as the clouds form over them and cloud shadows blot out the sun. The sky gets darker and darker as if the lights were being dimmed on the stage, there is lightning like probings of strong spotlights, thunder the sound of drums, and a curtain of rain, slanting with the wind, joining the sky and Earth so that you cannot tell where one begins and the other leaves off....

There is beauty in the storm. The great thunderheads of summer have a massiveness and a grandeur never found in other cloud formations. They form, they pour their moisture to the Earth, and then they break up and scatter....

Evening thunderstorm over Tucson.
Robert Campbell
(Following panel) Storm clouds reaching skyward over Mesa. Bruce Vanderhaar

Grand Canyon Storm

The clouds show the way of the wind. There are no clouds and no wind as a long summer day begins at Grand Canyon. The sky is dark blue overhead, light blue, almost white, at the horizon as if there was not enough blue to go around. It is a big sky, this sky that covers the Canyon. The shadows in the Canyon are long and cool, crazy shaped shadows as if the turrets and pinnacles that cast them are stretching and twisting in grotesque postures after a night's repose. Giants with sleep and dreams in their eyes....

Mid-morning! The Sun rides his chariot higher into the sky. Shadows grow shorter. The hot breath of the Sun weakens the color in sky and Earth. The river digging in the bottom of the Canyon becomes a streak of glinting silver...

The four-o'clock sky over the Canyon is a dark, brooding sky, heavy with moisture. The fitful gusts of wind will shake the patient cedars on the rim and kick up dust along the trails that crawl down steep rock walls. Flashes of lightning leap out of the dark sky. The cloud gods are flailing the Earth with angry whips. Thunder echoes in the depths of the Canyon.

Then out in the Canyon it begins to rain. Patches here and there, moving about, curtains of water spilling out of the sky, and as you watch you cannot see where Earth begins and the dark sky ends. Lightning continues the mad dance, and the thunder is a great wave of noise flooding the Canyon. The Sun, defiant of the storm, breaks through the clouded sky and, to show what a clever fellow he is, hangs a rainbow out in the Canyon for all the world to see.

The storm is short-lived. The Sun parts the clouds and the rain stops. The dark sky breaks up in little pieces and each little piece becomes a white cloud and the white clouds hitch a ride with the wind and go tumbling along to other places. The newly-washed Canyon is clean and bright after the rain. The Sun seems to be brighter than ever and then with a triumphant smile and satisfied with a good day's work he decides to call it a day. Before he leaves, he fills the Canyon with gold that gradually turns to deep purple. The evening sky is clear and studded with bright, twinkling gems called stars and a summer day and a summer storm end at Grand Canyon.

Storm in the Grand Canyon. Kathleen Norris Cook

Our Southwest

The name "Southwest" could start a lot of arguments. It is conceivable that residents of Chickasha or Big Cabin, Oklahoma, could consider themselves true Southwesterners or that folks living in Dallas, Sugar Land, Big Spring, Muleshoe, Mesquite or Sherman, Texas, would claim they were deep in the heart of the Southwest. It is further conceivable that a geographer would scoff at such claims and by merely pointing to a map say the true Southwest is Southern California, but, to us, that doesn't seem to ring a bell. Maybe the "Southwest" is more a state of mind than an explicit geographical fact.

Our Southwest is a large piece of landscape of which Arizona is the center and which would encompass strips of our neighboring states— California, Nevada, Utah, Southwestern Colorado, New Mexico and, for good measure, our neighbor to the south, Sonora, Mexico.

Our Southwest is hemmed in between the Coastal range on the west and the high Rockies on the east. It is a generally barren, arid, empty land, harsh in some ways, fantastically colorful in others, a land that seems to be swallowed in distance, canopied with the endless blue of endless skies in which seasonal storms drift in to add a spice of contrast and change, giving by their presence respite from what can become a monotonous Sun.

Our Southwest, as we describe it, is by far the most scenic area in these United States. It takes in within its boundaries numerous national parks, and many national monuments, national recreational areas, national historical shrines, state parks, national forests, and Indian reservations. It is difficult to keep a count of all that have been set aside for our pleasure and the pleasure of future generations.

One of the oldest inhabited parts of our country, Our Southwest is essentially the least inhabited. By square mile count, our population is so small the land could almost be called empty, but there are enough folks around so that one does not lack for neighbors.

That's how we describe Our Southwest.

Saguaro Lake, one of four major lakes on the Salt River east of Phoenix. James Tallon

A Dam & a Lake

Glen Canyon Dam holds back the water of Lake Powell for over 185 miles. James Tallon photos

First there was the Earth, a sodden mudball Divinely created.... Then the mud hardened, and eventually crevices were formed on Earth's obdurate crust, and little trickles of water began to dig the crevices deeper and deeper. One of these crevices became known as Glen Canyon, and the trickle of water that formed it became known as the Colorado, one of the great rivers of America.

Glen Canyon! Remote, lonely, and hauntingly beautiful, was known to ancient people, to the Navajos, to a few early-day explorers, and then in modern times to a few hardy and adventuresome river enthusiasts forever seeking the lonely and out-of-the-way places. The mighty river flowed on and on through the silent Canyon.

Then to harness the strength of the river, a dam was built....

Comes Autumn:
the Gentle, Welcome Intruder...

But if I'd ever leave you,
It couldn't be in autumn...

Autumn along Oak Creek, Steve Bruno

Autumn. You will find autumn in the mountains along the road through the aspen. The leaves, a few weeks ago so green and shiny and sparkling in the sunlight, have turned to yellow, gold, red, and brown. For the touch of autumn is a magic touch, and autumn is in the air. The wind tugs at the leaves. They fall to the ground to dance before the wind, and they are crisp and crunchy underfoot. Soon all the leaves will be gone from the aspen, and the branches, so white and delicate, will hum a different tune to the music of the wind.

All the flowers are gone now...insects, whose voices were raised to summer's song are gone, too. Summer is over, and it is time to rest. The colors have faded from Earth's covering; a warmer carpet has been spread, a thick brown carpet deep enough and warm enough to keep out the cold of winter.

The days of autumn are shorter, and they hurry along as if they had more important business elsewhere. There is frost on the ground in the morning, and the air has a bite and a nip. Night falls swiftly, and there is not that lingering twilight that marks the days of summer. The stars have a steely look, as if they, too, felt the season's change.

Yet not even spring is more beautiful in the mountains than autumn. The colors of the leaves turning before autumn's touch are extravagantly rich, a profusion of gold coin, turning to more solemn tones, flung over the land. Against the color of the turning leaves, the green of the pine and spruce stand out, and even the blue of the sky takes on a depth and character it does not possess at any other time during the year.

Autumn brings a hush to the mountain world, as if all the world were tensed and waiting. The gossipy, chattering birds have taken their gossip and chatter to other places. What you hear is the sound of crispy brown leaves dancing before the wind.

(Right) Log watering trough in the White Mountains. Jerry Jacka
(Below) Detail of aspen leaves. Kathleen Norris Cook

Mountain Music

There is persuasion in the invitation of the cool, green silence of the mountains while summer's heat still envelops the lowlands. In just a couple of whiles from the desert one can find streams, lakes, meadows, and the eternal music of the pines telling their age-old secrets to the wind.

Hannagan Meadow along the Coronado Trail.
Jerry Jacka

September

September's arrival on the Arizona calendar is always an auspicious one. The month heralds the coming of autumn and finds summer beginning to pack up the more dazzling items of her wardrobe. Out here in Arizona the changing of the seasons is not something that takes place overnight but is a gradual, almost imperceptible process, not harsh or impatient, but gentle and calm. So summer is still with us in September, you understand, but autumn is in the air. September's weather is just about perfect.

For the traveler, September and October are perfect travel months. All Arizona beckons, and it would be hard to find two months more perfect for the adventurer to follow the open road. You will like September, in our land.

(Right) Frosty dawn greets the ghost town of Jerome.
Willard Clay
(Below) Mule deer and ground squirrel get ready for
winter. James Tallon photos

The Mellow Month

If you are like us, you love ice cream, fried chicken, and October. October is a dreamy month, a mellow month, when the summer Sun has been toned down in its intensity, and the rather frigid blasts of winter, not too far over the horizon, have not arrived to force one to turn on the heating system. October is a month one doesn't have to hide from. The month beckons one to follow the sorceress trail to the highland and the woodland where October's beauty proclaims old Mother Nature at her colorful best.

(Above) Enjoying the last warm days of autumn.
Tom Canby
(Left) Country road through an aspen glade near
Flagstaff. Dick Dietrich

October

October in Arizona has a split personality. On the desert, the weather is warm and mild, as if summer had taken a liking to the place and was very reluctant to leave. In the higher country, however, it is definitely autumn. The leaves are turning, and there is a chill in the air both morning and evening.

(Left and below) Maple trees in Maple Canyon, Chiricahua Mountains. Willard Clay photos
(Right) An old cabin nestles in an autumn forest. Dick Canby

So the Seasons Change

Out of the north and across the wide expanse comes autumn, the gentle, welcome intruder, dispelling the last caress of summer, carefree truant in the carefree land. The leaves have lost their bright green, turning to brown, orange, red, yellow, touched by the season's enchantment. So gradual and casual is the change in dress in these proud high mountain dwellers that it seems as if they hardly change at all—yet one day the change is complete, and the leaves fall dry and brown and crisp to the ground....They came from the Earth, and they return to the Earth, so completing their life's span...and a life well-spent.

Autumn is a new world. The Sublime Stagehand has shifted the scenery. The seasons change. It is time to think long thoughts of the high mountains and aspen groves and the leaves brown and dry and crisp hurrying along the ground before the wind from the north that autumn brings....

Along the road to Escudilla Mountain near Alpine.
Jerry Jacka

November

Of all the months in the year, November in Arizona can lay claim to being the most beautiful. Autumn is still about in the mountains with warm days and chilly nights. The heat of summer has gone from the Earth, where the serenity of evening skies and placid days foretell the winter season, when all the world, it seems, comes knocking at our door. Welcome stranger!

Autumn reflections on the Mogollon Rim. Jerry Jacka

Heart of the Forest

A man, for his own well-being, for peace of mind, and for the good of his immortal soul, should spend a couple of weeks each year deep in the heart of the forest. There the soft murmur of the breeze in the pines, the most beautiful music on earth, will calm jumpy nerves, and a few hours a day tramping along a trout stream, will not only whet the appetite but will clear the cobwebs from the mind.

(Left) Colorful maples in West Fork of Oak Creek.
Bob Clemenz
(Below) Autumn leaves in the Kaibab Forest on the
Grand Canyon's North Rim. Josef Muench

We take you to a forest...and we probe with you into the many things, large and small, that compose one of Nature's most impressive creations. A leisurely forest stroll, we assure you, can not only be fun but very revealing.

In the Kaibab National Forest north of Grand Canyon...is a very special fellow, the Kaibab squirrel. When you travel a highway from Jacob Lake to the Canyon's North Rim, please take a couple of hours off and go wandering off into a pine grove. Your wandering can be very rewarding. You might, if you are patient and observant enough, meet his honor, the Kaibab squirrel. He's unique. There's not another like him on Earth.

Autumn Leaves

Autumn is that period of the year that falls between summer and winter. The season features such wonderful nonsense as school, football, little boys reluctantly raking leaves, pumpkins, Halloween, headliners back on the radio and television programs, turkeys, Thanksgiving, the clank of radiators and the repair of furnaces...thoughts of Christmas gifts, pumpkin pie and cranberry sauce, fireplaces, evening slippers, the comforting pipe, and—oh, yes!—comely young ladies trying to make evening gowns fit in such a way so summer tans, laboriously acquired, won't show in the wrong places.

Autumn is the season, first and foremost, when we glorify leaves—just plain, old leaves.... In the spring, we are more concerned with blooms and blossoms. Our world in autumn is a world of leaves. The season makes us leaf conscious. There is no greater miracle than a leaf...a large cottonwood would probably have as many as 80,000....

Look twice, think twice, when you meet autumn on a mountainside. There is sorcery in the season.

The magic of life in an autumn forest. (Left) Tree frog.
Peter Kresan
(Right) A new tree amid a colorful summer past.
Dick Canby photos

Winds and Mummies

Canyon de Chelly and its famous tributary Canyon del Muerto rise in the Chuska Mountains that form in part the northeastern boundary of Arizona. The canyons cleave through red and yellow and gray sandstone that towers in sheer cliffs and pinnacles and domes hundreds of feet above narrow sandy floors. The twin gorges, characterized by "cliff dwellings like mud-daubers nests, and foot holes in solid rock, leading mysteriously upward," are on the Navajo Indian Reservation and are included in the Canyon de Chelly National Monument....

Here, guarded by overhanging cliffs, protected from decay by dry Arizona air, are found ruined houses, graves, mortuary offerings, and refuse middens; veritable galleries of pictographs carved on cliff rocks; subterranean ceremonial chambers; turquoise pendants with intricate mosaic designs...finely woven baskets; stone-tipped lances...mummies who whisper the story of a succession of cultures....

Autumn comes to Canyon de Chelly National Monument. David Muench

Nature's Paint

Nowhere on Earth's surface does Nature paint with more vivid colors, erect and mould on a more grandiose scale than in our Southwest. To describe the scenic wonders of this area would be a puny gesture. How can mortals with their grimy ink pots catch the mood and the grandeur and the rugged nobility of time's ageless carvings? Can cold words on cold paper, guided by a human's narrow vision and narrower intellect, portray the warmth, the depth, the all-encompassing, the all-powerful message written in stone by the mad winds, the riotous storms, and changing seasons of the tired centuries, punctuated by the sardonic laughter of a bright Sun, whose aeons are but a fleeting paragraph scrawled in the dust?

We can only point to these temples of time and the river in awe and reverent silence. How diaphanous and evanescent, how unimportant the events of our life and times, when we stand before these pillars of forever! The headlines of our day fade into nothing when viewed in surroundings which bear in bold outline a million years of history's story. It is good for the soul to pause occasionally and give heed to these sermons in colored stone, listen to the gentle symphonies of wind mellowed by the blue sky and bright sunshine, or shiver in the wild cacophony of storm in these cathedrals of agelessness.

How amusing it must be to Nature, and her faithful servants, time and the weather, to view man's monument to tomorrow and his tribute to the past and present on either side of this continent! We can imagine the raucous laughter and high mirth as Nature views these piles of glass, iron, and concrete. "I have builded and destroyed for fifty million years. I will build and destroy long after your puny fairs and expositions have vanished into dust and forgetfulness. Only I can tell of past; only I build for tomorrow."

Autumn gold in Canyon del Muerto. Wayne Davis

Pintail ducks flush in morning light. James Tallon

May the Song of Birds Be with Us Always...

Without the song of birds our battered old planet would be very dull indeed!

Without the color of birds our tired old planet would be less colorful and considerably drabber than it is now!

A bird is a creature of God, perhaps one of His most delicate and exquisite creations. Those bumbling old bipeds, Homo sapiens, who think they're the Lords of all creation... can't do what a bird can do—they can't fly. At least they can't without the use of mechanical props, gasoline, aerodynamics, and jet fuel. Ha! Those old vainglorious stumble-bums still have a lot to learn from birds...we dedicate these pages with warmest affection to bird lovers everywhere and especially to those members of the National Audubon Society....

The Philosophic Saguaro

The nights are cool in the desert, and the mornings are crisp and clear. November has caressed the mountains with frosty fingers, and the aspen leaves, like flakes of burnished gold, have carpeted the ground, awaiting winter's covering of snow.

The desert becomes alive in November, peopled by travelers from afar who seek the rest and the peace and contentment to be found there. The desert roads and desert trails resound again with the happy voices of people engaged in the delightful occupation of killing time in a place where time stands still. There is no hurry in the desert. The philosophic saguaro, ageless and mute, gives eloquent testimony to the utter uselessness of the modern individual's fuss and furor. Truly the person beset with the problems of a too transient existence and a too complicated world can learn lessons on the Arizona desert that will never be learned in books.

The November Sun on the desert, as it is throughout the fall and winter months here in Arizona, is warm and restful and invigorating. The desert, clothed in this garb of sunshine—its atmosphere the concoction of the very gods themselves—becomes a religion that will stay with a person forever....

Wintry clouds settle onto the foothills
of Sabino Canyon near Tucson.
Willard Clay

Where the Lions Dwell

The hills and mountains of Arizona are apparitions on the horizon—jagged and sawtoothed. The Sun and clouds play a symphony of color on them, and at night, starlit and eerie, they loom in the moonlight, strange and far-away, dim in distance and mystery.

Sunrise over the hills and mountains of Arizona is a sight to behold. In the east, the rising Sun builds a halo of soft gold, as if gentle, unseen fingers were enveloping the crests with burnished cloth. The color becomes more intense as the fire god rises in the heavens, and soon the east is aflame, and the hills and mountains are aglow with fire—leaping fire of red and living gold.

Then the fires fade into cold purple-blue embers as morning shadows cling to the outline, and soon the hills and mountains are cold and clear in the bright Sun, and above is the clear blue sky with an errant white cloud loitering by, going no place in a hurry, a sleepyhead with dreams of yestereve still lingering.

When the storms come, the sky is black and heavy over the hills and mountains, and the lightning flashes break through the blackness, livid and repellent. After the storm passes, the mountains glisten in the clear sunlight, so bright and clear they seem, that the unwary traveler will think they are only a few miles away, and then they will taunt you in high mirth as they seem to be farther away the longer you travel toward them....

In the evening, the mountains of Arizona wear robes of rose and garnet, ruby and crimson, as the worn old Sun sinks slowly in the west like a tired old man, happy and proud of his pious centuries, going to bed. The million shades of red over the mountains deepen into fantastic purples before night pulls its magic curtain, and the world sleeps.

These are the high rugged mountains where the lions dwell, where come the winds and the storms, and from where on clear days you see new horizons far, far away....

Arizona high country, where the lions dwell.
First snow comes to San Francisco Peaks. Wesley Holden

Arizona's Winter: a Synonym for Sunshine...

And could I leave you
Running merrily through the snow?

Winter scene on the range land near Elgin. Willard Clay

When you spend your winter in the Old West you have all of southern and central Arizona to choose from; and much of northern Arizona has that delightful winter climate that beckons.

Winter of snow and cold comes only to our high mountains. Only our loftier peaks and higher elevations wear coats of ermine, and they do so proudly, for theirs is a noble mission. They seem to stand like mighty guardians against the storms that come with winter, and in their strong arms they seize the storms' challenge and struggle ever-victoriously to protect the pleasant valleys and the desert below.

Here is the snowdrift on the mountainside, whose silence is broken by the breaking of a snow-heavy twig on the pine tree or the happy shout of a figure on skies gliding rhythmically through the alabaster of snow and sunlight.

Down below, but an hour or so away, is that glorious admixture of winter, spring, summer, and along a trail rides a couple of carefree people whose wide hats shade their faces from the Sun, their horses munching occasional patches of grass, their faces reflecting the joyousness of their surroundings and the exhilaration of bright, sun-drenched out-of-doors in the Old West.

From the high mountains in morning comes the zestful freshness in the air, invigorating and enlivening to the valleys and desert below. This is the kind of air one would like to bottle and have for all time; for no other air on Earth is quite like it. It is the desert and the mountains and the sky and sunlight all mixed up, and its label is "Arizona."

Arizona cattle country between Flagstaff and Winslow. Jerry Jacka
(Right) Southern Arizona visitors enjoy a trail ride on a wintry afternoon. J. Peter Mortimer
(Right, below) Home for the holidays. Val Stannard

A bit of Arctic

The business of winter sets in early in the northern part of this land, and with winter comes the snow, hard and bright and clean. 'Way up in the San Francisco Peaks near Flagstaff you might find snow any time after the first day of November. And sometimes it remains on the rocky slopes of the mountain until July. But this is just a little bit of the Arctic in a land where summer and spring are mostly in season. In these mountains and in the higher elevations where snow comes early and is piled deep, people with skis seek the snow and plunge down mountainsides on the wings of winter. And to these people snow is sport.

Snow is many things to many people in this land, where, to very, very few, snow is a hardship.

Snow is a fearful thing to many people in colder climes, with its attendant evil companions: cold and sleet and freezing weather. But here winter's white garment loses its terror. It becomes something different for nearly every person who lives in or near it.

Lonesome winter scene south of Flagstaff. Jerry Jacka

Winter Serenade

Night was a whirling mass of darkness, with savage voice and with savage fingers clawing at the mountain. There were no stars. Creatures of the night eschewed familiar paths and haunts to wisely remain warm and secure in sequestered places. There was only the wind and the voice of the night. The trees were bent wraiths, flinching before the anger of the wind.

The storm was on a high lonesome on the lonely mountainside.

Far below, feeble lights flickering in the darkness revealed the presence of people. Houses were barred against the storm. The wind rattled loose gates and window shutters, raging to be denied the warmth within the houses. The broad highway skirting the base of the mountain, with a dark pathway in the night over which an occasional automobile cautiously picked its way. Not a pleasant night to be traveling about in, but fate and destiny decree not all God's creatures shall be warm and secure on cold winter nights.

By morning the storm had blown itself away. There were no clouds, only a sky of blue ice. There was no wind on the mountainside, only silence of a white winter world broken every now and then by the crackling of a limb weighed down with snow. Mountain animals ventured forth from their sequestered places leaving marks in the snow where they walked.

The sunshine straining through the cold, crisp air was bright but not warm so early in the morning, and where the light snow caught the sunshine there was the flash of diamonds, gleaming precious jewels flung about with the spendthrift's grace. The trees on the mountainside threw long shadows, but even there light was reflected so that the snow crystals were blue diamonds. Never were the mountains more beautiful, never was the air more clear.

Snowy boughs unburden themselves into Oak Creek.
Suzanne Clemenz

The Many Mansions of Winter

Winter lives in many mansions in Arizona. There is the winter people in more inclement climates expect and are accustomed to—the winter of white silence in high forests; trees bowed with the weight of the ermine robes they wear; the song of the birds stilled; tracks in the snow, furtive signatures left by small creatures in their comings and goings—the only signs that life exists in a dormant, sleeping world....

Snows fall lightly and gently at the Grand Canyon during the winter, and when they do, the effect is beautiful to behold....

In a land where there is so little snow, snow in Arizona is a thing of beauty, that shining white curtain of cleanliness with which winter creates a wonderland. In the mountain regions of our state, snow comes early and lies deep to feed mountain streams in the spring, which in turn bring moisture to the great reservoirs. Farmers who may never see snow owe their crops to it....

Only very rarely does snow come to the desert. An inch or two will fall some stormy night, and the next morning the desert will blink with the new day on whiteness all around. A saguaro will look the world over, startled by the unexpected and will wear a "See, what a bright fellow I am!" expression. No, snow is not for the desert. An hour or two after the storm comes in the night, the snow will begin to fade, apologetic for the intrusion. And in the sunlight the next noon all the snow will be gone from the desert, and dampness and freshness will remain.

(Right) Winter snow patterns on the South Rim of the Grand Canyon. David Muench
(Below) Pack train emerging from the Grand Canyon. Dick Canby
(Following panel) After a stormy night, first light finds the desert foothills near Tucson covered with snow. Joe Carrder

The Year It Snowed

So the storm passed, and the world wore a cloak of white. The morning sun in a clear, cold sky turned snow crystals into glistening jewels. The cold breath of the storm could still be felt, challenging the Sun. It was as if the furnaces of the Sun had lost their fire, for there was no warmth in the bright light of the sunshine. The wind, which accompanied the storm during the night, left marks of its passing on the sculptured mounds and patterns of clean, white snow, a mantle of sparkling ermine which the Earth wore with proud grace and beauty....

There was drama, majesty, and beauty wrought by the big storm that came the year it snowed, the year it snowed real big.

Winter's fury in the red rock country near Sedona.
Tom Canby

Skiers' Paradise

This is the winter that sports enthusiasts, living in lower and warmer elevations of the state, claim as their personal domain. (A visitor would be surprised to see how many sporting goods stores there are in the desert oases cities of Phoenix and Tucson, for instance, which do a thriving business catering to winter sports needs and whims of Arizonans.) This, too, is the winter that meteorologists and hydrologists study with intense concern because snow in the mountains means spring runoffs, spring runoffs mean water for thirsty lands, and water for thirsty lands means the good life, the assured life, and well-being for so many in so many ways. Knowing that winter has brought snow to the mountains is pleasant knowledge to those who live in the dry and arid land....

That skiing should flourish in a state not ordinarily associated with snow is merely another of those tantalizing contrasts that are to be found here. Visitors to the Sun country can loll about an orange grove in the morning and by noon hurtle a mountainside on a pair of skis. This is probably the only place on Earth where you can have your cake and eat it too....

Cross-country skiing near northern Arizona's Snow Bowl.
Tom Bean

Beyond Where the Roads End

And what, you may ask, is a wilderness area? Well, according to Webster, a wilderness is a "tract of land, or a region, whether a forest or a wide, barren plain, uncultivated and uninhabited by human beings; a wild waste...an area of national forest land set aside by the government for preservation of natural conditions, either for scientific or recreational purposes."

Now we are getting someplace. Our wilderness areas (nine in number) are portions of our seven national forests set aside and protected by the U.S. Forest Service to remain for all time as close as possible to what they were when the Good Lord first made them. Technically we have wilderness, wild and primitive areas,

according to size, but for our purpose "wilderness area" will suffice.

They begin beyond where the roads end. The only sign of man ever passing their way are a few trails for the convenience of the hiker or the person riding a horse. No roads, no automobiles, no Jeeps, no motorcycles, no scooters, nothing mechanized. Here, in these isolated areas, one can at last be free from the odor of carbon monoxide. Fresh air! It's wonderful!

We owe a lot to the Forest Service for setting up such areas for us to enjoy, places where we can be by ourselves if we wish. The debt...for these wilderness areas will be even greater for the generations to come....

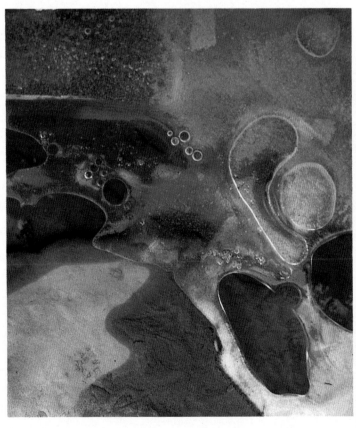

(Left) Silent winter symphony in blue and white.
George McCullough
(Right) The Coconino National Forest in winter dress.
George McCullough
(Below) Nature's artwork in ice. Tom Canby

Children of Nature

In the Navajo hogan, as the storm passed, all was secure and warm, the family sleeping serenely in their beds of sheepskins and heavy, woolen blankets. All night the coals of the fire glowed in friendly comfort, giving warmth against the cold of night.

When the first rays of the Sun appeared above the horizon, the Navajo father went out to greet the new day. The world that greeted him was a world of winter white, winter bright, the Sun turning the newly fallen snow into a carpet of glistening diamonds. His sheep were huddled together in mutual warmth against the cold. The Navajo found his world good.

On his return to the hogan, he told the Navajo mother, who was busy with the morning meal, "Last night the snow came!" She answered, "That is good! When the snow comes in winter, the grass will come in the spring, and the sheep will grow big, fat and healthy."

The high, barren plateau regions...here live the Navajos, with the weather—good, bad, but never indifferent—their constant companion. They are children of Nature. Nature in many ways has moulded them as it has moulded the land in which they live. They accept the buffets of wind and storm and Sun stoically. Bad weather—as well as good weather—is decreed by their gods. Their respect for the weather is shown in the names they give the months of the year.

December, in Navajo, is "Nitch'l Tson," The Month of Increasing Cold and Wind. January is "Yas Nilt'ees," The Month of Crusting or Icing of Snow; and February is "Atsa Bujaazh," The Month of the Young Eagles Hatching. Names of beauty that fit.

Navajo hogan in winter, Chuska Mountains background.
David Muench
(Following panel) Wintery contrast between the desert and 7645 foot high Four Peaks northeast of Phoenix.
Jerry Jacka

The Beautiful Season

Many, many, many years ago—just yesterday, in fact—the firm light of a bright new star guided three wise and kindly men through another and faraway desert seeking a newborn in a simple manger. Since then, through the placid and turbulent centuries, during this season the stars shine with greater warmth, greetings between friends are more friendly, man is more considerate and thoughtful of the needs and afflictions of man.

During this season we think not only of ourselves. More so than at any other time of the year those of well-being think of others, the selfish are less selfish, the miser less a miser. Our loved ones, near and far, are closer to us than before, the blessings we enjoy and our happiness we wish to share with those less favored.

The light that illuminated the newborn in that simple manger so many, many, many years ago shines more brightly today. The centuries proclaim the wisdom of His message of peace on Earth and of human righteousness and decency.

Let the bells ring out the message of the season. Never do bells sound so inspiring. Let voices be raised in the season's songs, the grandest songs ever sung on Earth.

This is Yule. This is the Beautiful Season.

(Right) A giant saguaro silhouetted against an Arizona sunset. Jerry Jacka
(Below) Mission San Xavier del Bac, Tucson. Willard Clay
(Following panel) Organ Pipe Cactus National Monument. Jody Forster

Look to the Skies

Look to the skies for beauty, for rest, for inspiration and quiet reverie. Look to the skies for those precious moments in your life when your mind and heart soar to higher and finer things, and you lift your eyes from the mundane. All the world is a cathedral and the sky the sacred dome of Heaven that covers it. Look to the skies, then, for guidance, for comfort, for understanding. Here is nourishment for the soul, pinched by the confinements and the harassments of everyday living. This is the way God made the world, and the sky is always with us. It is our fault that we look down and follow little footsteps in the dust. And if all we get is dust in our eyes only we are to blame. Behold the skies! Course of the Sun and pathway of the Moon and clouds! Behold the skies!

Sonoran Desert sunset. Alan Benoit

Spring Brings God's Blossoms...

If ever I would leave you,
How could it be in springtime,

A late snow caps blooms on Hopi peach trees
in northern Arizona. Jerry Jacka

Spring, enchanting sorceress, brings the flowers to the desert and puts the bloom and color in our desert bouquet. The desert is always a thing of beauty, but in spring it primps and poses and takes on a loveliness that to the beholder bespeaks the stroke of some magic wand. No matter how often you see it, our desert bouquet, with its myriad flowers, is a memorable sight....

Those who live in the desert or those whose leisure moments are spent in following its lazy, dusty trails say that generally desert flowers bloom from Washington's Birthday to the Fourth of July. The flowering season will vary with the year but if you seek your bouquet April, May, and June are delightful months for your search. At this time you are sure to find the desert wearing the gayest of corsages.

If you should be lucky enough to wander into the desert during what desert folks call a "wet" spring, then you will see the desert at its best. A green carpet of grass is stretched invitingly before you. Poppies and many other small flowers dance their dance in the sun. In places they are so thick they make up the patterned floor covering that rolls out before you almost as far as you can see. During a "dry" spring, the seeds that hold these flowers lie dormant in the desert soil, holding their charm for more favorable weather.

During a "wet" spring you will discover the cacti vying with each other to produce the largest blossoms in greatest numbers, spendthrifts spending their beauty with lavish recklessness. Rain is the miracle worker in the desert....

Regardless of the whims of the rain gods, the desert always pays fitting tribute to the smiling season. The flowers may not be so numerous, but they are just as exquisite and bewitching, their colors as vivid and luminous, their petals as waxy and delicate, the craftsmanship that formed them just as exacting and elegant.

The aimless roads follow their aimless ways into the desert, inviting you to the purple hills not so far ahead. You who seek will have no trouble finding your desert bouquet this spring. The flowers are there awaiting you....

Spring in Organ Pipe Cactus National Monument. Kaz Hagiwara

The Days of Spring

Those were the days of spring—the bright Sun in the desert, the warm and friendly Sun, a lazy and languorous Sun popping out of a clear sky, full of blue and punctuated with a lazy cloud or so.

For all people sometime will return to the desert in spring...whatever missions call them to whatever lands and islands beyond the seas....

There is color in the desert in spring and music and the fragrance of a world new and clean and bright, a world redolent with charm and sunshine...a lazy world but a lovely one, and a world of peace....

Spring will miss many of her companions in the desert this year, their destinies having taken them to far places or are keeping them in far places busy with tasks important to their fate and to their nation, far from the desert in spring. But the desert people will return some other spring when peace comes again to the land....

And that spring the desert shut you out from all the world, and soon you felt how removed the world was and how far away the little joys and troubles that people describe as life, how far away was yesterday. In the desert time stands still, as if it, too, in its inexorable march to eternity has found a pleasant place to pause and linger a bit. The hours spin themselves out slowly, and a day stretches on and on for an endless age to blend like soft music with the softer music of a desert evening in spring.

In the desert you leave the world and your own thoughts behind you. The ways of man and his madness and his moneymaking find no accord in such a place. The scheme of the desert is but a pattern for reveries, for self-searching. Here undisclosed depths reveal themselves with startling clarity, and it is good for a man to see into his own soul.

Editor's note: Raymond wrote this as he departed for combat duty in World War II.

Cholla and saguaro cacti on the Sonoran Desert.
David Muench

Desert Moods

The desert has many faces, and it shows a different face to each and every person. The beholder, on meeting the desert for the first time, will find it almost drab in its simplicity but on better acquaintance will find it fascinating in its complexity, moody and mysterious in the varied and forever-changing facets of its personality.

The desert will never be all things to all people. To some it represents a sweeping emptiness of subtle coloring embracing the sky and the purple mountains, the ageless drapery of shadowed rock that forms the horizon. These people find the desert almost an empty void, cameo clear in the bright, light air, tantalizing in its invitation for further exploration.

The desert is a mighty instrument which records all the nuances and subtle changes of weather, sky, Sun, and cloud shadow. That is why desert lovers never find their beloved land a tale of twice-told monotony. In its agelessness, it is vitally youthful. The better you come to know it, the more you learn of its strange and surprising ways, and that is why true desert lovers never tire of it and find other lands dull in comparison....

"You will be rewarded well for whatever efforts, no matter how meager, you expand in my behalf. My secrets are many. No man can know them all, but those I reveal will in some way enrich your life. You will find me full of moods, full of mysteries, strange in all ways, but ever wise in the ways of the Sun. If you approach me with understanding and a loving heart, you will not find me unfriendly. Come with warm welcome, stranger. My treasures are many, and these I will gladly share with you."

(Right) The saguaro blossom, Arizona's state flower.
Jerry Jacka
(Below) The pineapple cactus in bloom. David Muench

Spring...Surprise!

Spring...the friendliest word in the language. Of all the seasons spring seems more intimate and delightful than any other. Throughout all the West—from Powder River in Wyoming to the San Pedro and the Gila in Arizona, from the ranges of Cochise County to Montana—spring is an awakening, something akin to a miraculous happening.

If you live to be nine and ninety or if you're only nine or deliciously nineteen, spring comes upon you all of a sudden as a surprise, bringing round-eyed admiration and wonder. Spring doesn't come in like a tiresome neighbor, full of innocent small talk, droning out the tiresome tales. Spring comes gushing in, bubbling and sprightly, full of laughter and merriment, new and full of music, exciting and thrilling....

But spring! Even when you get into the desert in our land, where seasons change so slowly you barely notice the change, you know that spring is here. The air is just a little bit lighter and the Sun has a particular glow. The skies are just a little bit bluer and the clouds a mite whiter and more billowy than at any other time. And then the flowers just seem to have popped up all about you, and they seem to dance in the breeze and shout laughingly, "Surprise! Surprise!"

Prickly pear cactus blossoms. Jerry Jacka

A Wondrous Thing

Life in the desert is a wondrous, miraculous thing, but, perhaps, most wondrous and miraculous of all is the transformation of drab desert land into a veritable flower garden when rains come in winter and early spring. This takes place not by happenstance or haphazard chance but by the careful blending of all Nature's wonderful nurturing tools to give and sustain life. The rains must come at the right time (some years they do not) to stir life's juices in dormant seeds. When dormant seeds have sprouted, hot, searing winds must take their mischief elsewhere (some years, alas, these mischievous winds are too much with us and our anticipated flower display comes to naught).

Ah! But when all things are right what beauty to behold when drab, desert land is transformed into a glorious flower garden under spring's gentle and magic touch. The usually dry, barren land is clothed in a garb of many hues, radiantly beautiful, almost awesome in its flowered splendor.

It doesn't happen every year, but when it does, it's worth waiting and watching for.

(Top) Hedgehog blossom detail. Jerry Jacka
(Left) Saguaro, ocotillo, prickly pear, and hedgehog along the Apache Trail east of Mesa. David Muench

Wild Flower Paradise

"In the wildest Nature, there is only the material of the most cultivated life, and a sort of anticipation of the last result, but a greater refinement already than is ever attained by man."
—Henry David Thoreau

...And that, dear reader, was the key that unlocked the cell in our mind wherein lived the botanist in our lives...to see botany as another vehicle on the road to the Beautiful Explanation of Life.

The Arizona desert is a perfect place to seek the great truths about Nature and especially about wild flowers.

Because of its geographical position, and range of altitude, in which are represented the five basic climate zones of the wild plant kingdom, Arizona is a paradise for almost 40 percent of the more than 12,000 known flowering plants of the world not grown under cultivation. More than 3438 species are known and listed in Kearney & Peebles' *Arizona Flora*, and they represent those of nearly every part of North America. There are still new species to be discovered in remote, and unexplored areas....

1957 was a peak year...so outstanding that more than 250 species were recorded which had not bloomed for 50 years prior. And they haven't been seen since....

In the Great Plan man is no match for Nature and the Great Spirit. At times Nature rebels, and for several years in succession the Great Spirit sends little rain. Then, when least expected, snows and rains recycle the process of life again. Nature never intended for humans to understand her, no more than we should ever understand the story of the Resurrection, and the mystery, miracle and wonder of life itself. whether it be manifest in plant and seed, mother and child, or the cycle of the seasons.

Yes, indeed, there is nothing like a day in a flower-carpeted desert to convince man that everything spiritual and material is born of the Earth, and man is no more important to God than the dormant seed waiting to be born again.

(Right) The bounty of spring near Bartlett Lake northeast of Phoenix.
Jerry Sieve

(Below)...discovering great truths about Nature.
Dick Dietrich

A Land that Takes Knowing

Our desert can be, to many people, the most forbidding, the harshest, the most uninviting portion of all God's not-so-green acres. It never has been nor ever will be the most comfortable and easiest portion of our planet on which to work, loaf, ruminate, dream, achieve ambitions, or build castles in the sky!

It is not a pretty, pretty wonderland! It is a land that takes knowing!

Now how do you come to know a desert land? Well, it takes living in, a lot of living in, that's how! It is not an easy land to know, as far as that is concerned. It is not a chummy-chummy land that gives its favors with gay frivolity or can be wooed with a careless toss of the head and an empty smile. It's hot, prickly, dry, ugly, repulsive, unkind, dangerous, rocky, totally without rhyme or reason! It is all of that unless you know it well. As we said it takes a lot of knowing, and then the desert is a different story.

A person coming to the desert for the first time from such places as the Pacific Northwest, the Midwest, the New England states or the deep South comes almost as if from another planet. Nothing in that person's experience has prepared him for the strange and arid land, warned him, we might say, of the weird and startlingly fantastic flora, so unlike anything he might have known in other climes, all shaped by the Sun, all equipped with the necessary armor not to defy the Sun but to live and flourish under all the strict impositions of that very Sun itself....These plants, who find themselves so well adapted to desert ways, are *xerophytic,* meaning, literally, the drier it is and the hotter it is the better they love it.

These are the things the visitor should know: The desert itself is of the Sun, and the creatures living therein are ruled by the Sun.

Gila blooms in May throughout Glen Canyon National Recreation Area in northern Arizona. Jeff Gnass (Following panel) Century plants blooming in south-eastern Arizona. Ed Cooper

Desert Trails

They wander into the desert, these desert trails, winding and twisting, lazily stepping aside now for a saguaro, now for a paloverde. Their destination is the desert edge where the foothills roll upward and lose themselves in the bluish haze of the distant mountain range. This winding path will take you to a ranch house in some small canyon in the foothills where a friendly cottonwood shields it from the sun. Another of these lazy desert trails will lead you to a prospector's camp and another to a small mine and another to a cottage in the desert where someone, shielded in the desert's bosom, is regaining lost health.

Each desert trail is an adventure, a glorious adventure into the sunshine and into the peaceful silence of a great outdoor cathedral. Not any place else on Earth can you be more alone, more immersed in your thoughts, more steeped in the beauty of simple Nature....

(Right) Sand verbena decorate a desert road near Yuma.
James Tallon
(Below) Golden blossoms crown the barrel cactus.
Jerry Jacka

Travelog to Spring

If your quest is spring, come to our land. Every highway in the state—east, west, north, south—will carry you to a happy rendezvous....

Spring's modish trademark is everywhere in our land. The Joshua forest to the west and north of Kingman; the Joshua forest to the west of Congress Junction; the great desert stretch between Chandler and Tucson; that wild remote area, the Organ Pipe Cactus National Monument, south of Ajo; Saguaro National Monument, near Tucson; all the countless miles of foothills and low mountains througout the state, half desert and half mountain: here is spring.

Spring in our land is many things. To the lover and student of cacti, it may be a tiny pincushion holding a large blossom, or it may be that intricate creation of Nature called the blossoming saguaro. To the painter it may be the desert landscape and the distant range of purple mountains, the vivid white clouds lazying above those mountains and the crystalline clearness beyond and above the clouds called blue sky. To the poet it may be the droning of the bees in the mesquite blossom, or the music of a clear, cold stream hurrying down from a snow bank of some high mountain. To the motorist spring may be the carpets of gold and blue wild flowers along the highway, and there are many miles of highway and many miles of wild flowers in our land.

To the rancher spring means the thick grass of the desert floor or the hillsides of grass you find in Santa Cruz County and Cochise County. Spring means to many the citrus trees in blossom, and to others dreamy afternoons just sitting in the Sun....

The dams along the Apache Trail...are this year churning full of water that has come boiling down the watershed to record an all-time mark for storage. Roosevelt Dam, a milepost in the history of reclamation, last spring but a mud-hole is filling to overflow capacity this spring.

Yes, it's spring! A happy, generous, colorful, fragrant spring!

(Above) Joshua blossom detail. John Cacheris
(Right) Joshua trees in spring near Kingman. Jerry Sieve

Arizona... an Enchantress!

Arizona! A magic word. Arizona! What visions of grandeur those seven letters conjure. Arizona! A symphony in mad, extravagant colors, shaded with the soft light of the desert in the evening, the purple mountains at twilight, the mauve sky of a rising sun.

Arizona! An enchantress, with rare and precious jewels worn lightly and gaily, like a new dress to the marketplace. An enchantress, whose jewels, sparkling in the bright sunshine, are more valuable than all the wealth of all the kings and kings' men ever to stride the Earth. Arizona! A tantalizing sorceress, whose charms are graciously and generously bestowed upon one and all alike, and yet whose secrets are held in unfathomable depths, ever-mysterious, ever-alluring.

Arizona! An adventure and a challenge, if you please. Stout men and stout hearts have followed her unending trails, climbed her unbending mountains, to bow at last in admiration and adoration. Arizona! Contradictions and contrasts! Arizona! Moods and majesty.

To all men and all women there is a different Arizona. But to all men as to all women there is one overwhelming Arizona—that is Arizona, the land of great beauty, and Arizona, the land of rich, magnificent color.

Arizona!...R.C.

Nowhere in the world is there anything quite like the fragrance of the desert after a fresh spring rain. Saguaro National Monument West. Thomas Ives
(Following panel) Perfect ending for a perfect day. Willard Clay

*Summer, autumn, winter, spring...the beauty of Arizona's
scenic seasons at Red Rock Crossing near Sedona. Dick Canby*